New/W

P9-CPV-088

3 9043 05425455 7

SUMNER REDSTONE

with Peter Knobler

A PASSION TO WIN

SIMON & SCHUSTER   *New York   London   Toronto   Sydney   Singapore*

W

SIMON & SCHUSTER
Rockefeller Center
1230 Avenue of the Americas
New York, NY 10020

Designed by Lisa Chovnick

A leatherbound first edition of this book has been published
by The Easton Press, a division of MBI, Inc.

Manufactured in the United States of America

1   3   5   7   9   10   8   6   4   2

Library of Congress Cataloging-in-Publication Data
Redstone, Sumner.
A passion to win / Sumner Redstone with Peter Knobler.
p.   cm.
1. Redstone, Sumner.   2. Viacom International.
I. Knobler, Peter.   II. Title.
PN1992.7.R38 A3 2001
384'.092—dc21
[B]   2001020663
ISBN 0-684-86224-7

ACKNOWLEDGMENTS

J ust as I did not build Viacom by myself, I have many people to thank
for their participation, good work and good wishes in the writing
of this book. My close friend Philippe Dauman spent extensive
time working with me directly, focusing the big picture, sharpening the
details, recalling stories and shaping insight. His help and dedication
were essential and greatly appreciated. Tom Freston, Jon Dolgen, Sherry
Lansing, John Antioco and Ken Miller all added their good will and rec-
ollections, providing important views from all corners of the Viacom
world. I am pleased to call them all my friends.

My family of colleagues at National Amusements—Jerry Magner,
Ed Knudson, Bill Towey, George Levitt and Jeff Aldrich—pitched in
with anecdotes and good humor, just like old times. I feel lucky to have
Jon Newcomb at Simon & Schuster—he has been doing a great job. Jack
Romanos was especially adept at piloting this project, and he, Carolyn
Reidy and David Rosenthal have been very supportive. Fred Hills edited
the manuscript thoughtfully with great attention to detail; Charlotte
Gross copyedited wisely, Leslie Ellen supervised with care, and Michael
Selleck, Victoria Meyer and Aileen Boyle provided their marketing and

public relations expertise. Nadine Wolf and Joycelyn Ferguson transcribed quickly and accurately. France Rovelli assisted ably.

My collaborator, Peter Knobler, has been of inestimable assistance to me in conveying the story of my life and the story of Viacom to the outside world. In the course of our collaboration, Peter has demonstrated enormous insight and intelligence and, at the same time, has become my friend.

We appreciate the work of Esther Newberg, who brought Peter to me.

Viacom is at the center of my life, and the board of directors that helped build Viacom is made up entirely of smart and excellent businesspeople. Bill Schwartz is a fine man and was dean of Boston University Law School, where it gave me so much pleasure to teach. He is now of counsel to Cadwalader Wickersham & Taft. Ivan Seidenberg possesses an extraordinarily sharp mind and continually impresses me, particularly in his building of NYNEX into Bell Atlantic, followed by that company's merger with GTE and the creation of Verizon. Fred Salerno, Seidenberg's second-in-command, has likewise been very successful and is now vice chairman and chief financial officer of Verizon. Ken Miller played a large role in the original acquisition of Viacom. I put so much trust and faith in my personal attorney, George Abrams, that I have almost literally placed my life in his hands.

And what excellent executives we have at Viacom. Carl Folta, senior vice president, corporate relations, has done a fantastic job in conveying the enormous success and growth of the company. He and his staff, particularly Lauren Cohen, were instrumental in providing and confirming many of the details on which this book is based. Marty Shea, along with Carl Folta, has traveled the world with me, from New York to Dubai, meeting with business associates and investors. Michael Fricklas has proved to be a worthy successor to the talented Philippe Dauman. And as for Bill Roskin, he is a master at dealing with all human resources issues.

My friends Marvin and Barbara Davis introduced me to almost

everyone I know in California and have been extremely good to me. Bob Evans, who has been so supportive over the years, is also a good friend.

Until recent years I knew Aaron Spelling only as a venerable legend, the single most prolific producer of television programming in history. But since Spelling Entertainment Group, Inc. (now Spelling Television, Inc.) became a part of Paramount, he has become one of my closest friends. Notwithstanding the mansion in which he lives with his beautiful wife, Candy, Aaron is a gentle, compassionate and laid-back man who doesn't take himself too seriously, all characteristics that appeal to me.

Herb Geller, who now acts as my assistant and driver in Boston, was the man who used to literally drag me into the car when I would travel back and forth between my home and the hospital after the fire, before I could really walk. There has never been anything I could ask of him that he would not do. Without Herb, life would have been far more difficult than it was. With the acquisition of Paramount, Frank Gomez became my driver and aide in New York, and he has proved to be a valuable asset.

My brokerage account at Bear Stearns is run by Steven Sweetwood, whose mother, Madeline (once my stockbroker), is married to my brother, Edward. Aside from being an able broker, Steven is the most loyal person I have ever met. Steven and his colleague Marvin Friedman are not only business acquaintances but also friends.

There are three women who play enormous roles in my life: Tilly Berman, Harriet Solo and Cathy Matera. All three have made my life far better than it would have been without them, and I appreciate their devotion. Tilly is my assistant in Boston and has been with me for many decades. She records all my financial turns, provides all the information for my accountants concerning my tax returns. She is wonderful, a close friend not only of me but also of my entire family. Tilly *is* family.

Harriet and Cathy are my New York assistants. Harriet has been with me at Viacom since the beginning. A highly skilled woman, she coordinates my hectic travel schedule, arranges all of my appointments and keeps the details of my life in order. I can't thank her enough. Cathy, a woman of great spirit and talent, worked tirelessly with me on the manuscript, spending hours as we reviewed every word. I value her energy, dedication and enthusiasm.

And I thank Viacom. It is my world.

—S. R.

This book is dedicated to my children, Shari and Brent,
to Brent's wife, Annie, and to the five people I adore the most:
my grandchildren, Brandon, Keryn, Kimberlee, Lauren and Tyler.

—*S. R.*

To Jane and Daniel

—*P. K.*

CONTENTS

PROLOGUE

The Fire This Time

I *don't splurge on much in my life.* My material desires have always been minimal. When I'm in Boston I live in the same suburban home I moved into forty years ago. For sixty years I bought suits off the rack (some would say not wisely). But I like a nice hotel. I feel I've worked hard and should be able to enjoy good food and stay at a nice place. If it's comfortable and the service is good, that's enough for me. I don't have to own it.

I was perfectly happy checking into Boston's Copley Plaza. As president of National Amusements, Inc., owner of a small chain of movie theaters, mainly drive-ins, I was there for a party to honor a branch manager of Warner Bros. Pictures. I was going to New York the next day. It was 1979 and we were in the planning stages of opening the Sunrise Multiplex, our first indoor operation in the New York metropolitan area, and between construction, booking and breaking into a new market, there was a lot of work to be done. The party at the hotel was going to run late. I would stay the night, get up early and be on my way.

I went to sleep thinking about work. It was well after midnight when I woke up and smelled smoke.

I don't recall ever being taught what to do when faced with smoke and fire in a hotel, or anywhere else for that matter. It's not something you think about when you check in. I smelled smoke and made the classic mistake; I opened the door. The branch manager, who was staying in the next room, made a bigger mistake. He opened his door wide and stepped into the hotel corridor. He died.

I was enveloped in flames. The fire shot up my legs. The pain was searing. I was being burned alive. But even in the middle of terror there is sometimes clarity. I thought, What a horrible way to die.

Somehow I staggered to the window. It was stuck, I couldn't budge it. I moved to another window and, I don't know how, got it open and clambered outside. I was kneeling on a tiny ledge, barely big enough to put one foot on. I was three floors up. If I jump, I'm dead. Flames were shooting out of the window head-high and I crouched there, hanging onto the windowsill, my fingers cupped, my right hand and arm in the fire and burning.

The sound of the inferno was terrifying. The heat and flames roaring out of the room burned off my pajamas and peeled away my skin. My legs had been burned to the arteries, now my arm was charring. The pain was excruciating but I refused to let go. That way was death. I began counting one to ten, one to ten, hoping that a fire engine would come save me.

But it didn't. The hotel people hadn't called the fire department right away because they didn't want anyone to know there was a problem. What a disgrace—an outrage. I hung on the ledge for what seemed like forever. Finally a hook-and-ladder truck arrived. A fireman climbed up, cradled me in his arms and carried me to the ground.

At City Hospital, I lay on a table and could hear the doctors say, Give him so much of this, give him so much of that. I'm sure some of what they gave me must have been morphine because the pain of fire is overwhelming. And then I passed out. My family all gathered at the hospital. They were told that I probably wouldn't live the night.

The next day when I woke up I had third-degree burns over 45 percent of my body; my right wrist had been almost severed and was literally hanging off my arm. But I had no idea of the extent of my injuries and I was feeling pretty good. It was great just to be alive! It must have been the drugs. Still, I was fifty-five years old and there was a significant question about whether or not I would live. Even if I did, there was a uniform belief that I would never walk again.

My personal physician was Dr. Samuel Proger, head of the New England Medical Center. He made a critical decision to move me to the Burn Center at Massachusetts General Hospital, the place of the highest competence in burn surgery. At Mass General they began to operate on me immediately. One operation the day I got there and then a day or two later, another. The pain was almost unbearable and my father demanded of the surgeon, "How can you operate on him again?" Dr. John Burke, the chief of the burn unit, told him, "If we don't operate, he's dead."

Forty-five percent of my body had been burned away, and to cover my wounds they had to painstakingly take live skin from other parts of my body, graft it to the rest of me and hope it regenerated. Skin will do that if it is successfully grafted. It was the only way that I could hope to have flesh cover my body. Now there is artificial skin, the research for which I helped finance, but in 1979 they had no choice but to flay me.

I didn't feel my burns anymore, all the nerves in those areas had been seared away, but the pain from having my skin removed from my body strip by strip was beyond imagining. If I lay still sometimes I could handle it, but when they changed my bandages it was hell on earth. I thought, I'd rather my children be dead than have them suffer the pain I am suffering. At first the nurses gave me morphine but I stopped taking it, not because I was heroic but because I got so little benefit from it. What was the sense of risking narcotic addiction when the pain shot through the drug as if it wasn't there?

I went through five operations, sixty hours in all, each involving teams of surgeons. I lay in the hospital for months. Finally, after the third operation, it seemed reasonably clear that I would live. The doctors gathered around for the final unwrapping of the gauze, the peeling of the bandages to see whether the grafts had taken and my skin had grown back. Success meant I had many months of rehabilitation in front of me; failure I didn't even want to think about. Dr. Burke peered down and said, "Congratulations."

"Congratulations?" By this time I had progressed to sitting up in bed. "You're congratulating *me*? You guys saved my life!"

"Listen, Sumner," Dr. Burke told me, "everything we know is on your body. Bone grafts, skin grafts"—my toes were nailed to my foot—"and the reason you're alive is you." Determination, physical or any other kind, is the key to survival. If I hadn't learned that lesson before, I knew it well now.

As I began my long, slow recovery, I was touched that the doctors who had taken care of me that first night at City Hospital were regular visitors at Massachusetts General. And the people who worked there were angels. Among the nurses who tenderly changed my bandages every day was an African-American woman named Dell. She was kind and friendly and I enjoyed her company. One night, just as she was talking to me and unwrapping my bandages, she was called away and a new nurse took her place. "What happened to my friend?" I asked. Her brother-in-law, I was told, had died suddenly and she had had to leave. As much pain as I was in, I had held tightly to the moments with Dell and I missed her when she was gone.

During my months of recuperation I had to learn how to walk again. Every morning they would literally drag me out of bed, and with a nurse on each side holding me upright, I would try to put one foot in front of the other. Usually I simply collapsed, but as the weeks went by my useless legs started to come back to life. I took one step before failing, then two, then several. I never felt strong, but after a while I moved from a teeter to a shuffle to a walk. One day, I was walking very slowly in slippers and a robe down the linoleum corridor when Dell suddenly appeared. I hadn't seen her in weeks. She had just experienced a family tragedy, but when she saw me her face lit up like a beacon and she cried, *"Mr. Redstone, you can walk!"*

Among the primary concerns, along with my skin grafts, was the risk of infection. So much of my body was raw and exposed that it was imperative that my environment be germ-free. The hospital couldn't keep my room absolutely sterile, that was impossible, but from the very beginning an old woman came in every day and mopped the floor. There are many ways to handle a job like that, many attitudes she might have taken toward her work. She chose compassion. "How are you feeling today, Mr. Redstone?" she would always ask kindly. I was lying in bed, each movement a moment of pain, but I'd summon enough strength to say, "Okay. Okay."

After months of surgery and rehabilitation I was finally well enough to go home. I walked out of Mass General.

A few weeks later I was carried back in.

I had just begun to regain my confidence and was walking on my own. I still couldn't pick up a piece of paper with my burned hand but otherwise I was feeling fairly capable. I thought that I had this thing beat. Then one night I started to bleed, blood pouring out of me. I was rushed to the hospital and the doctors discovered that I had a double pulmonary embolism. Two blood clots had hit my lungs. That was pretty serious, but if they had hit my heart I would have been dead.

Forget the physical discomfort from the plumbing of my veins and arteries. That was painful, but I'd been subjected to worse. After living through all the operations and the therapy and the excruciating uncertainty of not knowing if I was going to live, now, to be back in the same hospital once again at the risk of my life was almost too much to bear.

I was hooked up to an intravenous system and wheeled up and down the hospital corridors for blood tests every day. The doctors injected me with one thinner after another, trying to find just the right medication and dosage to eliminate the clotting. I was always aware that one fast-moving clot could be the end of me. The drain was overwhelming. What else could happen? Finally they thought they had it under control. And about two months after the clots had been dissolved, I began to feel okay again.

A year or so after I recovered, I went back to Mass General to tell the staff thank you. I had sued the Copley Plaza for negligence and I donated the settlement, several million dollars, to the Burn Center. Most of the same people were still there. One in particular. The woman who had mopped my room every day saw me, walked over, put her arms around me and started to cry.

By that time I had been elected president of the Theatre Owners of America, an organization which represented exhibitors in their extremely adversarial relationship with the movie studios, and I was scheduled to deliver the keynote speech to a giant meeting of theater operators in Los Angeles.

"You can't go," my doctor informed me.

"I'm going," I told him. "If I don't show up, people in this industry will say, 'This guy's dead, he's gone, he's out of it.' "

I traveled with a healthy supply of blood thinners and a nurse who gave me injections. My doctor made arrangements with a hospital in Los Angeles to see me in case of an emergency. No one knew this when I walked to the lectern and made what people later told me was a spectacular speech in support of motion picture exhibitors. I stayed the night in a nice hotel, got injected with blood thinners, walked onto a plane the next morning and flew home to Boston.

Now, was this ordeal a seminal event in my life? Was it some sort of cleansing fire in which I was transformed by a powerful encounter with death? Knowing how precious life is, did I grab it with more gusto than ever before?

Absolutely not. Some people may want to believe that's what happened—it's convenient, it's psychologically satisfying, it's an easy hook —but I don't buy it. It's nonsense. I hadn't changed. I had the same value system after the fire that I had before. Whether in high school or college or law school or building a theater circuit, I have always been driven. I have a passion to win, and the will to win is the will to survive.

And my love of family will always be the same. I remember how my wife, Phyllis, and my children, Shari and Brent, would sit at my bedside until the late hours of the night, hoping they would see me alive and better the next day. I love my children. They are my best friends, both of them now intimately involved in my business and personal life.

There are doctors who claim that your mental attitude will help you get through cancer. I don't know about that, but I can say with certainty that my will to win, my tenacity, had a lot to do with my recovery.

The most exciting things that have happened to me in my professional life have occurred after the fire but not because of it. It doesn't take near death to bring you to life. Life begins whenever *you* want it to begin.

BLOCKBUSTER TANKS

Viacom is me. I have a love affair with this business and this company. The global competitive struggle, the creation of the most successful books and movies and television—and the creation of audiences for all of them—is exhilarating. My industry reaches the hearts and minds of tremendous numbers of people, and no one matches Viacom for its effect on lives all over the world. It is exciting to think that our brands—MTV, Nickelodeon, VH1, CBS, Simon & Schuster, Paramount Pictures, Showtime, Blockbuster, Comedy Central, Nick at Nite, TV Land—have far-reaching social as well as business dimensions. I love Viacom's successes and I am stung by its failures. I enjoy being part of it every day. In 1987, when I acquired the company, I had bet my life on it and so far I was winning.

I had a vision of creating the premier software-driven media company in the world, and in 1993, Viacom had the opportunity to acquire one of the world's premier movie studios, Paramount Pictures. However, I was locked in a titanic bidding war with Barry Diller, the chairman of QVC Network, Inc., that was jacking up the price unconscionably. I needed cash. In order to acquire Paramount I needed to acquire the world's leading video rental company, Blockbuster. Its cash flow was extraordinary. I was looking for another $600 million and Blockbuster had it.

Taking on Paramount without Blockbuster would have been extremely difficult. Could we have done it? Possibly, but the acquisition of Paramount would saddle Viacom with a significant debt, and we needed a source of cash to service it. Otherwise, once we acquired the company, we would have had to sell off many of its assets, which would have defeated the point of the acquisition in the first place. I wanted all of Paramount's important assets, including the movie and television studios and its library of films, Simon & Schuster publishers, Paramount Parks, several TV stations and hundreds of theater screens.

I was not interested in buying the company to liquidate it. Besides, there was no guarantee, in the event we did gain control, that we would be able to sell any of these assets at an acceptable price. We would be under significant pressure to divest and potential buyers could use that pressure to their advantage. We also needed cash flow in order to grow the company. A merger with Blockbuster, as part of my vision of Viacom's future, was critically important.

Blockbuster, however, was not without its downside. The concept of video-on-demand via cable and computer brought the possibility that one day the video rental business might become obsolete. One Wall Street analyst, who spoke to *The New York Times* only on the promise of anonymity, said, "Do you want Blockbuster? If you're buying into this thing for the brave new world of convergence in the entertainment world, it looks like these guys are going to kind of get converged out."

We took all that into account, but when we evaluated Blockbuster we didn't think we were making a big sacrifice. According to the company's figures, its cash flow was terrific, it was offering continuity in management, it was the leader in its industry, the company was expanding rapidly, and money was streaming into its coffers. We saw Blockbuster as a growing company, worth the investment whether we ended up with Paramount or not.

We merged with Blockbuster and, after a tough fight, we got Paramount.

I put Blockbuster's founder and chairman, H. Wayne Huizenga, and its vice chairman, Steven Berrard, on the Viacom board of directors. Huizenga was the visible leader, the business visionary who got and deserved all the credit for creating Blockbuster, but a tremendous amount of the work had been done by Berrard. I suspect, because of my age, Huizenga thought he was going to run Viacom someday. I had no intention of retiring, however. I would call and update him on company matters—he was a stockholder with a big position—but he frequently complained that he was left out of important decisions. That bothered me because it was not at all my intention, but in the daily stress of running Viacom, I was not focused on keeping him up to date on every aspect of what was going on.

About a year after the merger, Huizenga left Viacom and founded Republic Industries, becoming its chairman. He clearly wanted a company to run. Several top Blockbuster managers would later leave Viacom to go with him. Berrard, Blockbuster's chief executive officer, stayed and was placed in charge. He indicated to us that because he would not make the move, he and Huizenga were no longer on speaking terms. He essentially told us, "I have no further relationship with Wayne Huizenga. I'm with you."

That was fine with us. Steve Berrard was extremely competent, offered the strong continuity of leadership necessary for Blockbuster's success and had been largely responsible for the company's operational workings. Plus, I liked him. Blockbuster had a vastly expanding store network, many newly exploited territories and markets, and a large cash flow which was used to build more stores, further the expansion and bring in more cash. It was a beautiful growth story and I relied on Berrard to continue Blockbuster's success. I paid him handsomely and placed great faith in him.

At the time of the merger, Blockbuster was involved in several expansion initiatives, all of which sounded good. A new Blockbuster store was opening every fourteen hours around the globe, 220 outside the United States including in countries new to Blockbuster like Colombia, Germany and Peru. There were plans for a Blockbuster credit card, a

Blockbuster move into the music retail business with the opening of a hundred Blockbuster Music stores to rival Tower Records, a system for electronic downloading of both music CDs and video games at Blockbuster outlets. Discovery Zone, a playground network for kids, was already in operation. Block Party virtual reality centers were going to be the Discovery Zone for grown-ups. Blockbuster Park, an entertainment, sports and retailing complex planned for Florida's Broward County, was going to compete with Disney World.

The first sign of trouble came when we began to see shortfalls in Blockbuster's performance in relation to its budgets. We asked for an explanation and got a lot of rationalizations. The new initiatives sounded great while Blockbuster was being sold to Viacom, but by their very nature they took time to unfold. And as each initiative got to the point where we could assess its success, it began to unravel. We went through them one by one and found that each was either falling short of projections or sucking up money and becoming an unmitigated disaster.

It was time to get more immersed in the guts of the Blockbuster operation. It had made sense to give Berrard great autonomy. After all, it was a business in which we had no experience. But we were astounded. The company had overexpanded and could not sustain its rate of development with the necessary intelligence and business acumen. Such a premium had been placed on simply opening new stores that all controls had fallen away. It was as if they'd had a quota to meet—"I've got to get eight stores up and running this week"—and no one had the time to process them correctly. *Is there enough traffic and business to sustain this location? Is the lease on the proper terms?* As we ultimately discovered, too often the answers were no.

We visited Discovery Zones and were horrified. The food was spoiled, the kids' milk was sour. The buildings were huge and the major business, birthday parties and other functions, was highly concentrated on weekends; during the week the places were empty. We had tremendous real estate expenses and no ability to amortize them. There simply wasn't enough consideration given to the day-to-day practicalities of running the business. In each case the people at Blockbuster were doing everything to build revenue. Revenue, however, is not profit. They were thinking of the top line, not the bottom line. The concepts were good, the execution was extremely poor. It turned out that this was Blockbuster in microcosm.

They were deal guys. Consolidators. Huizenga and his managers were great builders but far from excellent operators. There was high-concept hype combined with a total lack of concern about the long term. Plus, their hiring policies left a lot to be desired. People who had been hired by Blockbuster straight out of college four years earlier were being put into positions of responsibility for which they weren't prepared. Because of the rapid expansion, there were so many new jobs to fill that bodies were being moved around without regard to qualifications.

How did they handle these difficulties? They didn't. If there was a problem, they swept it under the rug and moved on to the next project. But as a natural consequence these problems started accumulating until they could no longer be ignored. Now we had to face them. There are very few people who can both make deals and operate, and at Viacom we prided ourselves on having that ability. We went to work.

We killed the plans for Blockbuster Park. The record companies rebelled against the idea of producing personalized CDs at Blockbuster Music stores; it turned out that the concept hadn't been vetted sufficiently and was withdrawn. We shelved the plans for Block Party, dissolved its entertainment division and sold its two locations to Discovery Zone, which itself soon filed for bankruptcy. We closed fifty unprofitable Blockbuster Music stores, cut back on video store expansion and tried to get Blockbuster back to being Blockbuster.

Around this time, Huizenga called and asked me to invest in his new company, Republic Industries. I decided, despite what I was finding at his former company, that it would serve Viacom best if I maintained a decent relationship with the man. I told him I'd buy $1 million worth of

Republic Industries stock. When the placement memorandum for the investment arrived, it listed other investors and there on the list was Steve Berrard, allocated something on the order of 600,000 shares. Neither Berrard nor Huizenga had disclosed this relationship to us.

Huizenga had left us with a leader who he said was going to stay and maintain continuity. Instead, the two men appeared to be engaged in some kind of seductive relationship which practically compelled Berrard and others to leave and for Huizenga to hire them. I felt betrayed.

Berrard had begun to seem disengaged from his job. Still, he was one of the people who had built the company and we needed him; we were married to his management, there was no one else. For a long period I tried very hard to keep him at Blockbuster. While we were at a management conference in Vail, Colorado, Berrard said he was considering leaving. But when I made several management changes and reminded him I had taken the role of Viacom CEO myself, which would put us in closer daily contact, he said it might lead him to change his mind. In fact, during an earnings teleconference, Berrard stated to the analysts that my assuming the role of CEO would quite probably lead him to remain. Berrard had a very attractive wife, and I told her, "You want to be a movie star? Get your husband to stay." She seemed to have aspirations in that direction and I was only half kidding. Berrard agreed he would stick around for a while and keep an open mind.

I had sat for considerable lengths of time with Philippe Dauman and Tom Dooley, then my deputies, discussing our options. I was on the fence. I liked Berrard. I thought he had not been given enough credit within the company for what he had accomplished at Blockbuster. I also thought it was extremely important to maintain a good working and personal relationship with him; if it was necessary we would at least be in position to woo him back.

Tom and Philippe had questioned Berrard's management. Now Philippe said, "Look, let's let him move on. He's not doing the job because his mind's not there, so forget about the consequences of his leaving. He's going to leave, and if he's not going to leave, we should say goodbye anyway." Tom was even more forceful. "The sooner he goes," he said, "the better."

We had a real problem: Who was going to lead Blockbuster forward? There was no natural successor within the company. We immediately contacted a corporate headhunter, but this was not a business in which we had any experience and it wasn't as if we could reach outside for an executive who was running another video rental company; Blockbuster *was* the video rental industry. There was no business like it from which to find parallel executives.

The stress was enormous and the search did not go smoothly. If Berrard had decided he wanted to stay, I would have let him. But finally, he told me he was definitely leaving. He would be CEO of AutoNation USA, a national chain of used-car showrooms, in which, *The Wall Street Journal* reported, he was already a major founding shareholder. Huizenga, of course, was also a major shareholder. We were rushing the headhunter to recruit a replacement and I asked Berrard to stay until we could find one.

I was looking for the preeminent man in retail and the name I heard most often was Bill Fields. Fields was second-in-command at Wal-Mart, among the largest retailers in the world, and was in line to get the top job. But along with his name came the phrase "You can't get this guy." I was told repeatedly, "This is the guy you should get, but you can't get him." So, of course, we went after the prize.

At first Fields wasn't very interested, but we pursued him. Philippe made the pitch: "Blockbuster is an exciting company, there's a great place for you, you'll do a lot better in terms of compensation, and we are very excited about the possibility of having you on board." Fields lived in Wal-Mart's hometown, Bentonville, Arkansas, and ultimately—this sounds as if it took months, but actually it was a matter of days—he came to New York and met with Philippe and our human resources people. Fields talked about his wife and kids; he seemed very family-oriented, which I liked. Philippe found his strong Arkansas accent hard to understand, but otherwise was impressed. Fields told us he would think about whether he wanted to make the move and then flew back to Arkansas. We pressed him and he agreed to return to New York a few days later and meet with me.

Fields, Philippe, Viacom's Human Resources Senior Vice President Bill Roskin and Steve Berrard met over lunch. They discussed compensation and responded to Fields's concerns. Berrard answered questions about what the job involved and then they walked him over to my apartment at the Carlyle Hotel.

Bill Fields is a great physical specimen, tall and lean. I can't say we exactly clicked on a personal level, but he had a remarkable résumé. He was the fourth college graduate Sam Walton had hired, he had been with Wal-Mart almost from the beginning and was widely credited with developing the company into the giant it is. While Berrard had Huizenga's entrepreneurial zeal, our feeling was that now that Blockbuster had become substantial, we needed a seasoned operating executive. I offered Fields the job and he accepted. Bill Fields had all the qualifications we needed. He was the heir apparent at Wal-Mart and he was leaving to come to us. He seemed like God's gift to Blockbuster.

Steve Berrard would not do us the courtesy of creating a smooth executive transition. I do not know whether Huizenga had pressured him, but on March 19, 1996, he announced that he was resigning from Blockbuster and going to join his old boss at AutoNation. He wouldn't even wait a couple of weeks while we buttoned things down with his successor. Many people, seeing that the company they are running is having trouble, would be motivated to stay. Berrard didn't appear to care.

I flew to Blockbuster's headquarters in Fort Lauderdale, Florida—also the home of Huizenga's new companies—and addressed our employees, telling them they were still a key part of Viacom's plans. Talk of a spin-off sale of Blockbuster had begun in the press almost immediately and I needed to quash that. It took nine days to iron out the details with Bill Fields, and for all that time Blockbuster was without a leader.

We gave Fields a lot of room. By reputation, he deserved it. "I think there's opportunity for great growth here," he told us, and brought in some of his former Wal-Mart executives, whom old Blockbuster hands referred to as Wal-Martians. He began to put in his own systems. He suggested moving corporate headquarters from Fort Lauderdale, where they had been since Huizenga founded the company, to Dallas, which was more centrally located to Blockbuster stores around the country, where the labor pool was far greater and where we could build a giant distribution center. It would also be a means of finally dissociating the company from Huizenga, who was then something of a hero in South Florida.

Despite the fact that he was no longer involved, Huizenga continued to have a strong impact on Blockbuster. He had hired many of our staff members and still had contact with them, his other businesses were located in close proximity to ours, and he was a strong presence in the community. I'm not suggesting that this was necessarily destructive, but he was no longer running the show and we could not truly take over Blockbuster in the full sense of the word, as we wanted to, because of his influence.

The move to Dallas was wrenching, and whether people stayed behind or relocated with us, it was not easy for them. In the end, however, the company was better off for it and the move was ultimately successful.

From the beginning, however, things did not go well with Fields. Wal-Mart sold everything under the sun and Fields began to remake Blockbuster as a concession stand. To utilize our sizable square footage of retail space, he stocked Blockbuster shelves with popcorn, T-shirts, games, bubble gum, excess videos and music that we couldn't sell—everything but ladies' underwear. Stores quickly became cluttered with all this retail merchandise, which had very little profit margin, while at the same time Blockbuster lost concentration on its basic business, which was video rental. In fact, the word "video" was deleted from the logo and taken off the marquees of our stores. Fields changed the focus of the company and he did it overnight.

He also changed our advertising slogan from "Make It a Blockbuster Night," which implied that the Blockbuster customer was going to go home with a videotape, to "One World, One Word: Blockbuster," which was so general it could have fit anything from organized religion to the United Nations to the circus. What *was* this company?

Maybe we should have been more aggressive in overseeing his initiatives, but this was Bill Fields, the guy we couldn't get, the heir apparent at Wal-Mart. That was why we were paying him the big dollars. We had just given him the top job in a field that was not our strength; even if we felt he was heading in an unusual direction, in view of his background and experience we had to give him the benefit of the doubt. We were not about to take away his self-confidence, certainly not in his first six months on the job. I held back. I am not usually like that.

Then there was the matter of Fields's demeanor. I never got the feeling that he was engaged at Blockbuster. He had a very good contract, he had more autonomy than almost any other Viacom executive, he had a large budget to bring his ideas to life, but I felt no commitment. He certainly didn't behave toward Blockbuster the way I and my other managers behaved toward Viacom.

I am often asked what I look for in an executive. In my experience, success has three essential ingredients: a passionate commitment to your goal, the courage to dream and to take risks, and the moral and intellectual character to realize the dreams worth pursuing and the best route to take to achieve them. Commitment, courage, character—a powerful combination of qualities that I believe you will find in every truly accomplished person. Fields was certainly accomplished, but he was showing me little else. He really didn't seem to want to be at Blockbuster.

Even the people who had known him previously perceived him to be behaving uncharacteristically. His family had remained in Arkansas, where his children were in school, and we felt it was understandable that he flew home on the weekends. But during the week he was a complete recluse. He didn't invite his executives to dinner; he would eat alone in his hotel dining room. I hadn't clicked with him on a personal level during our interview but had let that pass in deference to his résumé. He had lived in Arkansas all his life and maybe he simply had a demeanor that we were not used to. We didn't know what to think.

We weren't alone. A high-ranking member of his management team who had known and worked with him at Wal-Mart walked into his office one day and asked, *"Where is the real Bill Fields?"* He never got an answer and neither did we.

Viacom holds a winter holiday party once a year to which we invite all our top executives and their spouses from around the country, perhaps 125 people at the uppermost rungs of the corporation like Jonathan Dolgen, Sherry Lansing and Tom McGrath of Paramount; Tom Freston and Mark Rosenthal of MTV Networks; Jon Newcomb of Simon & Schuster; Philippe Dauman and Tom Dooley; Judy McGrath of MTV; Herb Scannell of Nickelodeon; John Sykes of VH1 and Matt Blank of Showtime. And from National Amusements, Jerry Magner, Ed Knudson, Bill Towey and George Levitt and, of course, my children, Brent and Shari. People important to the company and to me. It's a way of fostering team unity and the sense that, despite each person's focus on his or her own division, we're all working toward one goal, the success of Viacom. It's an elegant affair with a holiday spirit and we all enjoy it. Fields arrived and instead of involving himself with his colleagues went off by himself somewhere. I found myself in another room, face-to-face with his wife. I didn't know her and was making conversation, but I wanted to say the right thing. "You know," I told her, "your husband is a really nice guy."

She looked at me. "You're the first person I've ever heard say *that!*"

When I was alone with Philippe and Tom, I asked them, "Was she kidding?" They didn't seem to know. But a short time later the Fieldses were divorced, so maybe she had it right.

Fields was hired in March 1996. By August, Blockbuster had been expected to produce approximately $1 billion in cash flow but instead came in at $800 million. We were $200 million short. Viacom stock dropped precipitately. We were paying the price for this failure. Fields was at the helm and we had run into an iceberg. In January 1997, when Blockbuster's fourth-quarter performance figures were available, Viacom stock fell 7.5 percent in ten days.

Business headline writers had a field day. "Stockbuster Video," cried *Variety.* "They have to deliver something," the trade paper quoted one analyst. "They have to show that Blockbuster is fixed."

Fields failed to understand that he was in the video business, not running a variety store. We were a specialty retailer and he didn't grasp the difference between general and specialty retail. Plus, he lacked commitment. We gave him six months and then it became clear that we had to do something. Otherwise the ship was going down.

I met with Philippe and Tom and we went through the same soul searching we'd gone through about Berrard. We had intensive debates concerning leadership. Were we better off to hang on to Fields or get rid of him, to have no leader or a leader whose capability and competence we were calling into question? I was exasperated that we had moved so quickly to find a replacement for Berrard; this was what happened when we operated in a rush. We had to make sure the next person was completely able. What would investors think? Fields had been in place less than a year. How many times could we replace Blockbuster's top executive without losing our credibility?

Philippe, Tom and I talked about the problem constantly; there was nothing more important. We went back and forth, searching for a solution. In the midst of this struggle, *The Wall Street Journal* arrived one morning with a front-page article titled "The Big Picture: How Viacom's Deal for Blockbuster Chain Went Sour So Fast." Wayne Huizenga's name was in the first paragraph. In the second the paper noted that Viacom stock was down 30 percent from its peak. In the third the *Journal* discussed what it called the "troubled aftermath" of the Viacom-Blockbuster deal. In the fourth Huizenga called me a liar.

"You can't lie to the Street," he said. He blamed Viacom, the *Journal* wrote, "for misleading Wall Street by not being more open about the impact of merger-related accounting changes that helped supercharge Blockbuster's financial performance in the first year after the deal closed." If Viacom "had stated their true numbers," Huizenga said, investors would have had a more realistic sense of Blockbuster's growth rate. According to him, we had cooked the books.

We had done nothing of the sort! To begin with, the numbers were fully disclosed and were accurate—carefully reviewed by Blockbuster, Viacom and our independent auditors. Even more unfair, though, was Huizenga's distancing himself from the figures. Whatever we told the Street we had gotten from Blockbuster. Blockbuster's accounting had been made more conservative since the time of the merger. We had done exactly what our accountants told us and had cleared the figures with Huizenga's staff, and now he had the utter gall to criticize us. Clearly he was trying to protect himself. He'd gotten out at the right time and now it certainly seemed to me that he didn't want to take the blame for the catastrophe that was occurring.

Huizenga had taken a paper loss of about $100 million in Viacom stock that year, and I didn't see how savaging us was going to help him regain that ground. If anything, he was harming himself as well. Plus, he hadn't sold the stock, he was holding on to it. Who was lying? I held my tongue, at least in public.

A *Business Week* writer had been spending a great amount of time with me during my workweek for a cover story that was scheduled to appear in the magazine in February. She had also spent several months interviewing dozens of my friends and business acquaintances, ranging from my teaching colleagues at Brandeis University and Harvard University Law School to television producer Aaron Spelling, Sherry Lansing and a host of Viacom executives. I was looking forward to the piece. At that time of corporate trial, I thought her story would be a shot in the arm for Viacom.

I should have suspected that something was up from the photograph of me on the cover looking tight-lipped and dour and the article's title, "Sumner's Last Stand." It began innocuously enough with descriptions of me as I took phone calls and did business with News Corporation chairman Rupert Murdoch and Tele-Communications, Inc., chairman John Malone. She reported on my conversations with Philippe concerning how to work our strategies for Viacom. It was established that she had access. She said I was "having the time of my life." True. Then she quoted an unidentified investment banker who said that I was "a mad genius. . . . At the moment, he's probably more mad" than genius. Having won Viacom and turned around Paramount Pictures, she wrote, I now "may be something of a liability."

What? "Redstone is unable to state a clear, realistic vision of what precisely he wants Viacom to be." Now, I may be many things but no one had ever accused me of being anything but clear and realistic. I "had trouble articulating a comprehensible strategy for the company." I spoke in platitudes, she said.

Then the writer launched into a series of attacks. There was a "widely held view that the company lacks executive depth." "Management gridlock." I ran Viacom "as if it were a mom-and-pop operation . . . all but living above the store." She quoted another investment banker as saying, "No strategic priority is emerging." She went on to talk about the "deterioration in Viacom's fundamentals. . . . Its stock has lost half its value since 1993, amid a roaring bull market."

I accepted responsibility for Viacom's difficulties—I control the company—but this was a personal profile and I was dismayed. According to the writer, I "was loath to give up much, if any, real authority." My "exacting, argumentative nature can also be a liability." Another investment banker, again unwilling to be named, said, "All things being equal, [other companies] would rather not deal with Sumner. . . . He's extremely difficult, litigious, not a partner of first choice."

The writer suggested intentional skulduggery on my part to account for the fall at Blockbuster, rehashing at length the accounting questions that had appeared in the *Journal*. She intimated that a turnaround, should it occur, would have "little to do with the very capable Fields" and much to do with the fact, she claimed, that we had manipulated the books to achieve certain price targets for our stock to prevent our having to pay guarantees to our stockholders.

These were serious, crushing allegations, which she backed up by quoting Huizenga telling me, "Blockbuster is doing fine. It's just the accounting. Blockbuster is being made the culprit when it shouldn't be."

The story was so vicious that the writer went so far as to question my account of the fire at the Copley Plaza. "A Boston Fire Dept. spokesman who was there that night says that Redstone was standing inside the room's large window, not dangling outside, when he was rescued." Had that been the case I would have been burned alive. Why had only one arm been burned—the arm from which I hung out of the window—and not the other? This was an outrage! Who was responsible for this hatchet job?

Thirty days earlier the same *Business Week* writer had written glowingly about Viacom's international operations, praising me alone among many others mentioned. In her research for the cover story she had spoken with dozens of people who had nothing but positive comments to make about me and the company, and she had clearly intended to write a positive piece—that much could be gleaned from the article's opening and structure. But after spending months interviewing academics, business associates and competitors from all over the United States, she failed to quote a single one of them. Huizenga, it was clear to me, had taken her in and turned her. It was apparent that after being subjected to Huizenga's distorted, self-serving presentation, she had jettisoned her initial position and gone with his.

Mass General's Dr. Burke and I both contacted *Business Week*'s editor, Stephen Shepard, concerning the article. Any moron could look at my body and see what had really happened; if I'd been standing in the fire I'd be dead. I told Shepard, "Anyone who would write something so contrary to the facts should have the rest of her judgments in the article questioned." *Business Week* retracted the paragraph about the fire, but the retraction did little to redress the damage done.

The article was extremely painful to me. It was not only an attack on my company, it was a ferocious attack on my personal integrity. I was being called a madman, a liability, a liar. My *competence* was questioned. I was ashamed, humiliated, desolate.

The week that the article appeared, I was invited to a party at Disney CEO Michael Eisner's home in southern California and I truly did not want to go. The place would be full of my colleagues and competitors, and I simply did not want to face them. My absence, however, would have been even more damaging, so I showed up. I walked in feeling embarrassed, knowing that everyone there had read the story, and the first thing Eisner said to me was, "Sumner, forget it. It will be trash a year from now." I appreciated his empathy and his kindness.

But three weeks later, Viacom's quarterly earnings appeared and we were in free fall. Blockbuster's flat sales growth and lower-than-expected cash flow sent us tumbling.

Blockbuster had tanked.

Viacom's stock lost nearly 10 percent of its value in one day. I am Viacom. I can't divorce myself from the company. For better or worse, it's my life, and when it went into the tank I went with it. I had come from nowhere, essentially an unknown in the business world, and worked hard all my life to achieve my position. Now everything was wiped out. All of my accomplishments were ignored. The fact that I had started with a few drive-in theaters and now controlled one of the major media companies in the world was also ignored. All of Viacom's many accomplishments were forgotten.

Viacom stock, which had risen as high as $63 a share, fell to a 52-week low of $25¾. With each setback for Blockbuster and Viacom, I was losing money, but money was not the issue. I've never cared about money. I realize that sounds strange coming from someone in a position of considerable wealth, but money is really only the report card on what you accomplish. I don't believe most truly successful people are driven by money; what they want is to be the best at what they do. Whether they're businessmen, educators, artists or actors, they want to win. For me, the issue was pride. I had become an idiot overnight. How had someone so smart suddenly become so stupid?

The media took after me. I was under siege. *The New York Times* asked, "How good an executive is he?" The paper noted "troubling new questions about whether Viacom really had a handle on its basic operations" and said, "It is Mr. Redstone who faces questions about his own skills." Under the headline "Those Sumner-Time Blues," *Variety* wrote, "Redstone, with all his brains and energy, has done little to make much of a difference in his empire." It quoted one industry executive as saying, again anonymously, "The perception in the market is that he is not running it for his net worth. He is running it for fame and glory. That is what is killing the stock. . . . Even if he were a good manager, [Wall Street] would still want somebody different."

Wall Street was punishing Viacom for Blockbuster's failure. This was a knockout blow, a catastrophe. Despite the fact that Blockbuster's rate of *growth* had declined, it was still earning hundreds of millions of dollars. Nevertheless, when Wall Street added up Viacom's assets to calculate the company's worth, Blockbuster was given a *negative* value. As far as the Street was concerned, Blockbuster was worth less than zero. It was a liability and so was I. And the sad fact was that, to the extent that there was failure on the part of Blockbuster, it was my failure. I was in charge, I had to take responsibility. It was a ruinous time to live through. The personal pain was enormous. I could hardly sleep at night. I saw my whole life not just slipping away but being pulled out from under me. In a way it was like a second fire.

Without actually saying it out loud, people within the company were extremely unhappy because their stock options were underwater and those who held stock as an investment in their future saw its value plunging. But even then I had great support from Viacom's top management. We have a different kind of company from any other in the world;

we are not just business associates, we are friends. I recognize that this sounds like Pollyanna piety, but it is true. I am uncomfortable with the word "employee." I can't use it, I don't think of anyone in the company that way; we are friends, we have affection and respect for each other. And we are passionately involved in the company, all collaborative, as we must be in a company as large and diversified as Viacom. This is what I always look for in an executive and it was abundantly present in the men and women around me now. "We are not going to be distracted by the press or by Wall Street," I told them. "We are going to focus on doing our job, exploiting our opportunities, solving our problems. We will perform, and when we perform we will prevail."

It was clear that we had to say goodbye to Bill Fields, and ultimately he and I agreed it was best for him to leave. At that point Blockbuster had no leadership, it was a headless horse. At our annual management meeting a few weeks later, I addressed our managers, discussing the series of events that had led to Blockbuster's downfall. In conclusion, I said, "Now, more than ever before, is the time we all need to embrace Blockbuster—to find new ways to help them drive their business, help them in any way we can through the power of our individual and combined businesses to get back on the growth track. . . . Let's get it done!"

I was determined to stay the course. It was a matter of principle. Facing physical pain, business disaster or personal trial, I was determined not only to stay the course but also to win. I knew that Blockbuster was facing catastrophe and was bringing Viacom down with it. The question I now had to ask was what to do about it. The answer: Go to Dallas and run Blockbuster myself. I had come too far in my life to accept defeat now.

BREAKING
THE CODES

My father and mother were both born in America. It was a source of considerable pride for them. In the tenement world of Jewish immigrants, they were native-born Americans.

My father, whose name was Max before he changed it to Michael, sold newspapers on the streets of Boston to help support his family when he was a boy. He was a street kid, not very well educated but smart in ways only kids who grow up on the street are smart. His father had come from Germany. My mother Bella's father had come from Russia, and when my parents married they moved in with him. I was born a few years later, in 1923. One of my earliest memories is of my maternal grandfather sitting in our kitchen drinking tea from a glass.

Our apartment in Charlesbank Homes in Boston's West End had no toilet; we had to walk down the corridor to use the pull-chain commode in the water closet we shared with the neighbors. That sort of living was all I knew and I never felt less privileged than anyone else.

My father peddled linoleum and I have a clear picture of him in my mind toting a huge roll over his shoulder and carrying it out to the truck. With the money he brought in he supported not only my mother, me and my younger brother, Edward, but his own parents and my mother's family as well.

My father and I had a close bond. When I was young he used to take me to the fights and to professional wrestling matches. A wrestler named Nick Lutz made such a strong impression on me that I remember him to this day. My father also liked to fish and he made every effort to pass this affection along to me. I couldn't have been more than fifteen years old when he and I were sitting in a small boat out in the middle of Lake Sebago in Maine, trying to land something. My father was sitting in the bow when he got a hit. This was exciting. For fifteen minutes he played it, all the while giving me instructions. When he finally reeled in his catch, he had fished up a log.

My father was a hardworking man, highly competent, and as he began to succeed in business, we moved from the West End to Bothwell Road in Brighton. In 1935, Brighton was an Irish neighborhood which didn't have much tolerance for Jews, and almost every morning on my way to James A. Garfield Intermediate School it was like taking my life in my hands. The level of violence was not nearly as high then as it is now and I saw no knives, but I would get smacked around, and along with my bruises I'd hear a lot of threats and name-calling. I fought back as best I could, but I often had to face five or six tough Irish kids and I was always pretty much outnumbered. Fortunately, I lived close to school, and although I got roughed up my ordeal was blessedly short. And when I got to school I found no anti-Semitism whatsoever.

While my father worked hard, my mother, whom he called Belle, was totally focused on her children. My father's increasing success allowed her not to work, and our education became her top priority. She instilled in me and my brother the absolute importance of diligence and concentration. For instance, she arranged for me to take classical piano lessons—a great luxury in working-class homes during the Depression—and if I was supposed to practice for one hour, she would sneak in and put the clock back thirty minutes so that I would actually play for an hour and a half. She could sometimes be a real pain, but my mother had one dedication in her life, which was my education.

I was a good student. In fact, I was the top student in my class at

Garfield. I was a great speller—you said a word and I could spell it—and as I won all the spelling bees I entered, I was climbing toward the nationals. This was a fierce competition and a great challenge; to be the national best at any- and everything was my mother's goal for me. Second best was not an option as far as Belle was concerned. She was a very good-looking woman but I'm not sure how much fun she got out of life. There was only one number one and that had to be me. My brother, while he was smart and did extremely well in school, was not the target of her passion; I was. I was her pride and her focus.

I reached the regionals, spelling all sorts of complicated and arcane words, and was fully expecting to go all the way to the finals. I could picture myself standing in front of the judges and a roaring crowd, a sash across my chest, as I was proclaimed Best Speller in America. The proctor said, "Spell 'tuberculosis.'" I knew that.

"Tuberculosis. T-u-b-e-r-c-u-s-i-s. Tuberculosis."

I had left out a syllable. It was a slip which had nothing to do with my knowledge, but one stupid mistake and I was eliminated. I was aghast and my mother was stricken. It was a horror. How important was this failure? It happened in 1935, and even in a new millennium I still remember the devastation as if it happened this morning.

I was accepted into Boston Latin School, the premier public school in the city if not the country, and the pressure on me to do well only got more intense. Boston Latin was a public school run like a private academy. For six years, from seventh through twelfth grade, I was surrounded by Boston's best students, many from the city's most disadvantaged neighborhoods. We had been chosen not because we were wealthy or connected but because we were smart.

As well as the Boston Irish there were Jews in the school, a fair number of black kids and some Asians. The only criterion for entrance into Boston Latin was competence. (Granted, it was an all-boys school, so at least one large segment of Boston's student population wasn't represented. In fact, it took fifty years to bring girls to Boston Latin, but now they're accepted as well.) Each student had been selected because he had superior grades, had worked extremely hard in the lower schools and was committed to the best possible education. Certainly I couldn't draw any uniform conclusion about every kid in my class, that wouldn't be realistic. But I thought we working-class kids were special because we were all underdogs.

The school demanded an obsessive, driving commitment to excellence from everyone. A passion to win. Nothing else mattered. I have always been driven to succeed, and in this critical situation I became even more driven because the competition was so fierce. Not only were we graded on our classwork and papers, indicating the amount of knowledge we had absorbed every semester, but each student was also placed into direct and rigorous competition with all others for the school's top honors and prizes. Every month of every year in every classroom, there was a prize given to the best student in modern studies and the best in the classics. At the end of the year overall awards were presented, and to win one of those awards was every student's goal. Each of us worked zealously to beat the others to that end. Nothing at Boston Latin School counted except ability and competence, commitment and achievement. Not race, not color, not family, not wealth, not religion. The competition was cruel, it seemed inhuman. But it was cruelty without discrimination; everybody felt it. And it taught us to pursue excellence for the rest of our lives.

I got up every morning, took a streetcar to school, and from that moment on I lived in terror. I wanted to be number one in my class and I did nothing but study. There was no such thing as a gentleman's C at Boston Latin. First, there were few if any gentlemen—this was a public school and most of us were from the streets. Second, to coast on intelligence alone was considered almost akin to committing a sin. It was at Boston Latin that I was first exposed to the idea that thinking, educated and disciplined people have the power within themselves to create a new and better world. That was the school's intention. We were being given a special opportunity and we would not be allowed to squander it.

My homeroom teacher was Wilfred O'Leary, who later became

headmaster of the school. He also ran the debating club, which I joined and where I thrived. My mother formed a bond with Mr. O'Leary and they met regularly to discuss my progress. My mother was a constant driving force in my life, and though I often resented her presence, I could never challenge her.

All I had going for me was an education. We certainly didn't have any money. The ten cents a day I spent on round-trip streetcar fare was a significant sacrifice for my family and I had to justify that sacrifice. I felt I had been put on this earth to get the most out of school and to be the best in it. *I had to be the best.* I had to know everything there was to know. I had to know my subjects cold, with not even the most minimal margin for error. There could be no slips now, no lapses, and there would be no mercy if I made them.

I had no social life. I had no friends. I knew people only because I sat next to them in class or because they were my closest competitors for the school awards. I remember a fellow by the name of Danny Gorenstein who had the number one score in America when he took the math SATs. Then there was Bill Ellis, a black kid who was terrifically smart and did extremely well on all the examinations.

Latin was taught all six years, as one would expect at Boston Latin; Greek was introduced in ninth grade. They were an important part of the curriculum, as Latin and Greek are the basis for almost every Western language and have always played a large role in our culture. One of our Greek teachers was Mr. Drummond. Of course we called him "Bulldog." He was all over us kids all the time. Whatever we did was not quite good enough. I went out of my way to please him. I immersed myself in my studies. I worked all day, then went home and worked some more. Morning, noon and night, in school, going to school, coming home from school and finally at home—I did nothing but study. Throughout high school I don't remember eating.

I was doing well my first few months at Boston Latin when I was stricken with scarlet fever. In the 1930s this was a dread disease among children. You could lose your hearing, you could lose your sight, you could lose your life. I was swept into the hospital and stayed for about a month. I don't remember any of the treatment I got there and I don't remember being scared of dying. I do remember being terrorized by the fact that I was missing classes. I felt that I was losing out even before I had begun. To be away from school was a disease in itself. Despite the fact that I was prescribed strict bed rest, books were brought to me— I'm sure by my mother—and I studied hard every day.

When I finally returned to school and finished the year I won the modern prize and the classics prize for my class. I won them both every year I was at Boston Latin.

While I was absorbing Latin and Greek and history and literature, I also learned a set of values which I continue to hold to this day. The primary lesson I learned at Boston Latin was that life is rough, that tension is frequently crushing, and that the only hope that counts is the hope that lies within each individual. I learned that one cannot retreat and survive; no one who retreated at Boston Latin could have graduated. All that matters is the ability to work at your highest level in the face of unrelenting competition. Because, let's face it, the winners are going to be the people who are committed and competent, and you don't succeed unless you can deal with and overcome the fiercest competition.

I graduated with the highest grade point average in the three-hundred-year history of Boston Latin. At the graduation ceremony I received the modern prize, the classics prize, the Benjamin Franklin Award for being first in my class, the Boston Latin School Scholarship to Harvard University—I can't remember them all, but medal after medal. My years on the debating team paid off; I was also chosen the Class of 1940's Best Speaker. With my parents in the audience I was called to the podium again and again and again. They were beaming and I felt terrific. I had won. As first in my class I was accepted at Harvard before I took the college boards. For my mother, her life's dream was coming true.

During the summer between my senior year of high school and my first year at college, my father changed the family name. I was born Sumner Murray Rothstein. And as we moved from place to place, we had belonged to a temple in each community where we had settled. At the same time I was going to Boston Latin, I spent many days at Hebrew school learning the Talmud and I approached those studies the same way I approached all my studies: religiously. Like most Jewish kids my age I had been bar mitzvahed, and I remember the rabbi bringing people in from outside our schul to hear me speak Hebrew. We weren't practicing Orthodox Jews but we went to temple on the holidays and were properly observant.

So I was very surprised when my father told me our name was now Redstone. "It's a much better name," he said. "An easier name. It's what our name should have been translated to by my father when he came here. Other people did it." When his parents came over to America from Germany their name had been Rohtstein, which indeed translated literally to Redstone. But immigration officials, in their infinite wisdom, registered them as Rothstein and that had been our family's name ever since.

But Redstone sounded so solidly American, so ecumenical, so Christian. I thought my father was trying to walk away from our being Jewish. It was 1940, Nazi Germany was rolling through Europe, taking over countries and packing the concentration camps. These were very bad days for the Jews. My father never denied being Jewish but he denied changing his name to hide the fact. It's possible that he was trying to hide our German ancestry to protect us from harassment, but the name change was a source of real embarrassment to me. It troubled me a lot. I talked to my father about it but he wouldn't be dissuaded. It was at the same time that he changed his own name from Max to Michael.

I was Belle and Michael's boy and I did what I was told. I don't know how many Jews there were at Harvard in 1940, probably not many, but I entered as Sumner Redstone.

I was excited to study at America's highest-echelon institution, but compared to Boston Latin, Harvard was a terrific letdown. There was no feeling of daily individual competition, no sense of intensity, no battle of intellects. Boston Latin's classes had been small; our teachers had been personalities in their own right. Many of my Harvard classes were held in large lecture halls and taught by graduate instructors. The great men whose names graced the course catalog rarely presided, certainly not on the undergraduate level. I was disappointed; the rigor I expected from the educational world was nowhere present.

I took a combined classics and government major, and much of my political science study led me back to the Greeks. (In those days I could read Greek lyric poetry in the original Greek.) Boston Latin had given me considerable experience in French and German, but when I attended Harvard's German classes they were so low-key they held no interest for me. I skipped almost all of them. When I had to prepare for an exam, I studied the German dictionary for nearly two days, practically memorizing it. I don't know what I retained two weeks later but I got an A. No one seemed to care.

I began the semester living at home but soon moved to a dormitory in Harvard Yard. What a different world that was! I had rarely dated—I knew that any girl I took out would not be good enough for my mother—and all of a sudden I began to have a social life. However, it didn't take long for me to get into hot water. At noon on the day of a Harvard football game, someone saw a young woman, fully clothed, standing at my dorm room window and turned me in. In those days, women were not allowed in dorms without special permission. What a difference from today's world. I was not engaged in untoward behavior but I was nevertheless called into the dean's office and issued a reprimand. Not a severe reprimand but enough to chastise me. My social life, though not entirely moribund, was still not flourishing.

During the summers I worked for my father. From his success selling linoleum he had gotten into the restaurant business. With several partners who put up the money, he ultimately owned one Boston restaurant and two nightclubs: the Townhouse, the Mayfair and the Latin Quarter, respectively. He bought the Latin Quarter from Lou Walters. Lou's daughter, Barbara, would go on to considerable fame in the television world, and she and I have become friends.

My father also owned two drive-in theaters. Very early in drive-in history, he bought a piece of land in Valley Stream on Long Island's Sunrise Highway and built the first drive-in in New York and maybe the third in the world. This was in the mid-1930s, before the advent of individual speakers for each car. The movies' sound was broadcast over outdoor speakers and my father's company, Northeast Theater Corporation, got sued regularly for creating a nuisance. At the time, drive-ins were considered sex pits but they were, in fact, family entertainment. The places were packed, kids got in free and the grounds were loaded with them. I worked one summer selling hot dogs at the little shack of a refreshment stand at the Sunrise Drive-In. This was my introduction to the high-powered world of media and entertainment.

At Harvard I studied all the time. Rather than simply take the required courses, I took many extras. I must have impressed someone in a position of authority because I was asked to enter a very intensive class in Japanese taught by Professor Edwin Reischauer. There was a war going on in Europe and the Far East, and while the United States was not yet a participant the possibility of entrance into World War II was not lost on the powers that be.

This course was a revelation. Much to my pleasure the studies were intense, the training rigorous, the pace fast. While I had considerable experience studying languages, I knew no Japanese when I sat down in class the first day but by the end of the year I had loaded several years' information into one. Professor Reischauer motivated and prodded us to great heights. He would have been well within his element at Boston Latin.

My second year at Harvard I joined the Reserve Officers Training Corps. The Harvard ROTC was a horse-drawn artillery unit, which at the time meant riding around on horses, dragging guns behind us. I had just turned eighteen and only that year become eligible for the armed forces, but I didn't consider myself much of a soldier. I entered ROTC to enhance my social life. I must have thought I looked good in uniform.

But mostly all I did was study and in a little over two years, while I had not fulfilled Harvard's residency requirement, I had passed all the required courses and amassed enough credits to graduate.

At the end of the first semester of my junior year, early January 1943, Professor Reischauer left Harvard to enter the military. The attack on Pearl Harbor had brought us into the war. The Japanese were now the enemy and the United States needed heightened intelligence about their military and diplomatic operations. Professor Reischauer was selected by the army to create and supervise the language division of an elaborate cryptography/cryptanalysis operation, and he took two or three of his most advanced students with him. I was honored to be among those chosen. I left Harvard without a degree, volunteered for the army and was assigned to his unit. When I arrived for duty in Washington, D.C., I spent the first night bivouacked on the floor of a fire station at a girls' school. Within a year the Arlington Hall installation held 10,000 people.

Our mission was to break the high-level military and diplomatic Japanese codes which protected the military and political information being transmitted back and forth by the Japanese high command. These were not the codes used in battle; those routinely lasted only a day or two and were nothing by comparison. The codes we were mandated to break contained information concerning troop movements and military and diplomatic strategies at the very highest levels. People's lives all over the world were in the balance and clearly this was among the most critical wartime jobs, but our unit had to learn our craft from a standing start.

We needed to learn and then use the Japanese language in all its arcane forms, but no Japanese-Americans were permitted in this installation. The treatment of Japanese-Americans during World War II seems to me tragic and unfair because most of them must have been extremely loyal citizens. And my background at Boston Latin made any form of discrimination even more unacceptable to me. The absence of Japanese-Americans from our unit also hindered our work, leaving the language analysis in the hands of neophytes like me or American missionaries in Japan who had been repatriated when the war broke out. We were learning on the job, and the job could not have been more crucial.

The army brought in senior experts and young upstarts from all over the country. They brought in mathematicians and calculating machine experts. This was, of course, pre-computer. It was a wide-ranging community of extremely smart people all gathered for a common purpose. But while our work was needed immediately, we were not permitted to enter the secure areas of the installation for a period of several months. I and all the others who had been recruited to the unit were subjected to a very intensive FBI investigation. Almost everyone I knew was questioned, from people who lived in our apartment building to my teachers, my schoolmates, my friends. They were asked about my schooling, my girlfriends, my associates. I'm sure the FBI found all of that pretty mundane and I was cleared for work.

Much of our time was spent trying to familiarize ourselves with the Japanese language and culture. I continued my studies under Reischauer almost as if I were in the classroom, learning to speak and read with proficiency. In an attempt to learn how Japanese people actually spoke we watched commercial Japanese movies. The work was so intensive that at some point I knew the meaning of more Japanese characters than the average Japanese on the street.

I sat at a desk all day and read intercepted messages, trying to piece together patterns which we could then use in decoding. The messages were numerical, and ultimately we compiled a book of 10,000 individual numerical units, each containing four digits, no words. For the longest time we didn't know what even one of them meant. The work was gut-grindingly tedious but crucially important.

The Japanese thought that their high command codes had never been broken and they were so convinced that they were invulnerable that they made critical mistakes out of sheer hubris. For instance, when making changes in the coding system, they would transmit the new code in the old, which meant that if we had already busted one we had automatically busted the other. But for the longest time this hubris was justified; we were nowhere close to discovering the meaning of their codes.

Much of our decoding operation had to do with the frequency of use of several units. When "words"—numbers corresponding to Japanese characters—appeared with regularity we made a concerted effort to key on them, assuming they held special significance. One major breakthrough came when we first identified the code for the word *maru*, or "ship." From that one word we were able to begin to decipher the basic code, gaining entry to their complex communications system and ultimately beginning to track the progression of the Japanese war effort.

On rare occasions we came into possession of Japanese codebooks captured in battle. This was a bonanza. For the most part we busted the codes without these texts, but there were always holes in our information and the ability to study a functional codebook was critical. I stayed up for three days and three nights without sleep poring over one particular captured codebook, sifting and analyzing its information.

During those times when the Japanese changed their codes and we had not yet broken the new one, we would track their movements by other means. We knew from experience that if a message originated in one location, was sent to a second and then forwarded to a third, this progression had a meaning: The fleet was leaving its initial position, picking up protection from a particular air squadron and going toward a battleground. Although we did not know what specifically was contained in the messages, their paths told us their content. This means of intelligence gathering was called traffic analysis and I headed the Traffic Analysis Group. There were periods, while we were in the process of deciphering the new code, when this method alone produced extraordinary results. All the while, since we broke the high-level diplomatic codes, the Japanese ambassador to Germany became an important source of intelligence for the United States. In January 1944, basically all the Japanese army codebooks were captured in New Guinea, which totally transformed our success against their codes.

Only the Special Branch Military Intelligence unit and the White House staff had access to the information we were gathering. President Franklin D. Roosevelt himself also had access and it was exciting to read a decoded Japanese message, distill it and pass the results along to our military. We would send it by special messenger in a pouch. I remember reading a message detailing the position of part of the Japanese fleet and then several days later reading in the newspaper that our submarines had intercepted and sunk it. Reischauer's unit was directly involved in obtaining information which played a significant role in several major battles, including one in the Gulf of Leyte in which a large part of the Japanese fleet was essentially demolished. When the United States reinvaded the Philippines, I stood in a room with generals and colonels, reading them intercepted Japanese messages like the one that said, "The American troops are advancing on our position and we are destroying our codebooks!" It felt as if we were there.

With the exception of the development of the atomic bomb, the number one secret in the United States was the ability to break German and Japanese codes. Nevertheless, the *Chicago Tribune* published an article revealing America's advance knowledge of the Japanese planes at Midway. You would think that an American newspaper would know better, and the navy began a prosecution of the paper for violations of the Espionage Act. Prosecution was dropped when it became clear that testimony on code-breaking would be required in court.

But the Japanese, if they ever saw the article, must not have paid attention to it because their codes were not altered. They considered their codes invincible.

If it was not quite evident to me at the time, it certainly is clear to me now: Everything you do has an effect upon the rest of your life. Education had been emphasized in my home, I had studied Latin and Greek rigorously in high school, then plunged into Japanese in college, and ultimately my studies had brought me to an important moment in history. Breaking the Japanese code was one of the turning points of the war and I was proud to have made a small contribution to the effort.

Our band of mathematicians and language specialists, all enlisted men, couldn't go to officers' training school to obtain a commission because we couldn't be spared, but the army did set up an officers' board to evaluate us for promotion. To become an officer you had to score well on a number of criteria, and when I walked into my interview the first question I was asked was, "What is the weight of a 70-millimeter round of ammunition?" My Harvard ROTC training paid off; I had dragged those rounds around on horseback and I damn well knew how much they weighed!

High among the criteria we were expected to fulfill was the ability to lead troops. That is, after all, what an officer does. But my time was fully devoted to desk-bound pursuits, and although I'd have been perfectly happy to try it, the likelihood of my leading men into battle was extremely small. Nevertheless, there I was, twenty years old, and what was I doing? I was out on a drill field one day commanding a company of men. I must have truly screwed up because the whole company was falling apart and I only saved myself by screaming, *"WHAT ARE YOU GUYS DOING? ARE YOU STUPID? GET BACK IN LINE!"*

All of us in the cryptography program at Arlington Hall had to rate each other, and you had to come out with a pretty good rating or else you were gone. Some of my fellow specialists were prickly individuals, better suited to solitary studies than group dynamics, and many truly terrific people, wonderful technicians who were doing outstanding work, were rejected as officers. I was directly commissioned by the secretary of war as a second lieutenant and later promoted to first lieutenant.

After the war but before I could muster out of the army, I was transferred to Special Services and put in charge of bringing in entertainment for army hospitals. Because my father was in the nightclub business I had met a few performers on the rare occasions during college when I had visited the clubs, so it seemed a natural assignment. I made some contacts and suddenly for a while I was an expert on booking bands. Usually all I had to say was, "Look, we've got wounded men at this hospital. You've got to come and play!" I was able to get Benny Goodman and many others to donate their time. I was happy to receive an army commendation for this work and felt a nice sense of satisfaction from this brief interlude. More important were the commendations I received from the army's Military Intelligence Division.

Once I got out of the army, I did not have to return to Harvard. By a special vote of the Board of Overseers I was awarded my degree even though I lacked the residency requirements.

During the long periods when I was working at Arlington Hall on either the four-to-midnight or midnight-to-eight shift, I attended law school during the day at Georgetown. Why did I choose the law? Because the law is based on reason and justice, two ideals I hold dear. Reason is what held Boston Latin together; it is what holds my life together. I will follow one idea to the next and then the next to attain my goals. The law is based on neutral principles that are constant and not result-oriented. Courts that act in this way, legal scholars say, act with legitimacy. I admire that constancy, that legitimacy.

Justice is equally important. The concept of fairness was ingrained in me. The use of reason in the service of injustice is, to me, intolerable. Lawyers are given little respect these days, largely because they are often seen as smart but unscrupulous. But I have a very firm belief in the use of law in the service of justice. It is the way Americans are supposed to live.

Given this deep and abiding respect for the law itself, combined with my obsessive study habits and unyielding need to win, I was first in my class at Georgetown. The law school prerequisites of discipline and logic came naturally to me, and when I got out of the army I was accepted directly into the second year of Harvard Law School.

Harvard Law was not unlike Boston Latin. While my undergraduate years had been disappointing, law school was an inspiration. Harvard was revered as the best law school in America and here, finally, I found myself in the presence of greatness. I walked into Professor Paul Freund's class on conflicts of law, and while his course may have seemed at first dry and dull, all of a sudden I could hear brilliance. I could hear it! What enormous possession the man had, what great intellect.

I took a course in taxation from the eminent Dean Erwin Griswold and was challenged by him the entire year. But after the final exam when I talked to the other students, I found that nobody else's answer to the question was anything like mine. We were asked how a certain tax matter might be adjudicated and I thought that I must have failed miserably. Nevertheless, I had to visit Professor Griswold's office because I wanted to take a course in labor and public policy at Harvard Business School and needed his consent. I hoped his secretary would bring out the documents because I was too embarrassed to see him. To my great surprise Dean Griswold came into the outer office, stuck out his hand and congratulated me. It turned out that in my answer to the exam question I had practically written the dissenting opinion. I think he gave me the highest grade in the class.

I had the highest grade in several of my classes but not everything went smoothly, particularly when I took a course in constitutional law from a very famous professor who was also a well-known drunk. He gave me a D. A *D!* That was impossible! I couldn't get the kind of grades I had in all my other courses and get a D in constitutional law. I had already taken the subject at Georgetown and gotten an A+. I knew the material and there was simply no explanation for this abject humiliation.

I should have done something about it. It's not in my nature to sit back and accept defeat. I should have gone to the dean and complained. My work was good and I would have gotten attention, at least enough to have someone else read the exam. But I didn't. I had fought for everything I had, but I didn't fight for myself then. Why I do not know. Such passivity was completely out of character. I do know that the feeling of disappointment—first for the grade itself and second, and more disturbing, for my own failure to do anything about it—has stayed with me throughout my life.

I studied labor law under Archibald Cox. This was during the heyday of the labor movement and my working-class background had given me a strong empathy with the have-nots of the world, people who weren't born into wealth and had to work for everything. Labor law was a field for which I felt not only intellectual excitement but also emotion. I received the highest grade in my class in labor law.

I graduated from Harvard Law School in 1947 among the top students in my class. The D in constitutional law eliminated whatever chance I had of being number one. It galls me to this day.

With the war over, as a veteran I was entitled to what was called veteran's preference in purchasing army surplus goods. I bought large quantities of screwdrivers, pots and pans and the like, and while I was still in law school I went from site to site in my broken-down $200 Plymouth, peddling them to Boston stores. I was a successful salesman and by the time I had my law degree I also had saved about $15,000.

I had met a lovely young woman named Phyllis Raphael at a temple dance in Brookline, Massachusetts, when I was a freshman at Harvard. She took me to her prom and we dated for several years. By the time I had graduated from Harvard Law School and was about to take the bar exam, it was clear we were going to get married. I said, "Look, you can have a choice. We can get married a week before I take the bar and then you can go home. After the exam we'll have a honeymoon and go out to California. Or we can wait to get married until after the exam." Phyllis didn't like the idea of going back to her parents' house after we were married. So I took the exam, we got married a few days later, then drove up to Niagara Falls and across country in that broken-down Plymouth.

When I got out of law school I was offered jobs at several major Wall Street firms as well as a teaching position at the University of Chicago Law School. However, I was not interested in either making a lot of money or limiting myself to academics; the postwar world was going in a million different directions and I wanted to make a difference. In those days a clerkship was the best law job you could get—for total immersion in the law there was no experience like it—and I was very pleased, with the help of my good friend and mentor Archibald Cox, to obtain a clerkship at the Ninth Circuit Court of Appeals in San Francisco under Judge William Orr. At the same time, also as a result of my association with Cox, I was offered a teaching position at the University of San Francisco Law School. This was perfect. My new wife and I moved to San Francisco, where I clerked during the day and taught labor law at night.

My years of clerkship were extremely exciting. Judge Orr was a pleasant man who gave me great leeway and allowed me to write first drafts of many of his opinions. Several of the cases he adjudicated were of major importance. I also had a continuing correspondence with Cox, who was very helpful to me in analyzing and understanding the world of labor law.

Sitting in San Francisco, the court was presented with all kinds of writs from prisoners at Alcatraz. Having nothing but time on their hands they would study the law and file petitions for habeas corpus on the grounds that they were unlawfully incarcerated. Most of the prison writs I read had no merit. While these jailhouse lawyers were often earnest and almost literally held their lives in their hands when they submitted their papers, their work product was rarely substantive enough to warrant more than a moment's consideration.

However, some of these men turned out to be very good lawyers. One, an inmate who had been convicted of armed robbery and had been in prison for twenty years, presented a compelling case. In his papers he complained that he had been deprived of counsel. He and a co-defendant had been indicted and tried together even though their stories were totally in conflict. The same attorney represented both men.

As I read this man's legal brief I realized, first, that he was presenting an issue that had not previously been acted upon—there was a live legal issue in play—and second, that this long-term prison inmate was absolutely right. By combining his case with his co-defendant's and trying two different men with two different stories under the same circumstances without separate representation, the state had indeed deprived him of counsel. "There's no question," I told Judge Orr, "this guy gets out!" The judge agreed and allowed me to write the first draft of this opinion.

What excitement in the court. We had informed the district attorney that the prisoner was going to walk and he told us he would not object. After twenty years this man was going to be freed. He had been denied counsel, a basic American right under the law. Now the law had set him free. My faith in the law had never been stronger.

Another case I remember well involved a Jewish teacher who had applied for American citizenship. In his application the man had presented a wide variety of character references testifying to his solidity, probity and good name. The government, in opposing the application, had countered by introducing evidence that the applicant had criticized the capitalist system. He was quoted as saying that while the rich were getting richer, the poor didn't have shoes. The government produced an affidavit claiming that someone had heard the Communist anthem, "The Internationale," sung at this man's house. He had been denied citizenship and the case came before the court of appeals.

I argued with Judge Orr long and hard on the man's behalf. The Constitution of the United States was being violated. The man's character references were outstanding, he had never been convicted of a crime, and there was nothing to justify the denial of citizenship except suspicions about his political beliefs. There was nothing in the Constitution that protected the capitalist system from criticism. To me it was clear: The basis for denial was totally wrong under our Constitution.

Judge Orr did not necessarily disagree with my argument on the point of law, but I could not get him to dissent. It was the beginning of McCarthyism and this was a relatively conservative court which Judge Orr simply could not influence. He just didn't have the guts to stand up and write a dissenting opinion, *which I was prepared to write.* It was an argument I did not win. The court decided to affirm the denial of citizenship.

After a year with Judge Orr, I applied and was accepted for a job in the United States Department of Justice as a special assistant to Attorney General Thomas Clark. This was one of the great experiences of my life. Working out of Washington, D.C., I traveled all over the country arguing cases for the government in the U.S. courts of appeals. Over the course of five years I must have argued fifty or sixty cases. In a lifetime, no lawyer in private practice has such an extensive opportunity, but I was avid to do the job. And my bosses seemed to like me, so I got many plum assignments.

I was a kid in my twenties just out of law school and I was arguing tax cases involving hundreds of millions of dollars, many of which concerned interesting and significant legal issues. For instance, I was handed a case in which a lawyer had guaranteed that his client would meet a certain obligation. When the lawyer did indeed pay the client's obligation, he then sought to deduct it as an "ordinary and necessary" business expense. The deduction was allowed by the district court but the government decided this was bad law and appealed. I argued the case in the United States Court of Appeals for the First Circuit, which is in Boston, my hometown.

The other side's position was that in the normal course of practicing law an assumption of financial obligation for a client can happen. Therefore, it can be considered a business expense. I argued in the negative, that the lawyer's guarantee was neither ordinary nor necessary, that he had undertaken the obligation of his own volition and the government should not be obligated to share the bill with him in the form of a tax write-off. The actual legal issue was simple. Under the tax code, one can deduct only "ordinary and necessary" expenditures. Was it either ordinary or necessary that a lawyer guarantee his client's obligations? The government obviously thought not.

I won the case and it is law today. But I also got a lot of flak—intense correspondence from several of my old Harvard Law professors, including Dean Griswold. Here I was only a couple of years out of law school and I was actually having a peer-to-peer practitioner's dialogue with these eminent scholars. In commenting on the case, as lawyers they had a natural empathy not with the government but with the attorney I had opposed. Dean Griswold wrote and criticized my role in the case, saying, "Well, Sumner, you won the case but it is bad law." I respectfully disagreed.

I won seventeen consecutive tax cases and the eighteenth was heard by the Ninth Circuit Court of Appeals in San Francisco, my old court. I had left as a law clerk and here, within a few months' time, I was back arguing a case for the government. I felt as if I'd gone from boy to man. I presented my case forcefully and with confidence. I was on a winning streak. I couldn't lose.

The case was decided by my judge, Judge Orr—and he found against me. He was wrong and I told him so. It didn't do me any good.

I was sitting in my office at the Department of Justice one day when I was told that the solicitor general wanted to chat with me. I went to his office.

"You were with the Ninth Circuit Court during a case involving the denial of citizenship to a teacher?" He mentioned the name of the case.

"For criticizing capitalism," I said. "Sure."

"What can you tell me about it?"

I told him the story.

"Well," he said, "we are going into court and admit error and ask for a reversal."

The Supreme Court has within its discretion to grant or not to grant an appeal from the lower court. In order to obtain such an appeal, the petitioner has to file what is called a petition for certiorari, which the teacher had done. These petitions are granted only when the Supreme Court not only agrees with the merits of the petitioner but also considers the issue to be extremely important, which is rare. In this case, the government had reviewed the issues and found it had been wrong.

I was astounded! This simply didn't happen. Imagine what the teacher must have felt. He probably thought he was never going to become a citizen when the circuit court ruled against him. Then all of a sudden the United States government—the same government he had been criticizing—said, "We're going to confess error and ask for a reversal." The law did work!

Judge Orr wrote me a letter when he heard about the reversal. "What a mistake I made," he said. "Why didn't I listen to you?"

I spent five years with the Department of Justice. The high stakes appealed to my sense of competition and reward, I was intellectually stimulated every day and I was working to capacity, just the way I liked it.

————————

In 1950, Deputy United States Attorney General Payton Ford, the head of the Department of Justice antitrust division, Herbert Bergson, and his assistant, Herbert Borkland, left to form a law firm. They invited a general practitioner named Bert Adams to join them. These were all senior guys. I was an ambitious young lawyer at Justice in whom they had taken an interest, and they invited me to join Ford Bergson Adams & Borkland as an associate. A year later they made me a partner in Ford Bergson Adams Borkland & Redstone.

Because its partners had a wide range of Justice Department contacts, the firm represented some very prestigious clients, ranging from the Minnesota Mining and Manufacturing Company to Lehman Brothers. We represented Paramount Pictures in its merger with ABC. Herb Bergson brought in enormous amounts of antitrust work and as junior partner I did the lion's share of it. Just from the number of hours involved, I went from being a tax attorney to quite a proficient antitrust lawyer.

My most important case came through a Midwestern congressman. He was representing two innkeepers, a husband and wife, friends of his who had been indicted and convicted of tax evasion largely on the basis of what is known as net worth evidence. Essentially, the government tells the taxpayer, "Your net worth has risen substantially. You had $50 in 1955, you have $500,000 in 1956, and you never reported it. You owe us taxes on this increase." Their conviction had been affirmed, which meant that the only possibility for reexamination of the case was to file a petition of certiorari before the Supreme Court.

However, this avenue did not look promising. A large number of petitions based on the use of net worth had already been filed, all of which the Supreme Court had rejected. I told my partners and the congressman, "Look, the odds are so bad against this case, we really shouldn't get involved."

"These people are really good friends of mine," the congressman replied. "They are good people. You have to do it. You really have to do it." I took the case. I had no illusions. This was a good payday for the law firm with no real possibility of victory. In Washington, D.C., you do this sort of thing for a congressman.

But that kind of case held no joy for me. I didn't want to do anyone a favor by taking the case and I wasn't concentrating on the firm's financial bottom line; I wanted to win. Still, I had no choice. I went to work. And as I started to immerse myself and study the details, a line of attack became clear.

The innkeepers had been asked where they had gotten all this newfound money and they had no real answer. But tax evasion is a criminal matter, and in a criminal case the burden of proof is on the government. To the extent that the government was saying to these people, "You tell us where you got the money," it was *reversing the burden of proof in a criminal case.* Here was a new legal strategy, one that had never been argued before. Rather than defend my clients' actions, I was putting the government on trial for its misuse of the law. I had an original concept and I worked on my certiorari petition feverishly. Lo and behold, the Supreme Court agreed to hear the case.

That was already a major victory. Almost all certioraris are turned down. Even if the Court thinks you are right, it can deny a petition because it doesn't think your issue is important enough for consideration. The very granting of our petition, even though it gave us no indication of how the law was going to be interpreted, was a big event. It meant our arguments were novel and sound and possibly determinative.

I was going to argue in front of the Supreme Court!

I walked into the Supreme Court building on the day of oral arguments feeling some degree of awe, some trepidation, but also quite a lot of self-confidence. I had argued tens of cases in the courts of appeals and I knew my material cold. Still, I was very excited by the opportunity to argue the law in the most important court in America.

The United States government was represented by the solicitor general, who had been my boss at the Department of Justice. The two Midwestern innkeepers were represented by me. I looked to my right and sensed the overwhelming power of government on the other side of the table arrayed against me, but I was not deterred.

I stood to speak and looked up at the bench. It was majestic. There in their robes were Chief Justice Earl Warren, Justices William O. Douglas, Felix Frankfurter, Thomas Clark, Harold Burton, Hugo Black, Sherman Minton, Stanley Reed and John Marshall Harlan. This was a formidable court. If I had allowed myself a moment to consider the awesomeness of this court and the sitting justices, I might have paused, but once I began to speak all nervousness was gone.

In the Supreme Court you don't get up and make a speech as if you're talking to a group of investors. The justices can interrupt you at any time, making you aware of your place because you are being hammered with questions. And from the start it seemed we were getting the better of the government. While I do not remember their colloquies verbatim, I do recall that Chief Justice Warren and Justices Frankfurter and Black were all over the issues, questioning the government strongly, asking essentially: "Isn't it a fact that you are reversing the burden of proof in a criminal case? This is a tax case. It is also a criminal case. The plaintiffs' arguments have not been made previously, there may be no precedent, but what of the issues in this case? When you come to a taxpayer and say, 'Tell us where you got the money or you are guilty of tax evasion. Why didn't you report it?' are you not reversing the burden of proof? What is your response?"

The justices were arguing my case for me! And as I listened, during the course of the argument the government began to back off its position. Government lawyers never admitted error, but they were getting mauled and they had no legitimate answers. The government was indeed putting the burden of proof on the defendants in a criminal trial. The law was on our side.

We won. The case was not reversed, however. The Court felt there was sufficient independent evidence other than net worth to support a conviction. Still representing the innkeepers, we cut a deal and they never went to prison. But a precedent had been established and had to be enforced. In fact, there had been three other previously denied net worth petitions presented to the Court that session by people already in prison. Most lawyers, including me, didn't know that after such a denial, the Supreme Court had the power to reopen a case if it was on the docket during that same session. Based on my petition for certiorari, many people ultimately were released from prison, including these three.

All of a sudden I was a famous tax attorney. The firm had more than enough business for me to handle and I spent several years thereafter trying major cases for major clients and developing our practice.

Sometime after the Supreme Court decision I found myself in Las Vegas representing a group that was building the Dunes Hotel and met a man who was working at the Flamingo. This was the mid-1950s, when the Las Vegas Strip was controlled by characters who didn't often show up in corporate boardrooms. "What do you do for a living?" the man asked me. I said I was a tax lawyer.

"You know," he told me, "something extraordinary happened. My brother was in Alcatraz and he just got out because of some case in the Supreme Court."

"What's your brother's name?" I asked. He was one of the three prisoners who had been released because of the ruling in my case. I told the man the story. And the next day I was sitting in the Flamingo Hotel at a meeting presided over by one Benjamin "Bugsy" Siegel.

Overnight, the men who ran the Flamingo had summoned their attorneys from one of the most eminent firms in San Francisco to meet with me. I knew this firm; it had argued cases before Judge Orr when I was a clerk in the court of appeals in San Francisco.

Notwithstanding who they were, Bugsy and his guys maintained an air of respectability. Las Vegas was pretty strict about appearances and you couldn't operate there without the patina of legitimacy. Bugsy himself seemed very smooth, no rough edges. I didn't hear anything that sounded like my impression of a mobster. He and everyone else conducted themselves as businessmen with an issue to discuss.

They wanted me to represent them. Their net worth was skyrocketing, for obvious reasons, and they needed someone to handle their legal work before the courts the same way I had defended the innkeepers. My expertise and their difficulties, in their eyes, dovetailed perfectly.

They offered me anything. Everything. All kinds of money—over the table, under the table, any way I wanted it.

I wasn't tempted. Money wasn't my vice and I saw my life in a very different way. I thought, What am I doing here? I told them how I viewed the law and what the issues of the case were, then I said, "Look, I'll give you my legal briefs, I'll help you as a lawyer in any way I can, but I don't want to get paid for it. I like what I'm doing. I want to practice law."

About a year later Bugsy Siegel was found in his girlfriend's house in Beverly Hills with five bullets in his head. The Flamingo carried on. His net worth was never clearly established.

T H R E E

NATIONAL
AMUSEMENTS

I *was making a ton of money* at my firm only six or seven years out of law school—about $100,000 in 1954, which is a lot more than $1 million today—but after a while my heart wasn't in it. A lot of kids who went to law school after the war graduated with the idealistic notion that as lawyers they might make some kind of contribution to society. This was particularly true of those of us who worked for the government. But during my term as a law clerk, then in the Department of Justice and finally at Ford Bergson, what became apparent was one of the realities of the profession: When you're practicing law it's just a business. It's not a crusade for humanity, it's a business. And when I reached that conclusion, I decided I was going to go into business for myself.

What better place to start than with my father? I left Ford Bergson and joined my father's company, Northeast Theater Corporation. My father was surprised. He was not a risk-taker. "You know I want the best for you," he said. "Why would you leave such an arrangement with your law firm and come to work for Northeast?" My initial annual salary at the company would be $5,000. I told him, "Dad, if I'm going to be in business, I want to be on my own. I want to play a role in building the company." While my father was happy we would be working together, he was not at all certain I was making the right decision. But all I saw was opportunity.

My father had become reasonably successful running nightclubs. Stars like Jerry Lewis and Dean Martin used to get paid $5,000 to $10,000 for a week's appearance, which made it feasible for a club to make a lot of money. (The reason there are no more Latin Quarter–style nightclubs is that you cannot hire the equivalent modern-day performers for equivalent prices. The talent priced itself out of the circuit and the circuit simply died.) My father was in the entertainment industry and he took a step forward, using his nightclub money and some from investors to buy land and build several drive-in theaters, which became even more successful.

My father, much to his credit, had the foresight to buy the land on which the theaters were built. He then went through the process of getting that land zoned for commercial use. When I was working at Ford Bergson in Washington, he was trying to build a drive-in in Fairfax County, Arlington, Virginia. I represented our company at the zoning hearing.

This was no easy task. Fairfax County didn't want these sex pits in its backyard and several other entrepreneurs before me had failed to get the necessary zoning. I would not be deterred. I sat in Fairfax County kitchens and explained to the neighbors why a drive-in was really family entertainment, that the other possible uses of the land would be far worse than a drive-in. There was a church across the street from the site and I convinced the minister to testify as a witness—for us. We got the approval.

My father bought a plot of land in Newark, New Jersey, and ran into all kinds of problems getting the permits to build a drive-in theater there. Why? The authorities were convinced that people driving on the New Jersey Turnpike would spot the screen, crane their necks to see the movie, and the state would have to contend with a continuing stream of pileups. A very practical concern. I finally got the permits, but the night that drive-in opened there were ambulances parked up and down the road just waiting for action. The only action that road saw was a steady stream of business.

One might think that the glamour of the motion picture industry had some effect on my decision to join my father. The entertainment business is exciting and fast-moving, and as a college student I had met some of the talent at my father's nightclubs, which I enjoyed. But I've never been a stargazer; to me it was a business.

My younger brother, Edward, was already working at Northeast. When I came on board, Edward handled the general operations and I handled both expansion and the film companies. The key to our business was our relationship with those film companies. We were a very small operation, a handful of drive-ins, not a factor at all. But dealing with film companies was the most exciting aspect of the drive-in business, whereas my brother felt that his job was more mundane. In fact, he did his job very well, but very quickly my father turned over the basic operation of the business to me. To my sorrow, this caused some tension between Edward and me, which was understandable, but my father clearly wanted me to run the company and be his successor. So essentially I took over.

In later years Edward came to me and said he wanted to leave our company and go into banking. I urged him to stay. I sat with my brother at a California hotel and pleaded with him. "Eddie, don't leave. You have everything to gain by staying. You want to go into the banking business? Start doing that while you are at our company. It will provide you with a base of operations." We were discussing, not arguing, but Edward said, "No, Sumner, if you wanted to leave I would help you, I would make it easy for you. I want you to do the same for me." He did go into banking and became very successful. And at some point along the way, his interest in Northeast was bought out by the company.

In the intervening years, stories have surfaced indicating that I eased my brother out of the business. It has always grieved me to see such stories since nothing could be further from the truth. I did everything in my power to prevail upon my brother to stay. Today, Eddie and his wife, Madeline, are my close friends. Eddie's son, my nephew Michael, was a difficult child and for many years was estranged from his parents. I had a lot to do with bringing Michael up, literally forcing him to go to college and then to get a business degree. Today Michael is a likable and productive employee of National Amusements. He is doing a great job and his parents and I are all proud him.

As soon as I arrived at Northeast, we started to expand our operations. First, we explored new territories. I scouted the locations myself. Forget real estate agents. I would get in a car and drive around looking for good potential sites. I always carried a pro forma contract in my jacket pocket in which I could fill in the price and description of the land, if we wanted to buy it. I had to act quickly because as we grew more successful, if it became known that we were interested in a particular location, all our competitors would flock there as well.

For instance, I flew into Louisville, Kentucky, drove around, saw several potential sites and finally found twenty acres of land at the intersection of two highways that would be perfect. I wanted to buy it. So I found out who owned the land, visited them, called in a secretary and a notary, modified the contract form as necessary and left with the deal. We called it the Kenwood Drive-In. Done. I did the same thing in Cincinnati. How did I know these were good sites? I just knew it! I operated as my own lawyer. Having handled the zoning for several of my father's theaters, I knew the deals had to be conditioned on getting planning and zoning permits. But you didn't have to be a zoning lawyer; you just had to know what you were doing.

We built a chain of between forty and fifty drive-in theaters. Pacific Theaters were the West Coast leaders; we were the industry leaders in the East. As we moved inland and opened drive-ins in Ohio, Virginia, Kentucky, Iowa, Illinois and Michigan, we changed our name to National Amusements, Inc. We were drive-ins, small potatoes compared to the indoor theater chains like Loews, RKO and Paramount. Still, we kept building more theaters.

Whatever cash flow National Amusements had we used for expansion. We borrowed very little and tried to stay out of debt, but eventually we needed financing. With plans to build a drive-in in Maryland and to expand the company further, I went to the Bank of New England and asked for $10 million, which was a huge amount of money for us at the time. The chief lending officer was a man by the name of Everett Smith. Mr. Smith came to our offices to turn us down personally, but he stayed to listen. We sat and talked for several hours, not only about our loan but also about trends and possibilities in the entertainment industry in general. A couple of days later he called back. "Could you come down and talk to all of our executives and tell them your view of the motion picture industry?" I went without question.

I gave them my pitch. We were a great growth opportunity. In the 1950s and early '60s the production end of the movie industry was growing faster than the exhibition end and there were more movies than places to show them. Demand was up and supply was racing to fill it. If you lived in the suburbs and wanted to see a movie, there were no luxurious theaters to go to. Combine that with the suburban car culture and you had thousands of movie fans driving to our theaters. With our scouting and expansion we were going into cities and areas that were absolutely dead and creating new markets. Notwithstanding the mosquitoes, cold, heat and rain, we were often the only game in town. As tiny an industry as the drive-ins were, we had the locations.

Then there were our specific economics. National, I told the bankers, would not be profligate in the way we handled their money. We also were growing our company in significantly different ways from our competitors. While others were building theaters in shopping centers, where someone else was responsible for the development and planning of the area and might not respond to their particular needs, we were buying and building on our own land. We controlled our environment.

What began as a request for a $10 million loan became the grant of a $50 million line of credit.

From the very beginning I was in the office at 6 a.m., getting the grosses from the night before. I had to be on top of the figures if I was going to be on top of the business. From then on, all day long, I was negotiating. My entire focus was on what movies we played, when we played them, what we paid for them, and where we were able to develop new theaters. I was on the phone with the movie studios' general managers, trying to get the best movies at the best prices. Barry Reardon at Warner Bros., Frank Mancuso, then the branch manager in Buffalo for Paramount, Jimmy Spitz at Columbia—these were the important people in my life. It was my job to convince these guys that we were on the cutting edge of the future of motion picture exhibition, and that we needed their help.

Nothing was easy. We were a small company trying to find our way in a world surrounded by much larger corporations that had more screens and therefore more clout. If we had the hot movie in Toledo we were making money; if our competition had it they were making the money and we weren't. We had a relatively small number of screens so we just didn't count with the film companies. We had to fight for the best pictures we could get for every location. We had a lot of merit on our side—good locations, good screens, good volume, a good business—but it was hard work to convince these people to license their films to us, particularly at a price somewhat lower than they might get elsewhere.

It was a tough, adversarial business but I found that making a deal turned not only on the merit of my arguments but also on the development of personal relationships with the men I dealt with daily. One major decision I made and held to consistently was that I didn't lie to them. I'm not saying other exhibitors did, only that National Amusements developed a reputation for credibility. If we made an agreement, we didn't need to put it in writing; it was bankable. My relationship with the movie studios was also based on admiration and respect. I found that to be a particularly valuable life lesson.

Which is not to say we didn't do a lot of screaming. That was part of the business too. "Look, Barry, stop giving me this! You know we're entitled to this movie in Cincinnati!" Today it may not seem important who played *Love Story* in Providence, Rhode Island, but we went through wild arguments to get it. We had the best theaters, I told the studios, and that's the only thing that should count. I told Wayne Lewellen at Paramount, "Wayne, you can't give that picture to General Cinema just because they're a bigger customer. We have to have that picture! We are entitled to it based on the merits." I had conversations like that on a picture-by-picture basis all day and part of the night. I often visited the studios in New York and Los Angeles, and whether it was from a general sales manager or anyone else, I would not accept no for an answer. As far as I was concerned I was making eminent sense, all my arguments had merit, and I topped them off with my obsessive desire to win. I treated every picture as life or death.

I didn't always get what I wanted but I never gave up. I'd have dinner with a general manager, we'd talk business, then I'd call him at home that night. "Listen, I forgot to mention . . ." I was relentless.

Frequently, sooner or later, I would win him over. "We'll give that picture to you in Cincinnati," he'd finally tell me. I suppose that was a victory. We were getting the picture. "But we're giving it to someone else in Louisville," he would add. "Equal allocation."

"No!" I wasn't interested in equal allocation. Why should I be? My competitors were in every city. We were the little guys, but I wasn't satisfied until I got everything I wanted. We were building a circuit, plowing the money we made straight back into the business, buying more land, building more theaters. We were not going to let somebody else take the important pictures away from us. It would undermine our entire organization, which made the loss of any important movie catastrophic.

And I must say I enjoyed the fight. There were times when I felt enough is enough, but not enough to disengage. This was a battlefield and I was going to win the war.

The war went on for twenty years.

One of the major problems we faced was that the larger companies were routinely offered first crack at the best pictures. They had the bulk of the locations, highly concentrated in the major population areas. All we had was a string of theaters. But we did excellent business, we made money for the studios by aggressive marketing and by putting the best possible theaters in the best possible locations. Still, despite our constant requests, the studios routinely refused to give us first-run movies. As a result we were prevented from making the kind of money a first-run hit generates.

I went to all the studios and pleaded my case. Their actions were totally unfair, I told them; they restrained trade, they would make as much money, if not more, if they gave the films to us for exhibition; their actions were outright discrimination against smaller exhibitors in favor of the major national chains.

All the studios turned me down. They refused to negotiate, refused to change the way they had been doing business for decades. They had a system that worked for them and they had no interest in seeing it change. I tried consistently for a long time to get the studios to give me product but they simply refused to budge. The sides were drawn, the issues were clear. Either we accepted the fact that we were going to be relegated to last-run status, with all the financial disadvantages that entailed, or we could fight to change the system.

In 1958 we filed a lawsuit.

This was dangerous. We were suing our suppliers, the people from whom we made our livelihood. We surely didn't want to make them angry with us. But faced with the prospect of a lifetime of unfair treatment, there was no other way to go. I had no choice but to sue.

Of course, I was aware that former assistant attorney general Herbert Bergson, one of the senior partners in my former law firm Ford Bergson et al., had several years earlier brought a climactic case, *United States* v. *Paramount,* against Paramount Pictures and a large number of other distributors. That case ended in a decree being entered against the studios which enjoined them from discriminating and held that they had to sell their product, picture by picture, theater by theater, without discrimination in favor of a circuit or otherwise. However, a decree is not a law, and although the court's decision represented basic commercial law, you cannot base a legal case on violation of a decree. The only body that can enforce a decree is the federal government. What I had was a wonderful decree but, on its face, unusable by a third party. How could I get that decree in front of a jury?

I came up with a concept I thought would work. While the exhibitors and distributors had restrained our trade, more importantly what they had done was to act in concert. We filed suit against Warner Bros., Loews, Twentieth Century–Fox, Columbia Pictures, United Artists, Universal, RKO and Paramount, alleging, among other things, a conspiracy to restrain trade and a conspiracy to violate the decree. We were, in fact, charging them with a broad conspiracy to exclude us from access to first-run films in a given area, in this case suburban Virginia.

Paramount et al. argued, as I had assumed they would, that the decree was not enforceable by anyone but the U.S. government and was not admissible. They moved that it should be excluded from the case. We held to our position. They were shocked when their motion was denied. My interpretation of the law held, and after several months of depositions and discovery we went to court and succeeded in putting the decree, which dealt with facts very similar to those in our own case, before a jury.

Our lead attorney was a local lawyer named John Caskey. He argued the case before a Fairfax County jury of his fellow Virginians, hands in his pockets like a father talking to family. He wasn't talking up or down to them; he was one of them, and about as sophisticated a lawyer as I had ever seen. His easy manner was a revelation; he didn't need bombast or bluster to win his points, only warmth and logic. I learned from watching him and I was impressed.

We argued that we were entitled to play day and day with the first-run theaters, a huge leap for a drive-in—usually we were given new movies only at the end of their runs—and that the defendants' actions had collectively prevented us from doing so. Caskey was doing so well that before the case went to the jury it was settled. We received essentially everything we sued for.

This was a giant victory for a little company, putting us on an even plane with the major circuits. It also continued my faith in the law as a place of resolution. The law is based on reason and justice; the studios' actions were discriminatory, unfair and unjust. We had a case to make and we made it.

I don't like to litigate. In fact, I hate it. I would rather handle disagreements through discussion and accommodation. But if that fails, and it often does, litigation is an appropriate tool. The world should understand that if anyone deals with you in an inappropriate manner he is going to get an aggressive response. I've never filed frivolous litigation and I would not want people to think I use litigation every time I fail to gain a business advantage. But I do want people to know that if they treat me unfairly, they are going to face the battle of their lives!

———————

By the early 1960s, the drive-in theater business had begun to change. The suburbs were growing rapidly and the indoor movie theater owners were expanding with them, building luxurious, state-of-the-art theaters for their increasing clientele. The economy was good, there was a lot of leisure time for entertainment to fill and a lot of money to pay for it. Competition for moviegoers grew fierce. Equally as important, as suburban land prices escalated, drive-in theater operations could not support the underlying value. Indoor theaters could generally put two, three or even six screens where a drive-in could put only one. Drive-in theater operators were being driven out of business by the carload. Drive-ins became like the horse and buggy, and as a force in the industry, their rationale for existence began to disappear.

We, at that time, had no indoor theaters but we were making money and I could see where the business was headed. In 1962, I sat at a lunch counter in Worcester, Massachusetts, with a guy who owned a little run-down local inner-city indoor theater and made a deal. We bought the Worcester theater for nothing because it was worth nothing. Then we went to work. We divided it into two screens, modernized it, and opened Cinema 1 and 2 with *Lawrence of Arabia*. We had a hit on our hands. Now we were indoor theater owners.

National's early decision to buy the land underneath our theaters and build on it turned out to be one of the major decisions of my life. The socioeconomic changes in suburban life actually increased our net worth and offered National not a career-ending crisis but a vast opportunity. We could build indoor theaters on our own land, and we had a lot of it.

As we converted drive-ins to indoor theaters, we increased our revenues and profits. We were then beginning to play five movies at a site where we had previously played only one. As important as it was to have more screens, it was even more important to me to have superior theaters. People want to be treated well and our customers were our primary concern. Some exhibitors in the theater industry built bandboxes they could walk away from, but that's the difference between owning the property and leasing. We were not going to walk away, so we built our theaters right, maintained them properly and developed a circuit with not only quality but also longevity. If we weren't the only game in town, we wanted to be the best game in town. Our theaters were well appointed, we were buying the pictures well, the business was growing.

We owned the Whitestone Drive-In, located in the South Bronx. Despite the fact that it was sitting in not exactly the best area of New York City, it was a very successful theater and we were knocking around the idea of building a major multi-screen theater on the site. I caucused the people who worked at important positions at National and they all thought it was a terrible idea. Too dangerous, too daunting for that many moviegoers to get to. "Eight votes 'no,' one 'yes,'" I said. "Mine is the one that counts and I'm saying 'yes'!" I rarely do this. I believed at National, and I believe at Viacom, in a team approach to both issues and opportunities. But it was and is my job to lead, and on those occasions when I am convinced I am right, I am prepared to override the consensus and make the critical decision. In this case I was convinced that we had a great location, and if we were making the film companies money, there was no way they would deny us their pictures. So we built it and the theater became a powerhouse. One of our competitors said, "Our circuit builds destroyers but National builds battleships!"

In order to attract a wide audience, if we had six screens at a location, we often played seven or eight pictures on them. We would mix up the times, run kids' films in the early afternoon and wider audience releases at night—any way to put the most people in the seats and maximize our revenues. The film companies really didn't like that at all; we were cutting down on the average number of showings of a given picture. However, we felt that although it might cost an individual picture some revenue, the total revenue reported to the film companies would be significantly larger.

The film companies, of course, monitored all local theater advertising. The newspapers run a directory of the films playing in the area and we listed our new theater as a sixplex. After the second week of our playing seven or eight pictures there, the film companies began to complain—loudly. I was sitting in my office one day trying to think of a word for a theater that showed more pictures than the number of screens without any specifics. The word "plex" was in the lexicon and I worked with that. I didn't want to say "eightplex" or "nineplex"—that would only get me in hot water again.

Then it came to me. "Multiplex!" I jotted the word down and said it out loud. That's what we had, a multiplex. Thus was born the Sunrise Multiplex.

Now, could we copyright the word? Trademark it? We hired lawyers and yes, it turned out, we could. National Amusements now owns the trademark to the word "multiplex." Although it has become common worldwide, when you see the word "multiplex" attached to a theater in the United States, it belongs to National Amusements.

We spent all of our time trying to attract people to our theaters and we used all of our ingenuity to get them there. We wanted people to think of us first. Movie theater listings are usually alphabetical, so if we knew we were going to open in Westchester County, New York, we didn't call it the Westchester Theater, which would be lost down at the bottom of the page. We came up with the All-Westchester Theater, which sat proudly at the top. We didn't want to be the Newark Theater for a number of reasons. So we opened as the All-Jersey.

The people at National were like a small family, working hard at the store every day. Booking, operations, site locations, construction, advertising, publicity—we were small enough for all of us to be involved in every phase of the business, and everyone was able to participate intelligently.

We would have booking meetings at 6 a.m. Fridays and Mondays to decide what was going to play in each theater. I'd already have seen the previous night's grosses. We would go over every picture in every theater in our entire chain, and every day was another adventure in getting product. I'd grill the bookers. "What's available in Toledo? What've you got in Lansing?" Drive-ins had their own list of legendary hits. "Let's play *Sisters Wedding Night* and *Chastity*. What about a double bill of *Eager Beavers* and *Student Nurses*? We'll bring that back." I wanted to know what pictures would draw in what theaters, I would agonize over second features, and the people around the table agonized with me.

I guess I wasn't the easiest person to get along with. "Let me see the ad schedules. What's on the radio? Let me see the ads." I didn't mean to be, but I was pretty tough on these guys whom I loved—Jerry Magner, Bill Towey, Lou Winer, Alex Castaldi, Sam Feldman, and later Eddie Knudson, George Levitt, Jeff Aldrich and others. They'd say, "He doesn't even have to be around to be around." But once they had earned my trust, I gave them a lot of room. They were the backbone of the company. All of us supported each other. We had affection for each other. We had confidence in each other's competence. That's the way it was at National.

I was chain-smoking cigars in those days and it wouldn't take long before I'd have a huge ashtray overflowing in front of me. As well as doing business at our meetings, I'd get to talking, just sort of digress into stories about our early days, and one morning as I was rhapsodizing, I unwrapped a new cigar and casually tossed the cellophane into the ashtray. There were about eight or ten of us crowded around a conference table in our small office. The way the guys tell it, the cellophane first smoked and smoldered and then caught fire, the flames shooting a foot straight up in the air. They just looked at each other. I didn't notice, I wasn't paying attention, I was telling a story. But they wouldn't interrupt—not one of them had the nerve to tell me I'd started an inferno. When I noticed the flames I jumped.

"What the hell's the matter with you guys?"

They all keeled over laughing, and this is now part of National Amusements family lore.

Because weekdays were filled with daily operations, we formed the practice of getting together on Saturday mornings to review the broader issues, set our goals and discuss what we should do to achieve them. Friday night was a big moviegoing night, so the figures that came in early Saturday morning were particularly important. Everyone was willing, no one balked at spending Saturday mornings doing business; it was part of the way our company grew. We were building a circuit.

We had started with a handful of screens and simply kept expanding. It went on that way for twenty years.

In the early 1960s, President John F. Kennedy invited about a hundred executives in the hotel, theater, restaurant and retail chain fields to a meeting in the Blue Room of the White House. I had become president of the Theatre Owners of America, then the major trade association in our industry, and was honored to attend. As a Bostonian, I was, of course, familiar with Kennedy, had contributed to his campaigns and admired his politics from the time he was a freshman congressman. He was about seven years older than I was and it would be quite an understatement to say he was a dynamic presence.

As it turned out, one of my bunkmates at Arlington Hall, where we were cracking the Japanese codes, was a fellow named Bay Manning. Bay went on to clerk for a Supreme Court judge and rose to the position of dean of Stanford University Law School. Another of my bunkmates had been named head of the civil rights division at the Department of Justice. He was also at the meeting and it was nice to see him again after so many years.

When we arrived, we were treated to an extremely forceful discussion of President Kennedy's position on civil rights. Each of us in the room, the president said, was in a unique and powerful position to effect real change in America. The South was in the midst of an upheaval, with lunch-counter sit-ins and protest marches and Freedom Rides turning daily life into a series of character-defining moments. Public accommodations were a major staging ground for civil rights demonstrations. Whites-only drinking fountains and rest rooms, colored sections in theaters, hotel room restrictions and stores where "we don't serve your kind" were symbols of segregation. Each person in that room owned or operated not just one but a series of establishments. We had it in our power, by simply declaring the facilities under our personal control to be desegregated, to move America forward. President Kennedy discussed the bills he was proposing to send to Congress which would bar racial discrimination in restaurants, theaters, hotels and other such establishments. He, his brother Attorney General Robert Kennedy and Vice President Lyndon Johnson all spoke to us, making it very clear that they felt action needed to be taken immediately, within a matter of days, to address this explosive issue. Then the president elicited our opinions.

I am no rabble-rouser. From my early days I have considered myself a liberal Democrat. The values I held then and the values I hold now are the ones I learned at home and at Boston Latin School: What counts is fairness and competence. Not race, not color, not gender. Competence. I returned from that meeting and made a significant attempt to enlist the support of theater operators all over the country in the civil rights effort. If access to hotel rooms and rest rooms and seating in restaurants and theaters could be opened to all races, I considered that a step in the right direction, and I was pleased to be in a position to make that gesture. Not everyone in that room that day agreed with me.

———————

There was only one reason I went to a Theatre Owners of America convention in Florida in the early '60s: to have a vacation. I had never attended a meeting of this trade association, I wasn't active in it and was, at best, peripherally involved. But when I got there I found myself a niche. We theater owners were being addressed by representatives of, of all things, the cable television industry. Cable was then in its infancy and they were telling the assembled theater operators that this new technology, capable of bringing films directly into the American home, would be good for the exhibition business. I listened to the presentation and was surprised that the heads of the big circuits—circuits like Loews and RKO—said nothing, voiced no objection.

Were the cable companies kidding? I approached the podium. "You know," I told the meeting, "if these people want to compete with us, fine. But don't insult our intelligence by telling us it's good for us." Cable was not the friend of exhibition; I could see from the outset that it was a direct competitor that would encourage potential moviegoers to stay home, eat popcorn and watch movies on the couch instead of in our theaters. "Your intelligence is being denigrated by these people," I warned the convention, "who are convincing you to go on a path of self-destruction!" I spoke extemporaneously but passionately.

That afternoon several of the major theater chain owners approached me. They didn't know who I was, I was a nobody with a small string of drive-ins and a couple of small indoor theaters, but they liked the way I had presented my case and they said, "We'd like you to become active in our organization." At the next meeting I was elected assistant to the president and within two years I was running the show.

As president of the TOA I had prominence but no economic clout. I didn't own enough theaters to be of any financial significance, but I was in a position to wield a lot of political influence. Although the TOA represented primarily the interests of the larger chains and the Allied States Association, another theater owners trade group, represented mainly those of the local operators, I quickly moved to forge an alliance between the two on the theory that a unified voice would speak more forcefully for our common interests. Discussions about creating such an organization had been going on within the industry for decades and it took several more years before we could come to an agreeable conclusion. But finally on January 1, 1966, we merged to form a new organization, the National Association of Theatre Owners (NATO—our own peacekeeping organization), which would speak with a single voice for the exhibitors who earned over 80 percent of film rentals in the United States. I was elected chairman of the board.

The first major issue NATO tackled was the process by which film exhibitors were forced to select and pay for the pictures they showed. This process was called blind bidding, as oppressive an operating system as had ever been seen in American business.

Put simply, blind bidding was the major motion picture studios' practice of compelling exhibitors to bid against each other in competitive situations on the studios' new releases, and to guarantee to show these films for extended amounts of time for given amounts of money, *without permitting exhibitors a chance to see them.* Paramount, Universal, Twentieth Century–Fox, all of them would tell us months in advance that their pictures were coming out. But they refused to screen them for us, insisting instead that each exhibitor bid on each movie sight unseen, often before the movie was even completed.

Whether it was *Love Story* or *Daktari, Bullitt* or *Shalako,* we had to commit our theaters, our advertising budgets and large amounts of guaranteed capital to these films without knowing whether they were any good, without really knowing if we stood a chance of recouping our investments, let alone making money. Had *West Side Story* or *Funny Girl* translated well from stage to screen? Was *Candy* a stiff? Which was the killer movie, *Coogan's Bluff* or *The Brotherhood?* We couldn't tell because we couldn't see them. Some films, because of their star or story, would be accompanied by huge hype, but would that help or hinder a movie? Would people flock to it opening weekend and then stay home in droves?

It's hard enough to make those predictions even when you've seen a picture—if the studios knew which movies were guaranteed hits, there would never be a flop—but we wouldn't know until after it opened, by which time it would be too late. We were going in blind! What investor would put his money in a product he'd never seen, based only on reports from the people who are selling it to him? As far as I could tell, the only industry in America being asked to do this was motion picture exhibition. You could lose a year's profit by bidding hundreds of thousands of dollars on a picture you thought was going to be good and have it turn out to be a disaster.

Of course the studios dismissed our objections out of hand. First they said, "It's our product, we can do what we want with it. You don't have to bid." Then they told us that because of production schedules they couldn't have the pictures ready in time to show us. Then they argued that exhibitors could get an early look at product by placing representatives at various sneak previews. But these arguments were all a smoke screen; they had a good thing going and they were of no mind to change it.

This was a gigantic issue. The forces of the studios were lined up against the forces of exhibition, and we exhibitors felt that our lives were at stake. We waged an extremely tough, adversarial battle over the course of many years, and as the head of the major trade association of our industry, I was at the forefront. We went from state to state lobbying lawmakers about the evils of blind bidding, explaining in detail why it was unfair and should be barred. Not bid? Each exhibitor depended on having access to top-quality movies, that was the way we made our living, and not to participate in the bidding process would simply mean that you were putting yourself out of business. No time? The studios were the ones who picked the release dates; they could build in as much lead time as they liked.

I argued in state legislature after state legislature, looking for laws to bar this practice. "If General Motors makes a car," I would testify, "they don't sell it until they put it in the showroom and you can see it. In this case, exhibitors are being called upon to take enormous risk; we're being forced not just to buy this car but to bid against each other without even seeing it. Name me one other place in the whole world where this kind of practice exists. We don't know what we're buying. Sometimes this car isn't even built yet."

I led that charge, and one by one, a large number of states began to outlaw blind bidding. Still, the industry persisted in this practice. At the same time we were lobbying against it, we met with the studios and negotiated a stipulation which would limit the number of pictures each would blind bid to three per company per year. Better, but not good enough. You could still very easily lose your shirt.

In 1965 we at the National Association of Theatre Owners interested the United States Justice Department in our cause and it held hearings. We were ultimately able to bring the matter before a federal court. The exhibitors asked me to present the case and I argued that blind bidding was a form of discrimination, since there were always some exhibitors who would know more about a motion picture than others. The more powerful the circuit, the more access it had to important information, putting it at a competitive advantage over the little guy. The fact that we had been reduced to the employment of every artifice and design to obtain the so-called coveted picture, most often when we didn't even know what it was and sometimes before it had even been produced, was a symptom of the real disease.

The studios, I argued, weren't making enough movies. Construction of new theaters had been the most healthy and exciting development in the motion picture industry of recent times, but construction of new theaters when the supply of motion pictures was inadequate to supply even the existing theaters would mean disaster, not only for exhibitors but ultimately for distributors.

But were the studios receptive? No. Was the government? Not very.

We could not get the federal government to move further, so we continued to work the states. By 1968, three years later, we finally appeared before Judge Edmund L. Palmieri, U.S. District Court in New York City, and filed a memorandum in connection with blind bidding and the 1965 stipulation. Rather than hire an outside attorney, NATO asked me to argue the case myself. I stood before the judge and said, "The turmoil and confusion brought about by blind bidding has in no sense been ameliorated [in the past three years], but has, on the contrary, attained a status of almost utter chaos. . . . It sometimes appears that an exhibitor's very existence depends upon his ability to correctly evaluate and then obtain by the competitive process the one, two, or three blockbuster pictures of the year."

The three variances per studio under the 1965 stipulation, I said, "may represent a small percentage of a company's total production, [but] it is very rare that an individual distributor has more than three blockbuster commercial productions in any given year. . . . The fact is that three or four important peak periods now exist in the motion picture industry—namely, the summer, Christmas, and to some extent Thanksgiving and Easter." Each company could therefore continue to blind bid its most important seasonal picture and still wreak havoc on exhibitors.

Shockingly, the court was unmoved. Judge Palmieri signed the stipulation and expressed his hope that it could be extended at the end of its two-year trial period. He said it would not be "wise" for the court to hold formal hearings on the subject because they would place a heavy burden on the Justice Department's time. Can you imagine? Rather than inconvenience the department and the court, Judge Palmieri let stand what our newsletter, *NATO News,* called a "legal hybrid of dubious character. It is not a decree nor an amendment to existing decrees; it provides no machinery, either for enforcement or for continuation; and no penalties." Apparently, as regards blind bidding, justice preferred being blind.

A year later, both *Newsweek* and *The Wall Street Journal* were writing about the economic decline of Hollywood. "Four to six studios," said *Newsweek*, "[were] responsible for 65 to 70 percent of all business in serious trouble." I told a NATO convention, "Wall Streeters are just catching on to what we have known for a long time—our business is run like a crap table. . . . Let's stop rolling the dice on every property—on every book and on every star. . . . Quality, not stardom, is the secret of motion picture success."

As one means of combating blind bidding, exhibitors had developed a practice called product splitting. Essentially, we met and agreed among ourselves that some exhibition companies would play, let's say, only Paramount, United Artists and Fox pictures while others would play only movies distributed by Warner Bros., Disney and Columbia. In this manner at least the competitors bidding blind against each other would be limited; it wouldn't be a constant free-for-all. On its face, this practice seemed like a clear violation of the antitrust laws. However, it had actually been encouraged by the Department of Justice as a way to allocate product fairly so that everyone had a shot at success. The film companies acquiesced and the practice had been going on for decades.

Then all of a sudden the Justice Department started cracking down. I don't know whether the impetus came from the studios, which did not appreciate our challenging them over blind bidding, but the government began to attack product splitting. I met with Justice Department representatives and told them, "This is a disaster! You are telling exhibitors they can't make arrangements by themselves, even if the film companies acquiesce? Who's being hurt? The consumer isn't being hurt. The studios whose product we are bidding on aren't being hurt." In fact, the studios were not complaining about the product splitting practice. We dug through our files and found previous government positions which supported us.

Nonetheless, the Justice Department persisted in an extremely inflammatory way to attack product splitting on antitrust grounds. It filed an aggressive lawsuit against an exhibitor—and won. With all the serious problems that plagued the United States in the late 1960s and early

'70s, one has to wonder about the Justice Department's involvement with a trade practice that had been accepted for as long as anyone could remember. Still, it started to impanel grand jurors all over the country, essentially for the purpose of indicting exhibitors.

A grand jury was impaneled in Massachusetts and began to subpoena exhibitors and their employees. Many of my industry friends and competitors were incensed and defiant. They decided to continue splitting product and wait for the court of appeals to reverse the decision. I disagreed, and thank God. As a lawyer, I saw the merits of the government's case; product splitting did violate antitrust laws, even though I thought it was an outrage, considering history, for the Justice Department to pursue it so aggressively. I got National's people together and told them, "From now on you will have nothing to do with our competition. I don't even want you to have social meetings." These were our friends, people in the industry whom I and my people had been having drinks with for years, if not decades. I said, "I know it's difficult, but I'm asking you to have nothing to do with anyone from General Cinema or any other competitor. You understand this?" I put it all in writing, hundreds of pages of notes and memoranda.

The Justice Department subpoenaed all our records, we shipped them literally tons of material, and sooner or later one of my guys was called to testify. He was sitting in front of a grand jury and was asked, "When was the last time you had a meeting with General Cinema relating to film?"

He replied, in effect, "I don't understand your question. Don't you know that we in our company were instructed not only not to discuss business of any kind with our competitors but not even to have lunch with them?"

The prosecutor was astounded. The government was probably about to indict me. When I heard what took place, I contacted our lawyer and said, "Do me a favor, will you? I can't believe these people got the material we sent them and still asked questions of this kind." It certainly looked as if National Amusements, if not I personally, would be indicted. "You have to be wrong, Sumner," the lawyer told me. "We sent it to them."

"Do me a favor. Just call them."

It turned out that the lawyer handling the case for the government had in his desk an unopened folder containing hundreds of pages of our material *which he had never looked at.* So much at stake—my company's reputation, our livelihood, jail time—and he hadn't even opened his mail. The paper trail led directly to our innocence, and that was the end of the U.S. government's investigation of National Amusements, but it was a hairy experience.

Several people in the exhibition industry were indicted. But their indictments were ultimately thrown out, and when the government did not prevail the issue disappeared from the scene.

My personal relations with the film companies were quite good, but this was an extremely adversarial time. The studios wanted to vacate even the ineffectual anti-blind-bidding decree; we opposed it. Even though we exhibitors brought in outside counsel, I participated personally throughout the battle and was continually involved in dealing with industry issues and the studios. I was at the Department of Justice much more often than I wanted to be. Yet blind bidding refused to die. We made the best of a bad situation, and despite the disadvantage at which blind bidding put us, National Amusements continued to make money.

For many years we had had a series of problems with Disney, which we felt was discriminating against us. The people who ran that company had fed us a string of turkeys, including *The Last Flight of Noah's Ark, Herbie Goes Bananas, Unidentified Flying Oddball* and *Tron,* and they were unrelenting in their demands for high advances. In 1979, in particular, they demanded that we bid blind and guarantee them the enormous sum of $427,500 for their film *The Black Hole.* They told us it was going to be bigger than *Star Wars.* They knew better and the movie stiffed. We were a little company, we couldn't afford to lose $400,000 based solely on their word. That was the last straw. In 1981, almost fifteen years after my days of testifying before the Justice Department, National Amusements sued Buena Vista Distribution Company, Inc., which is Disney, for treble damages, lawyers' fees and an end to the practice of blind bidding entirely.

In our complaint, we named Columbia Pictures, Universal, United Artists, Paramount, Twentieth Century–Fox and Warner Bros. as co-conspirators. We accused them all of participating in a "combination, conspiracy, unlawful agreement and understanding to engage in an illegal system of 'blind bidding.' " If we had sued one film company for unilateral action, we wouldn't have had a case. But with Disney as the point man we essentially sued the entire industry.

We alleged four purposes of the conspiracy:

- to maintain high rentals for the film companies;
- to eliminate competition among themselves;
- to restrain and prevent exhibitors from competing based upon the free exercise of our own judgment;
- to prevent and discourage new and independent film distributors from competing against them.

Over the years the film companies had come up with some new excuses for their behavior. One was the "Everybody's doing it" defense. No film company could unilaterally stop blind bidding, they held, essentially, because "Well, I'd be happy to give it up, but the others are all doing it and if I wait until my picture is ready to be screened, they'll get their pictures sold earlier and freeze me off the circuits." That was a straw man. They each could claim competitive disadvantage if they alone didn't engage in blind bidding, protected in the knowledge that all of their competitors would back them up: "We'd screw them in a second if we could. Definitely." But not one major distributor had made a single attempt to change the way the business was operated. In fact, notwithstanding their professed individual aversion to the practice, all had joined together in a concerted effort to oppose any action on the part of exhibitors to end it.

We asked for a jury trial—trial by moviegoers. Let the public decide whether they wanted good movies or not.

Our basic premise was that the requirement of equal information among buyers and sellers is essential to the workings of the competitive marketplace. Blind bidding, I held, seemed to be an anomaly in a system which is based upon open competition and free choice. In fact, it flew in the face of that system. Under the practice, we told the court, a distributor of a film had materially superior information concerning that film which was withheld from exhibitors at the time the film was licensed. Disney had told us and had distributed press kits claiming that *The Black Hole* was a sophisticated $20-million dramatic epic whose story line, special effects and acting performances would exceed those of *Star Wars,* and that the film would surpass "the mind's conception of even the most extraordinary of science-fiction extravaganzas." When the picture came out, it was panned ferociously by the critics on all levels. Moviegoers agreed by staying home. In our action we claimed that Disney "exceeded the boundaries of permissible 'puffing,'" that its misrepresentations were so wantonly reckless and grossly inaccurate when compared to the actual film that they amounted to an intentional fraud perpetrated to separate us from our money.

Disney and its co-conspirators constituted an oligopoly, and blind bidding was their rule of law. While we did not have the smoking gun of a signed agreement between the film distributors, we had documents subpoenaed from the Motion Picture Producers Association showing meetings between producers and studio representatives at which they together discussed the blind bidding practice, we averred, "with frequency and regularity in close proximity to each other."

As well as increasing prices, the practice of blind bidding most of the first-run product also freed the major distributors from the necessity of having their films compete on the merits. Instead of our viewing one picture after another and making informed judgments on their profit potential, we were, in effect, forced to pay substantial sums of money for bad films. This, we argued, decreased the incentive for competitive productions of quality films throughout the entire industry. Not only did this practice cost us money, it also deprived the public of superior pictures. That argument was somewhat of a stretch, but not entirely. And because it had great implications for the general public, we included it.

We developed another interesting concept. Because small, independent distributors don't have track records or reputations to assure exhibitors that their pictures will be either of sufficiently high quality or delivered on time—the criteria on which exhibitors always base their bids and make their rental decisions—they have to finish their films and screen them before those films can be licensed. They can't get away with what a United Artists or a Disney can get away with. Meanwhile, by the time these pictures are ready for release, the most desirable play dates have already been booked with films that were bid blind. Small, independent distributors, we argued, are harmed or even disenfranchised and the public again suffers.

All of these forces combined to create an asymmetry of information in the marketplace. The major distributors, we claimed, didn't disseminate information; they intentionally suppressed it. The entire industry had adopted blind bidding not only with great rapidity, but almost simultaneously. This was not a situation of mutual dependence recognized; on the contrary, it was a situation of a previously reached but implicit or explicit understanding. This was the conspiracy we were alleging. And because the pictures crossed state lines, the distributors' transgressions affected interstate commerce, making this a federal antitrust case.

Why did National and not another exhibitor institute this litigation? I just felt the practice of blind bidding was unfair. It was a disgrace, it harmed us, and we shouldn't have to live with it. I didn't want to sue Disney, that was the last thing I wanted to do. I wanted to do business with Disney! But Disney's executives had cost us hundreds of thousands of dollars on this one picture, their behavior on others was so consistently egregious, and their position was so indefensible that it was worth suing the company.

Plus, forget the legalities, it was a totally immoral practice—unprecedented in our entire economy. And the film distributors had gotten away with it because, even if they didn't talk to each other about specific pictures, they were a tight oligopoly, all depending on each other to make it work. It was an ideal test case.

The complaint was filed, material subpoenaed, depositions taken. Jack Valenti, now one of my best friends, and the Motion Picture Producers Association, of which he was president, filed an amicus curiae brief on behalf of the studios. But this was a case with serious damage and policy implications for the entire industry, and we were going all out to win.

While the charges were pending, Disney underwent a management change. Replacing the old regime, with whom I'd had very tendentious relations, were longtime friends Frank Wells and Michael Eisner and several members of the Disney family with whom I also had a very friendly relationship. In fact, years earlier, Wells had approached me to join with him in launching a bid to take control of Disney. I don't know where he thought we were going to get the wherewithal to do it, but we had this history together.

I was now in a rather difficult position. I had a meritorious case but suddenly found the defendants, instead of being hostile adversaries, to be my friends. I used to argue with Wells, "What do you want me to do with this, Frank? I didn't tell you to go buy the company!"

Ultimately, we settled the case. Disney changed the manner in which it did business, no longer demanding huge advances for loser movies, and there was a management in place whom I could trust. This had been a private case; I had not sued on behalf of the entire film exhibitors' industry, and I made the settlement privately. I didn't let Disney off the hook, but I decided not to take any profit personally. In fact,

I was never even compensated for the legal fees we incurred, but Disney, as part of the settlement, agreed to make a very substantial contribution to Mass General Hospital.

The exhibitors continued to fight blind bidding in the courts, in the state legislatures and in the public press, and ultimately justice won out and blind bidding disappeared from the scene.

As a derivation of the word "grandpa," my grandchildren call me "Grumpy." Many years later, at a banquet in my honor at which Frank Wells was the toastmaster, he accused me of violating the copyright laws by infringing on a Disney character. It was a joke. So sue me.

When Frank Wells died in a helicopter crash in 1994, it was an enormous tragedy and a great loss—a loss to his friends, like me; a loss to our industry, where he had been one of its preeminent leaders and statesmen; and an even greater loss to Disney and Michael Eisner. Indeed, had Wells not died, the bitter confrontation between Eisner and Jeffrey Katzenberg probably would never have occurred, since the battle had its origins in the issue of succession.

FOUR

STICK TO WHAT
YOU KNOW

For twenty years I went about my business. And it was a good business. National Amusements grew and did well. I plowed our profits back into the company, expanding, buying more land, building more theaters.

As head of NATO I did a lot of public speaking. I've always enjoyed that. I was often the keynote speaker at industry events, my training before the bar being put to good use, and I was the ritual presenter of any number of industry awards, which put me in contact with many of Hollywood's leading stars. But even when my father was running nightclubs in Boston, I never spent a lot of time hanging out with celebrities; their deals were more interesting to me. As I grew older I had more opportunities to mix in their company but I rarely took advantage of them. It was not something I would do for self-aggrandizement, and hobnobbing with movie stars really didn't relate to what I did for my company.

However, on the occasions that I did find myself in the company of some celebrities, the experience was kind of exhilarating. I was in my thirties when I presented Angie Dickinson with the exhibitors' award for Most Exciting New Star of 1963. Newspaper photographs showed me poker-faced and Ms. Dickinson, her hair swept up in a stylish bouffant, looking positively radiant. I was presenting a Best Actress award to Julie Andrews when I found myself onstage with Jerry Lewis, Dean

Martin, Gregory Peck and John Wayne. And Wayne was stone drunk. Staggering. The tension was amazing—such a major star so inebriated in front of so many industry people. I was impressed when Lewis adroitly and gracefully, in a very affectionate way, got him off the stage.

Perhaps the most memorable of the functions I attended was a convention organized by the trade newspaper *Variety* at the British Royal Naval Academy. I was invited to represent my country and give an address. My co-speaker was Lord Mountbatten. It was a huge gathering. The dining room was elegant—carved wood and silver service. My wife sat at the table as Lord Mountbatten's dinner partner, which was a great honor. Then the evening started with a battery of trumpets. It was something out of the Knights of the Round Table. And as each course was served, the trumpets sounded once again. Appetizer. *Trumpets!* Salad. *Trumpets!* Entree. *Trumpets!* Sorbet. *Trumpets!* I had never experienced anything like it in my life. It was an event of pomp and splendor.

Lord Mountbatten addressed the convention. He welcomed us to Great Britain and spoke at length about the variety of relationships between his country and ours, including the entertainment business. He was quite eloquent. Then it was my turn to respond on behalf of America. This was not something I could have prepared for. I had no prior knowledge of what he was going to say. With my country's good name and my own reputation on the line, I spoke extemporaneously and apparently I did well, since from then on I was in greater demand for speaking engagements. I was too busy running National to accept many of those requests, but I gained some prominence representing my industry.

In the mid-1960s the motion picture business was under heavy attack from many forces because of what they felt was inappropriate content. The Catholic Legion of Decency, conservative congressmen and other so-called guardians of public morals were arguing loudly that America was going straight to hell because of what people were seeing at the movies. The industry was under fire just as it is today, being blamed by the politicians and others for all of the nation's moral ills. I had recently become head of the exhibitors' organization and Jack Valenti, whom I had met when he was in the Kennedy White House, had just left the Lyndon Johnson administration to lead the Motion Picture Producers Association, and between us we recognized that something had to be done.

There were several avenues of action to consider. At one extreme, based on the First Amendment protection of free speech, we could argue that censorship was a blight on an open society and we could fight for the industry's right to make and distribute any picture it chose. At the other extreme, we could cave in to the demands of these self-appointed guardians of decency and submit all pictures to a government-run or privately controlled board of censors. Valenti and I met in my room at New York's Plaza Hotel and thought it out.

Clearly, we weren't going to put control of the content of the motion picture industry in either government or outsiders' hands. That way lay tyranny. I suppose we could have tried to weather the storm based on First Amendment grounds—the purists' position—but that wasn't the issue. The issue was to take the heat off the motion picture industry and at the same time come up with some form of self-regulation our critics would accept so we could all go back to making a living. Sitting in my hotel room, Jack and I agreed that it would be better to adopt a system of *self*-regulation than to leave ourselves vulnerable to public policy attacks, litigation and congressional inquiry. Ideally, we didn't need or want anyone supervising the content of our industry. Pragmatically, better us supervising it than them.

We would create a code. The industry itself would rate each film, give the public a sense of the general range of the picture and keep children under a certain age out of movies that might be inappropriate for them. Rather than cede the responsibility to others, we would take it on ourselves. This offered the added benefit of having the motion picture industry respond to a perceived problem directly, a proactive example of our public involvement rather than a passive exercise in public humiliation. By the time Jack and I finished our meeting that afternoon, we had come up with the basic code concept, even down to the categories to be used, which ultimately was institutionalized as the Motion Picture Rating System.

Jack Valenti was also instrumental in getting me interested in electoral politics. A Democratic partisan, he was intimately involved in the presidential campaign of Maine senator Edward Muskie, who had been Hubert Humphrey's running mate in the losing 1968 presidential race against Richard Nixon and was the front-runner for the 1972 Democratic nomination. Gene Picker of United Artists was also heavily involved as a chairman of the Muskie campaign, and between them they arranged an introduction.

I was aware of Senator Muskie's politics, which I supported. He also had a reputation for absolute honesty and integrity, which when I met the man I sensed was well justified. I liked him immediately. He had a direct way about him. "Senator," I said, "I'm glad to help but I don't know anything about campaigning."

"That's good," he told me. "That's what I need."

I learned quickly that politicians have a tough job. A large portion of their time is spent not formulating and discussing policy but raising money. They are constantly criticized for it, but you can't run a campaign without capital. I attended meeting after meeting where the basic purpose was to source funds. The senator would never ask for it directly, of course, but he would speak and the invited guests would be encouraged to give large donations to the campaign. Candidates have to tell prospective donors that they really want to hear their views on the issues, but the bottom line was the donation. I supported Muskie's basic view of the world; I wasn't so arrogant as to tell him how to run it. When I was asked I said, "Come on, Senator. You're interested in money. You don't need my views."

I began by running some fund-raising affairs in Massachusetts. At the Pine Brook Country Club in Weston, first I spoke, then the senator spoke, and if we raised $50,000 that was a lot. But the functions were successful and after a short time I was asked to become national co-chairman of the Muskie for President campaign. I accepted the post.

As national co-chairman I found sympathetic and enthusiastic audiences for the senator to address, I arranged events and got him exposure. I put my contacts in the motion picture industry to good use and we were off and running. We raised a lot of money and positioned the senator in the spotlight.

However, this was Dick Nixon we were running against. We arrived at one very substantial fund-raising dinner in Ohio to find no one there. Why? "You canceled it." Of course we hadn't. Nixon's "dirty tricks" squad had been working in overdrive and had sabotaged us.

I don't mean to suggest that I had absolutely no impact on the intellectual side of the campaign. I did spend time with the senator. One day, we sat together on the porch of my home in Newton, Massachusetts, and discussed why he wanted to be president. I'd never had the opportunity to speak with a man who might actually become President of the United States about why he wanted the job. Muskie talked in general terms about the issues. He had a bona fide sense that he could make a positive contribution to America, and he told me some of the specifics. Then he leaned back in his chair. He was a tall man and his legs stretched across the floor of the porch. "Sumner," he said, "when I get off a plane in some foreign country and I see the way I'm treated, it gives me such a great feeling. I like the sense of power."

Muskie impressed me by being so honest! Politicians always talk about contribution and service. Here was a man straightforward enough to say what he meant. I thought that demonstrated great character and I trusted him even more.

Senator Muskie and I also had some very heated discussions. I liked the man, he was strongly motivated, but he tended to waffle. This was 1972, the war in Vietnam was still being fought, abortion was among several significant issues facing the country and *Roe* v. *Wade* was before the Supreme Court. But rather than come out and take forthright positions on these issues, Muskie was talking around them.

I said, "Here's the point, Senator." I did not stand on ceremony in our discussions. Muskie encouraged comment from the people around him and I obliged. "The people will vote for a person even if they disagree with him on some issues. What the people want is a great leader. You can be wrong in people's minds on an issue but if they see you as a forthright, aggressive leader who believes in what he says, they'll vote for you for president." At one staff meeting when I pressed Senator Muskie in this way, his staff actually broke out into applause. The senator seemed about ready to take that advice to heart.

During the campaign Senator Ted Kennedy frequently called to compliment me on the job I was doing for Muskie. I just as frequently said, "Fine, Senator, but how about endorsing him? How about giving us your people to work for him?" That never quite happened.

Apparently some people had noticed my involvement in the Muskie campaign and thought I knew something about politics because a short time later I was invited to a small meeting of seven or eight business executives, at which I first met Senator Kennedy. We were all sitting around talking and everyone was lauding him when I said simply, "Look, I don't want to disagree with everybody, but Senator, the problem is that you believe—or these people believe—that you can solve any problem by just throwing money at it. It doesn't work that way."

Conversation ceased, glances were exchanged. Everyone was appalled. Then Senator Kennedy said, "Sumner's right." He was clearly a man who relished an exchange of ideas, not one who insisted upon being agreed with. I think we appreciated that trait in each other. After that, Senator Kennedy called me regularly when he came to Boston and we developed a lasting friendship.

The Muskie campaign was flourishing. He was running strongly in Massachusetts and looked like the man to beat. Then came his downfall. During the New Hampshire primary Senator Muskie spoke emotionally in a driving snowstorm about William Loeb, the extremely right-wing publisher of the *Manchester Union Leader,* and the next day all the papers said he had been crying. Supposedly the senator's wife's reputation had been attacked in Loeb's paper and Muskie had responded by bursting into tears.

Presidential candidates simply do not cry. It's not seen as strong, as manly, as presidential. In 1972 a man really couldn't cry in public and run for president. That sort of behavior disqualified him. Muskie's campaign effectively ended that day.

I had dinner in Boston with the senator the very next night. "What were you doing?" I asked. "You got so caught up in all this stuff about your wife that you started crying?" It didn't make any sense.

"No, Sumner," he said, "honest to God, I wasn't crying. There were snowflakes on my face." I believe that was true, but no one in the press believed it. Nixon's dirty tricks squad, aided and abetted by the press, spread the story like gale-force winds and Muskie was blown away. When people were polled after the primary, the single biggest reason given for voting against him was "emotional instability." This strong, upright, honorable man was simply undone. Incredibly, he lost on the issue of character.

To Richard Nixon!

I had no respect for Nixon. I had disliked him from his days running a smear campaign for Congress against Helen Gahagan Douglas. I usually voted Democratic on the issues, although I would vote for a person from any party if I thought he or she was the better candidate. But Nixon was a man totally lacking in character. My efforts on Senator Muskie's behalf apparently landed me on Nixon's notorious "enemies list." I took that as a badge of honor. And, of course, it was character that ultimately brought Richard Nixon down.

In the 1970s and into the '80s, National Amusements' growth began to slow. From year to year, despite the fact that we were continuing to find good locations and build state-of-the-art theaters, the same number of people went to the movies and across the country, from decade to decade, sales of movie tickets did not increase significantly. Exhibitors' income increased as we raised admission and concession prices but there was no bona fide growth in motion picture exhibition. *"Motion picture exhibition is not a growth business,"* I often said to the press, and was accused by my competitors—unfairly, I might add—of downing the industry while we continued to build. I was just stating the facts. Circuits like ours built multiple-screen theaters, and while we thrived, everyone with one or two screens went out of business. The industry was consolidating.

National was finally making some money; what we needed now was a way to grow the company.

Cable television was beginning to change the entertainment landscape. I believed strongly that cable's new technology was a tremendous threat to motion picture exhibition. I saw *content* as the growth industry. With a growing number of free and pay channels to choose from, the people who had been our customers were increasingly staying home. But they were still watching movies.

What did we know? Movies. National Amusements began investing in motion picture companies. We made substantial investments in Warner Communications, Disney, Loews and, ultimately, Fox and Columbia. This strategy was no secret; it seems, in retrospect, to have been very obvious, but we were the only ones who were pursuing it.

It was part of an investment strategy that I have always followed: Stick to what you know. Many investors are counseled to diversify, to take positions in a wide variety of areas of the market. I think people should invest in what they know most about, rather than spreading their money around. This requires both an active mind and a great deal of self-confidence, which you will need to sustain you in difficult times. I don't do anything unless I have confidence that I can do it well. Of course, there are times, no matter how much you think you know what you're doing, when things go wrong. This may be the result of your own mistakes or of circumstances entirely outside your control. But you must have confidence that you will ultimately prevail, which will help you mentally and psychologically to get the job done. If you start to lose confidence in your ability, you had better quit.

In those days, there was almost a direct correlation between the success of individual films and the success of the film studios that released them. Unlike today, when most studios are only one part of large multimedia conglomerates, back then studios were studios. Their only business was movies, and the success or failure of those movies could have an enormous impact on a company's profits. I had confidence in my ability to judge the quality of movies and I was willing to invest in my judgment. I saw movies at previews but not so very much earlier than the general public. In 1961 no broker referred us to Disney, but when I saw *101 Dalmatians* we bought a lot of Disney stock. I saw a screening of *Star Wars,* left the theater, walked across the street to a gas station and used the pay phone to buy 25,000 shares of Twentieth Century–Fox. I kept increasing my position and ultimately owned 5 percent of the company. When Marvin Davis bought Fox, we sold for $30 million. I was also impressed with the strong product coming out of Columbia Pictures, so National took a large position in its stock. We owned approximately 10 percent on the day Columbia's CEO at the time, Fay Vincent, called me. "Sumner, are you sitting down? We have a deal to sell to Coca-Cola." Our holdings were then worth $52.7 million; our profit: approximately $26 million.

But not all deals went smoothly. In 1982 we bought a considerable amount of stock in the MGM/UA Home Entertainment Group, based on the quality of its movies. The company had been spun off from its parent, MGM/UA Entertainment Company, essentially to control the worldwide marketing of the 4,600 movies in the MGM/United Artists library. With the growth of cable, the wildly expanding number of channels and the huge number of program hours to fill, the pay television and home video rights to these pictures were tremendously valuable, making our position clearly worth taking. MGM/UA had sold only 15 percent of its stock to the public, indicating and promoting the fact that this stock would remain outstanding, that in contrast to a film production company it was low-risk in nature, and that it was therefore appropriate for long-term investment. Of that stock we ended up owning almost 50 percent, spending tens of millions of dollars to become the largest individual shareholder. And because the subsidiary had provided most of the parent company's operating profits for several years, we did very well. Then, in 1984, MGM/UA announced its intention to buy back the outstanding stock and merge Home Entertainment back into its parent.

What it had promised investors was a long-term investment MGM/UA was now calling in only two years later. Why? Because of all the stock in the company, Home Entertainment was the most valuable and MGM/UA wanted that stock for itself. MGM/UA had spun off part of the company originally to get cash, but that cash had failed to alleviate MGM/UA's financial and operational problems. In contrast to Home Entertainment, MGM/UA was highly leveraged and carried a heavy debt burden. It had suffered a series of poor earning reports and for the first quarter of fiscal 1985 net income fell to $1.7 million from $11 million the year before. (The fall would have been worse were it not for MGM/UA's earnings from Home Entertainment.) The company's film releases had performed poorly and it had suffered high executive turnover. In addition, MGM/UA was self-dealing, using Home Entertainment's assets to further its own interests. This was fine for MGM/UA stockholders, but for investors in Home Entertainment it was a disaster. Now that Home Entertainment was almost the sole element of the corporation doing well, MGM/UA was taking it back. I didn't want to sell—the company was right in the first place, this was a good investment—but the manner in which MGM/UA orchestrated the sale made it necessary.

It was what we called a cram-down merger. Because MGM/UA held 85 percent of Home Entertainment stock and was prepared to vote as a bloc, the company could cram down the throats of all Home Entertainment stockholders any price it saw fit. Essentially, unless someone stopped it, MGM/UA was going to buy out the entire public interest of Home Entertainment at a price the company itself determined. And that price was insultingly low: $28 per share in subordinated debentures, likely to be junk bonds worth between $22 and $23 in cash.

MGM/UA was controlled by Kirk Kerkorian. I had admired Kerkorian's success over the years. He started with nothing, and I have a special affection for people who start with nothing and create empires. He is an extremely charming and personable man. A decent guy, someone you would like as your friend. There was no personal animosity between us. But this was business.

Today, Kirk Kerkorian and I are friends. Not long ago, I had a lunch date with him at Spago. He arrived late and apologized, explaining that he and a beautiful young woman had just become the parents of a new baby. Not bad!

One of the things that infuriated me in particular was the fact that only a short time before the merger announcement, Kerkorian's general counsel, Frank Rothman, had told me, "You know, Sumner, you are in great shape because this stock is worth . . ." and gave me a figure. The amount they were offering in the merger was substantially less than the figure Rothman had named. They were, plain and simple, trying to screw us.

I demanded a higher price for our stock and after several rounds of negotiation thought we had struck an acceptable compromise. Their banks approved it, MGM/UA stopped trading on the stock, and I thought it was a done deal. I was shocked when they reneged. Shocked at high volume.

I tried to talk them out of it. I personally wrote to Rothman. "Frank, I urge you . . . do not permit an agreement entered into in good faith to become a disaster." When they persisted, when I couldn't negotiate my way into a decent deal, I filed a lawsuit. I went to the Securities and Exchange Commission as well as the courts, charging fraud, misrepresentation and waste of corporate assets. We went through months of discovery and preparation, and as so often happens, just before we were scheduled for trial they settled. As I said, MGM/UA had initially tried to cram down the price at between $22 and $23 a share. They settled at $28 cash. Multiply that by our two million shares and my unwillingness to be taken advantage of produced a significant profit. The filing of the lawsuit was not only appropriate and in the interest of our company, it was also in the interest of all the stockholders of MGM Home Entertainment.

Was the Home Entertainment library worth the battle? Ted Turner clearly thought so. He subsequently bought the entire MGM/UA library and created the cable networks TNT and TBS from it.

I know that people think I sue too readily. That is not true and I resent it. The suit was the catalyst, but the bottom line was that what MGM/UA was doing was wrong and I wouldn't stand for it. As a result of tenacity, by refusing to accept an unfair deal, I and all the other Home Entertainment shareholders benefited significantly. I'll say it again: I hate litigation. It is just as bad for the plaintiff as for the defendant: the same tension, the same risks, the same distraction and monopoly of one's time and attention. You only file suit if you think the issue is very important and if you are convinced that you are right. Ten million dollars and the issue of fairness were extremely important to us.

F I V E

VIACOM—THE OPENING

mong the companies I invested in was Viacom International. In 1985 and 1986 the media company had gone on an acquisition binge, picking up full interest in the premium cable television network Showtime/The Movie Channel, the Puget Sound cable system in the state of Washington, KMOV-TV in St. Louis, and the MTV Networks, including MTV, VH1, Nickelodeon and Nick at Nite. In May '86, Viacom had attracted the attention of corporate raider Carl Icahn, and this spending spree had been seen by Wall Street as an attempt to fight off a potential unfriendly takeover bid by saddling the company with debt and thus making it more expensive to acquire. Icahn talked about paying stockholders $75 a share, but the stock, then trading at $65, went up only fifty cents, which meant the investment community didn't take him seriously. Otherwise, it would have gone up several dollars. *The New York Times* quoted an anonymous portfolio manager as saying, "A lot of arbitrageurs [stock speculators] just don't believe he's a player." Although he owned a considerable block of Viacom stock, I tended to agree with them. From the beginning Icahn's interest was probably a calculated greenmail move.

Significantly, however, if Wall Street didn't think he was a player, the people managing Viacom certainly did. In addition to their buying spree, they engaged in a series of defensive moves, including a Securities and Exchange Commission filing for a bond offering which would have contained restrictive covenants making it very difficult for Icahn to raise any money by increasing debt for the company if he acquired it. Icahn's group of investors said they had "not received any encouragement" from Viacom's management, which was putting it mildly. The net result was that Viacom bought Icahn's stock. Although the company said it wouldn't, it did. Icahn went home with a handsome profit and management maintained control.

Viacom International was a highly diversified entertainment company. It had been spun off from CBS and became a public company in 1971 after the Federal Communications Commission ruled that the three major television networks could not syndicate their own programming. Among Viacom's holdings aside from Showtime/The Movie Channel and MTV Networks were an interest in the cable TV Lifetime network; five television stations; eight radio stations; eighteen cable TV systems serving about 930,000 subscribers in seven states; Viacom Productions, which produced television's *Matlock, Jake and the Fatman,* the *Perry Mason* made-for-TV movies, and the *Father Dowling Mysteries;* Viacom Enterprises, which syndicated TV programs and feature films to television and had syndication rights to *The Cosby Show* and *The Honeymooners,* among other shows; and Viacom Worldwide, which explored media and communications business opportunities overseas.

Viacom was the flip side of the movie exhibition industry. I had warned my fellow exhibitors about the powerful threat of cable at my first Theatre Owners of America convention, and here it was all rolled up in one company. Viacom in 1986 was essentially in the cable and television programming business.

All the Wall Street analysts attributed Viacom's value to its hard assets—the cable systems and radio and TV stations, the delivery systems—but what attracted my interest was the software. The content. Showtime and MTV were fully capable of creating a wide variety of programming, and that prospect excited me. My experience as an exhibitor had brought home one major lesson: It is the software that counts. You can have the most beautiful theater in the world, but if you don't have a hot picture, forget it. If your competitor has an inferior theater and the hot show, he is going to do better than you. People don't watch technology, they watch what technology brings into their homes. *They watch what's on it, not what it's on!* And what is on it is software. Here was a true growth industry and I, an outsider, had figured that out. Content was and is indeed king.

I said at the time that Viacom was "a sleeping giant about to explode." Of course, that was a ridiculous image and terrible English, but my point was on target. The company had gigantic potential that had not yet been realized. My instincts told me to go for it.

For example, from the start I could see the value of MTV Networks. The business community was in almost complete agreement that MTV was nothing more than a fad, just a big radio with pictures. But something inside told me this wasn't true. MTV wasn't simply spewing music, it had special importance for young people. I was sixty-three years old and I wasn't certain whether my grandchildren watched it or not, but I had a sense that MTV was capturing the minds and hearts of a whole generation. I saw that early.

We bought Viacom stock, not expansively at first, but increasingly, at prices ranging from $26 to $34.50 a share. (It has been split several times since.) National Amusements owned approximately three million shares, or around 8.7 percent of Viacom, when I woke up on the morning of September 17, 1986, and read in *The New York Times* that an investment group, including several members of Viacom's board of directors, led by Viacom's chief executive officer Terrence A. Elkes, had made an offer of $2.7 billion to buy the company and take it private. The stock opened that morning at $35.35 and they were offering $40.50 a share, which consisted of $37 in cash and $3.50 in preferred stock. That was entirely too low.

Terry Elkes was trying to steal the company.

This bold move brought two reactions: It increased my interest in Viacom and it stimulated my competitive instincts. National Amusements' previous positions in Columbia and Fox had turned out very well, giving me greater confidence in my investment strategy. I liked our investment in Viacom and now they were trying to take it away from me. I was not going to let Terry Elkes or anyone else get away with that. It was not going to happen! I liked Elkes on a personal basis. I consider him a friend today. He had managed Viacom reasonably well, but he was not going to steal it.

Media analyst Paul Kagan noted that Viacom was following a trend in which other, smaller media companies had recently been taken private. He also estimated the company's breakup value at around $51 a share, which meant that, without factoring in the potential for growth, the Elkes group's leveraged buyout offer was not only low, it was flagrantly insulting. The board was trying to keep the company all to itself. Plus, the LBO was being financed by the sale of junk bonds. After buying several companies in the past year, Viacom was already $1 billion in debt and the interest on those bonds would more than double it. A significant portion of the company's assets would have to be sold to service that debt.

Anyone interested in raising money to bid against Elkes faced another problem. He and his management group had retained most of the heavyweight investment banks. Analyst Mark Riely said, "They've been clever here in tying up all the desirable dance partners." But they had missed one: Merrill Lynch. That was a big mistake.

The very next day we bought more stock and filed a Schedule 13D form with the Federal Trade Commission under the Hart-Scott-Rodino Antitrust Improvement Act of 1976, disclosing that we had raised our stake in Viacom to just under 10 percent. I arranged with Merrill Lynch to represent us in our attempts to raise money for what I was certain, if I were to get involved in a takeover attempt, would be a costly fight. Coniston Partners, an investment group, disclosed that it held 12.4 percent of Viacom stock. I called and arranged a meeting. Coniston was represented by one of the partners, Paul Tierney, and we had a frank exchange of ideas about my purchase of Coniston's relatively large volume of Viacom stock.

In every negotiation it is vital to understand the other side's goals. In this way you can tailor your offers to your counterpart's objectives and not unnecessarily part with something of value to you but not to him or her. Coniston was more sophisticated in the world of finance than I was, but I was not concerned that I couldn't hold my own. Although clearly some premium was in order for so large a purchase, I did not want to make it substantial. I wanted to buy as close as I could to the price I was paying for Viacom stock on the open market.

Moreover, I did not want to buy all the Coniston stock. "Poison pill" plans had come into fashion in the 1980s as anti-takeover devices, and the Elkes group had inserted one into Viacom's bylaws. As we investigated, we found this plan controversial and quite possibly illegal. The poison pill would be activated when any stockholder owned 20 percent or more of Viacom, at which time every other stockholder would receive additional shares, diluting the large stockholder's position to an insignificant percentage. The poison pill plan could be waived only by Viacom's board of directors, giving it absolute control of the situation, the same board of directors that was trying to buy the company on such low-ball terms. This anti-competitive measure, designed to scare away takeover investors willing to pay more for Viacom stock, was clearly not in the best interest of the stockholders, who would have been better off if various suitors were allowed to compete for the company, bid up the price and offer them the most value. I had to limit my holdings in the company to under 20 percent. To cross that threshold would be devastating.

During this time I received particular help from a young attorney named Philippe Dauman from the law firm of Shearman & Sterling, which had been brought to us by Merrill Lynch. As with most law firms, senior partners bring in the business and younger people do most of the hands-on work. Philippe was thirty-two years old, had been putting in a hundred hours a week and was up for partner when we were introduced by the head of Shearman & Sterling's mergers and acquisitions group, Steve Volk. All Philippe had been told was, "There's a theater owner from Boston who needs a little help on 13D and Hart-Scott-Rodino." Philippe was quick, smart, insightful. He spoke easily, with sharp intelligence and an understated wit. I evaluate people based on their ability, judgment and confidence, and he topped the list on all three counts.

Philippe and I hit it off almost instantly. We spoke on the phone five or six times daily about the details of the Viacom situation, and when I invited him to meet with me he properly suggested accompanying his boss, Steve Volk. "You don't need to bring him," I said. "Just you come." Despite the fact that he was almost exactly half my age, I placed a great deal of confidence in Philippe and he did not disappoint me. I was up every morning getting the overnight motion picture figures and I would call Philippe at 5 a.m., ready to go. Finally he told me, "Sumner, I don't get up at five like you do. You're waking my wife every morning, including Saturdays and Sundays." I appreciated the candor. From then on I waited until seven.

Coniston's Paul Tierney was pleasant, smart, firm. He and I were totally aboveboard with each other. There were no games played. "Sumner," he said, "you're in this thing for the company, we're in it for the money. We ought to be able to make a deal." It was the best kind of negotiating. Coniston had apparently bought early, seeing the same growth potential in Viacom as we did, and at a very good price. (We managed to elicit that information, which sometimes helps in a negotiation, but not necessarily. In fact, people sell for what things are worth. The idea that, in negotiating, you're going to predicate a deal on what the other person paid for it will lead to no deal. You will only outnegotiate and outsmart yourself. What is the deal worth *to them*? That's the question you have to answer.)

At that point, I hadn't made up my mind about whether I was going to make an all-out effort to take control of Viacom. We were simply accumulating stock to make our position more substantial in a negotiation, but if the Coniston people wanted to believe we were about to launch a takeover, we did not disabuse them of that notion.

My session with Tierney lasted almost all night. When it was over, we had struck a deal acceptable to both of us—2.9 million shares for $43 apiece—and National owned 18.3 percent of Viacom's stock.

In the next few days, I met with Terry Elkes twice. He was a relatively young man and very well spoken. I had admired Elkes's conduct at Viacom up to that point. He had run the company well and had made a significant number of productive moves to enhance the value for its stockholders. MTV and Showtime had been excellent acquisitions. But he was low-balling, and ultimately his bid, if accepted, would cost his shareholders, including me, a lot of money. Was his allegiance to the shareholders who had chosen him CEO to maximize their investment or to his own group of private investors who were trying to take over the company on the cheap?

"Terry," I told him, "I have no hostile intentions toward you. I would be very pleased if you continue to run the company in the manner in which you have been running it, as long as Viacom stays public." If Elkes had been content to let me continue to be an investor and share in the enhancements he had made for the company, I would have been satisfied with his performance. However, he turned me down. Elkes said that, with all due respect, he had no intention of rescinding his proposal and he was going to actively pursue his acquisition of Viacom. Not only that, he was averse to sweetening the deal. Now it was clear: Terry Elkes had been doing the right things to enhance the value of a company that he intended to take over for himself.

I suppose I could have backed off at that point. Despite the fact that their bid was low, I still stood to make a nice profit on my investment. I had made similar investments in Fox and Columbia, and I could walk away again with a substantial amount of money.

But this was not about money. Most people who succeed in significant areas do not succeed because of a desire for money. There are other more important motivations: the desire to be the best and the desire to win. And for better or worse, the desire for power. Winning is power. You can't divorce the desire for power from the desire to win.

I realize that many people do work for money, but I would wager that those who become extremely successful are more strongly motivated by the desire to achieve, by a commitment to excellence and an obsessive drive to win. There's nothing wrong with power. I'm sure you've heard that power corrupts. I don't buy that at all. Men become corrupt by their misuse of power. The issue more properly is whether or not you use power responsibly. In the business world, behaving responsibly with power means that while the bottom line is important, it is not the end-all. That may sound hypocritical coming from a wealthy man, but there are situations in which you have to look deeper than the bottom line. You have to stand for something more than making money. I believed that the Viacom board was using its power irresponsibly and I was not going to be muscled out.

In order to insulate themselves from charges of self-dealing and protect against suits by shareholders for agreeing to sell the company at too low a price, Elkes and the board appointed a special committee of "outside directors," people with ostensibly no ties to the management, whose function was theoretically to evaluate the bids for Viacom. The special committee, in turn, selected the investment banking firm of Goldman Sachs & Company to act as its financial advisor with respect to the fairness of all bids to the Viacom shareholders. Reviewing the Elkes group's first and then sweetened second bid, Goldman Sachs called the offers "outside the range of fairness" and recommended their rejection. The special committee, arms twisted by this recommendation, turned down an offer of $44 a share. Big deal. I had just bought 2.9 million shares from Coniston at $43 each. If the company was worth only $44 a share, would I have been buying at $43? It didn't make sense. The Elkes group's offer was still unconscionably low.

I met with Joseph Condon of the special committee and two of its advisors. I again stressed that I felt the company's future prospects were very strong, that it would be in the long-range strategic interest of Viacom and all the shareholders that the company remain public, and that Elkes's offer was clearly well below any conceivable level of acceptability. By this time, however, I was not only annoyed by the proposed coup, my competitive instincts had been further aroused. The more I looked at Viacom the more convinced I became that, with the proper management, the growth of the company could be explosive. Again and again we had made investments and been content to go along with management when the time came to reap the benefits. I had always been a passive investor and that strategy had been successful. While I stressed to Condon that my first choice would be to sit back and watch my investment in Viacom grow under Elkes's management, I told him I also had a second choice. Viacom was no longer simply an investment. Viacom was a company that I wanted to own.

What made me think I could run a major international media company? I was living two lives, one as an entrepreneur, another as an investor, and I was successful in both. Even as a passive investor, I had to be pretty nimble when making decisions. As an entrepreneur, I had begun at National Amusements with only a couple of drive-ins, run the company hands on, involved myself in every detail, and now we were a major circuit with four hundred screens. I was proud of that accomplishment. It was the entrepreneur who built National, not the investor who bought and sold stock, who was making a play for Viacom.

Condon listened respectfully to me and then left. What he did not tell me was that he had ducked out of a special committee meeting to see me, then proceeded to walk down the hall and duck back in. This board meeting had been convened specifically to consider and approve Terry Elkes's LBO bid. Condon's polite interest in my position was, to my mind, clearly a sham; in his stroll down the hall to return to his meeting he could not possibly have given it careful consideration. His conduct was of questionable propriety. It was clear to me: Those "outside directors" were plenty inside.

I woke up on the morning of October 18 to find that Goldman Sachs, the special committee and the Viacom board of directors had all approved the Elkes bid: $44 a share plus 20 percent of the new corporation that would be formed to run the business.

So the special committee was in Terry Elkes's pocket.

I felt the brunt of that impropriety. I owned more than 18 percent of the company and management had given very short shrift to my views. I didn't like the board's attitude, I didn't like Terry Elkes's attitude, and I didn't like the way we were being treated. But whether or not I liked their behavior was immaterial. I would have lived with that if the deal had been acceptable. It wasn't. And the more I examined Viacom, the more I became convinced the company could become a major force in its field.

To understand the value of a business, you must be able to anticipate success. You can't evaluate a company based simply on the present worth of its assets and operations; you need to understand the growth dynamic, the potential and your own participation in it. You have to be confident that if its value is ten you can make it twenty.

I was convinced that Viacom's future lay in software, not only in the United States but also around the world. Experience was showing me that exhibition was a nongrowth area, and that in entertainment, television was the name of the game. And the name of television was Viacom. I was particularly taken with the potential of MTV Networks, though certainly not because I had any particular affinity with the music played on MTV. My favorites were Benny Goodman, Tony Bennett and Artie Shaw. In fact, MTV wasn't making much money at all at that point; it was just sitting there, barely getting by.

MTV was geared to teenagers, but I didn't have to be of that generation to appreciate its power and potential. I believed that MTV could be a cultural force in America. I also believed that there was an insatiable desire for American entertainment overseas and that MTV could be expanded around the globe. Some found American teenagers a bunch of slackers. But I saw that a bond in that generation was beginning to form. Kids in the streets of Tokyo had more in common with kids in Paris and

New York than they did with their parents, of that I was certain. This generation had a powerful voice that was as yet unheard. Very early in the game, they had been yelling to their cable systems, "I Want My MTV!" They had been successfully rallied around that flag, so clearly they could be mobilized. I felt this was a powerful generation whose power would only increase. And they would grow up. Young people twelve to twenty were going to become adults of thirty to forty, then forty to fifty. If we attracted them early, we could keep them forever.

I felt much the same way about Nickelodeon and the possibilities in creating a children's brand. Nickelodeon at least had Disney as an extremely attractive precursor and a goal. MTV was much more a leap of faith.

Viacom's assets were primarily hardware and I believed that software was king. Yet I instinctively knew the incredible potential of the company. My background in theaters had taught me that the only thing that counted was what was on the screen. Why shouldn't that be true on TV screens throughout the world?

How could I know the value of the businesses I might be competing for, having never been in any one of them? I was operating on instinct. What is instinct? Business instinct is a combination of experience and the intellectual capacity to come up with the right answer to a question, the right solution to a problem.

How did I know about the value of Viacom? I just knew.

That morning I said, "To hell with this, I'm going for it!"

Just because a bid had been accepted didn't mean it was a done deal. I don't care how much you're in somebody's pocket, no board can ignore a better bid. I went to work.

Did I want a partner in this acquisition? It certainly would have alleviated some of the financial strain of buying and then running such a large corporation, and I was contacted by several companies that said they would be willing to join with me in a takeover bid. Cable operator Charles Dolan called to say he would make life easy for us by taking

Viacom's cable system off our hands—for about a quarter of the going price. Can't blame him for trying. Coca-Cola and Disney were interested and we had some very preliminary, highly tentative discussions.

What I quickly came to realize, however, was that at the end of the day all of them would want to sell some of Viacom's assets in order to pay down the debt involved in borrowing money to buy the company. I've never been a dismantler; I've been essentially an acquirer and I did not want to part with assets that I considered critical to the success of the company once I owned it. The company I was after would not be the company I'd get. I wanted to grow Viacom, not cut it up into pieces and sell it.

Around this time I ran into Laurence Tisch in the lobby of a Beverly Hills hotel. He was chairman of Loews Corporation, and other than the Tisches, we were that company's largest stockholders. Tisch and I had been friendly for many years because of our mutual interest in film exhibition and naturally we talked about my intention to acquire Viacom. Listening is always a good thing; you never know so much that you can afford to ignore advice from smart people whom you respect. "Forget this partner business," he told me. "Viacom is a great company. All of its assets are interesting. No partners." I had already reached that same conclusion.

So I was going to go after it. I must say I enjoyed the idea. Why? First, because the prize was of real value. This would not be a battle over a trifle. Viacom was a company worth fighting for. Second, it's fair to say that I would enjoy the contest. If you get involved in a major competitive struggle and the stress that inevitably comes with it, you'd better have some sense of satisfaction and enjoyment about entering the fray. If you feel only stress, you have less chance of success than if you are excited about engaging in what was almost literally, when you're talking about control of a company like Viacom, business warfare. I enjoy the give-and-take of negotiating. Certainly, I would always rather talk than fight. That's my first choice: discuss things rationally and settle agreeably. But if you do get into a fight, you have to enjoy the battle to win it.

I was prepared to put National Amusements' entire holdings in Viacom plus other stocks we owned (worth about $400 million) toward the purchase of Viacom. My father was a builder, not a risk-taker, and I was putting up the company we had spent our lives building. He never said, "Don't do it." He said, "Sumner, we have a good company. Why would you want to risk it all?" I answered, "My instincts tell me this is the way to go." My father, much to his credit, supported the decision.

But even including National Amusements' holdings, that still left several billion dollars unaccounted for. We had to borrow it. To put together the necessary financing, I brought in bankers and lawyers and began working seriously with advisors from Merrill Lynch, who pointed us toward Citibank and Bank of America. While Citibank was the more established institution, BOA offered the better rates.

I was unused to borrowing large amounts of money and had very little experience with big banks. We basically financed National from its internal growth, socking our earnings right back into the company, and as a result our need for outside capital was minimal. Borrowing $10 million was a big deal for us. Now I sat with the bankers and said "million" when I meant "billion." I just wasn't accustomed to using that word. From time to time Philippe had to correct me.

Our contacts at Merrill Lynch were Ken Miller and James Mason. Mason was a hamburger eater. We would schedule a lunch meeting and, first thing, Mason would walk in, get on the phone to room service and order six hamburgers. He also had a prodigious appetite for work.

Ken Miller was a Merrill Lynch investment banker who took up our cause to acquire Viacom as an advisor on the deal. Miller, Mason, Philippe and I spent endless hours and many late nights in arduous negotiations with bankers and lawyers. The most critical area had to do with covenants which related to the level of debt we would be permitted to put on the company. The banks had to agree on what would be defined as an acceptable level. From their perspective it would be pointless to lend us money to buy this company and then find that our financial position prevented us from making the money to pay it back. As a result, they kept pushing for a frame of obligations on our part to sell specific assets of the company. Should we finally end up with Viacom, they wanted us to gut it. They didn't share my vision; they didn't understand that the components which they wanted us to get rid of were the very ones vital to the company's success.

They specifically wanted us to sell MTV. I refused.

Since this would be a highly leveraged acquisition and there was not a lot of coverage in the earnings of Viacom, the banks tried to impose very tough conditions. Their extreme starting position was that they had to control every operating decision. They also wanted to control which assets would be sold. They wanted to dictate to us on every level. This was clearly unacceptable. If you are running a company, it is ridiculous to have to consult a bank every time you make an important decision. You never want to be at the mercy of banks. Your passion is not their bottom line. They don't care.

Banks will routinely throw all their restrictive clauses into an opening agreement if you have no choice but to deal with them. But why, we argued, would we run the business in a way that would jeopardize their investment? I was going to put $400 million of my own money in Viacom; that should be comfort enough. When that line of reasoning did not move them, we threatened to go to other banks. The only leverage we had was to take our business elsewhere or refuse to go ahead with the deal, in which case they wouldn't get any fees.

Our meetings went on twenty hours a day, painfully, back and forth and back again, even negotiating over individual words. We were scrounging to get money but I simply refused to commit to buying Viacom in order to tear it apart. Someone had to have a clear vision of the priorities of value for the company, and I would be damned if the banks were going to establish those priorities.

Finally we settled on a package of Viacom holdings, including but not limited to MTV Networks, from which we would, if necessary, select sufficient assets to sell and pay down the debt. The decision as to which of these assets would be sold remained ours, not theirs. This was satisfactory and it ultimately saved MTV for us. As our banker we selected Bank of America, which agreed to syndicate the loan.

In December we bought more Viacom stock from Coniston, raising our stake to 19.6 percent, pulling close to activating the poison pill. With such a huge position in the company, there was no turning back. But from the start, the people in management were extremely hostile to our interest. They did everything they could to keep our understanding of the company at a minimum. When after much delay we finally got access to Viacom's internal information for due diligence, Elkes's colleague, Viacom executive vice president Kenneth Gorman, refused to shake Ken Miller's hand.

Finally, at their invitation, we sat down with Elkes and his contingent. They had a proposition for us. They offered me 50 percent of the deal for a mere $25 million. That meant that their entire investment would be only $50 million, which, in turn, meant that they would necessarily be liquidating the company.

I'm sure they thought that if they were not being generous, they were at least offering me something I would find appealing. Their single important demand was that I had to be a totally passive investor.

Their research left a lot to be desired. No doubt they had looked at my past investment history and thought I was in this for the money. From one vantage point, I suppose, that might have been a reasonable supposition, and by their lights they had offered me what they thought I wanted. From their perspective, it appeared, Viacom could be acquired so cheaply that there was enough to go around. But they were pursuing a false goal. Passive? Me? Had Condon not been listening when I told him I wanted to be actively involved? Had he simply put that aside as he walked on down the hall?

I was an unknown, just some theater owner who had struck it rich with a couple of stock purchases. Elkes and his group didn't know me and they never took the time to find out who I was. I believe they underestimated me, never for a minute took me seriously. That's a grave negotiating flaw and a cardinal mistake. Never underestimate your competition. Always do your research. I heard through sources that Elkes had walked through the hallways of Viacom muttering, "Who is this peasant from Boston?"

It didn't take him long to find out.

I told the group that their offer was completely unacceptable. I wanted Viacom. I wanted to run Viacom. They seemed shocked, but they were ready to play hardball.

Included in the Elkes buyout group was Donaldson, Lufkin & Jenrette Securities Corporation. Apparently one of the DLJ representatives was their designated hit man. He sat across the table and intoned, "Sumner, you have no choice but to accept this proposal. I want you to know that for every act you plan, we have an anecdote."

Everyone on our side of the table looked at each other. "Excuse me?" Shearman & Sterling's Steve Volk could hardly contain himself. "Did I hear you right?" he said. We were all snickering and tittering. Were they going to tell us amusing little stories until we caved? "You couldn't have meant antidote, could you?" Volk said. I didn't want to underestimate our adversaries, but clearly we weren't going up against geniuses.

We turned down their proposal, the meeting ended, and the battle for control of Viacom was fully engaged.

SIX

VIACOM—THE BATTLE

I t took several months to get the financing together, but the other side had regulatory clearances to gather and we were not worried that the deal would be finalized before we could act. I spent many hours in excruciating consideration and debate over how to proceed and exactly how far to go. I had run a private company all my life. Now I asked Ken Miller and others, "What is it like to run a public company? Where do you see the problems and the opportunities? In short, recognizing that we are in the early stages of this transaction, what do you think we can anticipate?" Once I found there was a way to answer to public shareholders and still exercise complete control of the company, I moved forward more comfortably.

On February 2, 1987, we filed a counteroffer. We mirrored management's bid but added more money: $44.75 a share in cash and preferred stock, fifty cents more than their proposal, or about $2.1 billion for the 80.4 percent of Viacom we didn't already own. Most significantly, we were backing up our proposal with National Amusements' $400 million equity and financing the debt through a bank. We offered the same 20 percent of the acquiring company, but management had offered equity of only $81 million and their deal depended on high-yield, high-risk junk bonds. Because we already owned 18.6 percent of Viacom, we would not have to borrow money to buy those shares and the company would not have to pay interest on that loan should we win. Our price was higher and included more cash and exchangeable preferred stock; the interest savings under our offer would be substantial, tens of millions of dollars per year, making it far preferable for Viacom stockholders. (If the debt is less onerous, the preferred stock is more valuable.) There would be no breakup fees and a more secure financial structure. Ours was clearly the better offer. Wall Street thought so. The Street looked at it and said, "Underneath all those public securities is real cash from a real operator with a lot of business sense. Management is just giving shareholders more of what they already own." Viacom stock went up $2.50 that day.

Did Elkes's management group still think we weren't serious? Our filing contained a letter to Allan R. Johnson, chairman of the special committee, which detailed the serious acts engaged in by the board that were contrary to the interests of the stockholders and "subjected the Company and its Board of Directors to serious claims of breach of fiduciary duty": the adoption of the poison pill plan, the payment of greenmail, the adoption of "golden parachutes" for Elkes and his cohorts in the millions of dollars which any new acquirer would have to pay out of company funds, the failure to solicit better bids for the company than the low management offer, the hoarding of information.

We asked for an answer from the board by five that Friday afternoon.

The transfer of television station licenses to a new company requires the approval of the Federal Communications Commission, and we offered to put our Viacom stock in a trust while that was taking place. But the real problem we faced was the bureaucratic nightmare of getting each individual local cable franchise authority to approve the transfer. That was a big order. It could take months. Our team went right to work.

We didn't expect our offer to be accepted. The board always managed to tip Elkes's group off as to our next bid so that they could raise their bid to our level.

Our bid was rejected.

Despite our superiority in price, equity and financing, the board found our offer less favorable than management's, ostensibly because of regulatory delays and the length of time it might take for us to get the necessary transfer approvals.

We immediately asked the board to provide us with sufficient information so that we could enhance our bid. A sensible strategy, but they were never forthcoming on anything. When the board finally did respond, John Tinker, an analyst with Bear Stearns at the time, saw the disclosure as a signal that management "may now be willing to sweeten its buyout offer." The press speculated that management might pay us a premium for our stock. Greenmail. Tinker said, "The question is, What's his price?"

Maybe that was the question in the financial community. Maybe it was the question among the people around management's table. But they continued to underestimate us. We were way beyond money now. It never entered my mind to let them buy us out. We weren't going to put up with any of that. *We were going to get this company!* Was there no limit to how far we would go? We would go far enough to dissuade Viacom's management from believing they could win.

I was becoming immersed in the affairs of Viacom. I now knew much more about it than when we bought our first shares, and each day I was becoming even more excited about its potential. Not only did I have confidence in the company, I had confidence in what I could do with the company once I got hold of it. It might be a stretch, but we were convinced that we could make every one of Viacom's businesses more valuable in the course of time.

The people in Viacom's management weren't letting us anywhere near their corporation, so I decided to go around them. I met with Bob Pittman, who had helped to create MTV before moving on to MCA, and picked his brain. He told me MTV had become a very unpopular place to work in the year since Viacom had bought it. Morale was extremely low and people were leaving in droves. He said the general feeling was, "They're not going to let us invest in programming. They're

trying to do this LBO, there's this takeover battle and we're gonna bail."
All the MTV people knew about me was that I was some mysterious
Boston millionaire who lived in hotels and had hung out of a window at
the Copley Plaza. Viacom management was dismissing me as a cranky
pest who was just trying to mess up its LBO.

Pittman was very engaging. I asked for an entry into MTV and he
called Tom Freston, who had started there with him at the very beginning and had risen to co-president after Pittman left. Freston was thinking of leaving the company, too.

"Listen, Tom, I just left the Carlyle Hotel. I had a meeting with Sumner Redstone, who had called me, and he wanted to know more about
the company. You should call him because he can't really get access to
any management. You know, those guys who are running the company
now, there's no future. Maybe this guy will be better. Maybe MTV can
prosper under him. Give him a call."

Freston called and he and Nickelodeon president Geraldine Laybourne came to see me. Over dinner I quizzed them about MTV Networks. "What's the future of these companies? What can they be?" I
asked. Both Freston and Laybourne were big MTV Networks boosters
and told me that even though the company was only about at break-
even, the MTV business was just getting started and was making $15
million on $80 million in revenues. I was at ground zero as far as knowl-
edge of these channels was concerned. A neophyte to the entire business, I was looking for a sign that an element of management in Viacom
might stay and also for some reasons to bolster my faith that the businesses in Viacom might grow.

I asked a lot of questions. Should I sell MTV? This, of course, was a
rhetorical question since I would never have considered selling MTV—
after all, content was king. "Oh, no," Freston and Laybourne told me.
"These consumer-based businesses are home runs. They need investment. We've created this unique culture, and if it's allowed to grow, we
could really have global brands."

"What's this about morale?" I asked. "We are at a dangerous time at the company," Freston said. "People have left and more are planning to leave. Morale has been down since we were sold by Time Warner. Our people would probably root for the guy they didn't know on the chance that he might be better than the people who are running the company right now. What have we got to lose?"

At the end of the meal Freston told me, "You ought to drop by sometime when you get a chance. You would get a kick out of the place." He was making a great leap of faith. Viacom management had made it clear that no one of importance in the corporation was supposed to talk to me. But MTV was in a different building than Viacom headquarters; its people were also of a different mind-set and Freston and Laybourne figured they could sneak me in.

The next morning at nine, I called from the MTV lobby at 1775 Broadway. "Tom, it's Sumner. I'm downstairs."

MTV looked like what you would imagine MTV would look like: a college dormitory. Freston preceded me down a hallway with videotapes stacked all over like used McDonald's boxes. CDs were everywhere, music was blaring, and there were posters on the walls. "Wow! This is fabulous!" I said. I felt as if I was in a creative factory. Even if I preferred Tony Bennett and Benny Goodman, it was possible to like rock and roll. And, of course, I loved the energy of the place.

I left MTV more determined than ever to acquire Viacom. Winning this battle became my life. All day and all night. In my apartment at the Carlyle Hotel with Philippe, Ken Miller, James Mason, the bankers et al., we plotted our strategy. Should we make a tender offer? Do we make a hostile tender offer? Do we try to nullify the poison pill? The only thing certain in our minds was that we were going to win. We would go far enough, be tenacious enough, relentless enough, competitive enough to BEAT THEM!

We had anticipated the regulatory objection and had a ready response. On February 23 we increased our bid by $5.75 a share and offered to pay interest on that money if the merger was not completed by April 30. We were up to $3.2 billion for the company.

John Tinker finally said, "This is a for-real offer." Now there was no way management could say their offer was better.

When the board failed to respond, I hoped the battle was over. But knowing that management had the board in their pocket, I was realistic. I wasn't taking anything for granted.

At sixty-three years old, I was in the fight of my life. I wasn't spending my day discussing the price of a movie with Warner Bros.; I wasn't going over the early-morning daily grosses from theaters around the country as I normally did. I was hardly running National Amusements at all. I was singularly focused on the acquisition of Viacom. What if the directors didn't yield to logic or even listen to reason? What was our recourse? How much money could we afford to raise in order to win this battle? While I was not the "peasant from Boston" that Terry Elkes assumed I was, I had never in my life been involved in anything like this. When I asked myself, Is it worth it? Are we doing the right thing? I never doubted my answer. I knew instinctively I was making the right move.

On February 26 the special committee met and said it would consider a new and sweetened offer by management of around $49 a share. Management hadn't beaten our offer, they had sidled up against it. We had a significantly superior offer still on the table—the committee hadn't acted on it—and yet this group of supposedly impartial men was prepared to consider and presumably accept a lesser offer by their board employers. It was not only unfair, it was intolerable. This so-called board, especially this special committee, was simply a tool of the management group and we were getting screwed.

I was livid. "I'm going to get this board!" I roared. "I'm not going to let those guys get away with it!"

"Sumner, relax . . . ," Philippe said, trying to calm me down.

It was no use. I was infuriated by the way we were being treated. The board was supposed to represent all the stockholders, but these men were clearly in management's pocket. I could see the scenario. This bidding war was just going to keep going and going. We would make an offer and Elkes and his guys would gain access to our information and then offer another ten cents.

And think about the comparative financial strength of the resulting companies. Whatever management's offer, they were only going to invest a minuscule amount of equity. We were putting in around $500 million, and once management controlled Viacom, they would have to sell off its assets, essentially destroying the company.

We were scrambling for money now. We were so tightly financed that every time we wanted to improve our bid we had to go back to our financial sources to see if they would cover it. We met at my apartment at the Carlyle and continued to hash it out with Bank of America. BOA had agreed to syndicate a $2.25 billion loan and we needed more. The meeting went late, with bankers and lawyers haggling over words and the fine points of law in such a huge and intricate deal. Bank of America was represented by a fellow named Eric Richards, and at one point we turned to him for information and found he was gone.

"Where's Richards?" I asked. Nobody knew. It wasn't as if the room was all that large; he couldn't get lost in it. He was the money source and he had disappeared. Had he simply walked out? Did this mean that Bank of America, our entire source of outside financing, had backed out of the deal? If so, we were done. There was no way, given the kind of time constraints we were under, that we or Merrill Lynch could institute and successfully conclude such high-level negotiations with another bank. Where was the man?

Two hours later he came back. Two hours! It turned out that, in the middle of this multi-billion-dollar transaction, Richards had left the meeting to change a tire on his wife's car. I'm sure he wins Husband of the Year for that one, but what could he have been thinking? The guys around the room caught their breath, rolled their eyes and then burst out laughing. Didn't he have Triple-A?

Bank of America increased its commitment to us to $2.28 billion and then stopped. We had reached its limit. We were raising every nickel we could to support the financing and interest payments. We were so close. Still, we needed more money.

In order to swing it, we had to raise capital through the issuance of what Merrill Lynch called high-yield bonds—junk bonds. At the time, they were the specialty of Michael Milken at Drexel Burnham (which had been working with the Elkes group), who was raising the financing for many a would-be mogul. Milken had a network of people he placed these bonds with, but as part of the deal he would demand and receive warrants—the right to buy shares in the company he was helping to finance. When these companies took off so did his net worth. This was the source of much of Milken's wealth. Essentially, warrants were what might discreetly be called incentives to him for raising the money.

We needed more money to stay in the bidding. One way to bridge the gap, which was in the neighborhood of $250 million, was this junk bond debt. We were discussing it when, out of the blue, one of the Merrill Lynch bankers tried to play Michael Milken Jr. He asked us for warrants. He wasn't going to line his own pockets. I'm not suggesting in any way that his request was personally inappropriate; the profits would fuel the return for that Merrill Lynch department. But we were being squeezed and I didn't like it. Merrill Lynch was our investment banker. These people represented us, and for them to try to get a piece of the action was wildly inappropriate. We expressed our deep discontent to the banker who raised the issue, and when he left I turned to Ken Miller and let him have it. Normally I discipline myself and use Harvard Law School language, but this time I shouted, *"This is an outrage!* You're breaching your duty to us. I think you've forgotten you're supposed to represent us, not Merrill Lynch. We're not going to put up with it! If you think you're the only people around, forget it. If we have to do other things, we'll do it with other people!"

Miller knew he was on a precipice. We needed Merrill Lynch, but this was a big deal and he could not afford to lose us. Miller impressed me. With us in the room he phoned his fellow investment banker and tried to straighten him out. We only heard Miller's side of the conversation, but he was instrumental in successfully smoothing over the difficulty. We didn't give Merrill Lynch warrants and the junk bonds were issued. Putting aside the bidding war going on outside our closed doors, even within our camp the atmosphere was stormy.

"What we've all learned here," I told Philippe, "is whenever we can be, we're our own investment banker. *We* carry the ball." It is useful for us to maintain relationships with the investment banks; they bring us ideas, their analysts follow the companies in the market, it's part of doing business. But to a large extent, after that experience, the negotiating was done in-house.

We raised our bid again. Now we were offering $42 per share in cash, $7.50 in exchangeable preferred stock and 20 percent of the $500 million acquiring company. *The New York Times* quoted one arbitrageur—who, interestingly, requested anonymity, presumably because he was afraid of Viacom's management—estimating that we were offering to pay about $3.3 billion for the whole company, $100 million more than management.

I wrote to the special committee's chairman, Allan Johnson:

> We had been given assurances that the Special Committee would follow a bidding process pursuant to which any proposal made by us or [the management group] would be kept confidential until a final determination had been made by the Special Committee on Sunday, March 1, and a merger agreement had been executed. Notwithstanding this fact, and notwithstanding the fact that the management group expressly stated that it had already made its final offer, we understood that the management group is attempting to pressure the Special Committee into disclosing to the management group the terms of our bid. We urge the Special Committee to maintain the integrity of the bidding process in a manner consistent with the assurances given to us.

Management, with what again appeared to be access to our information, came up to $3.23 billion. It was obvious to us that Elkes and his group were being given the time and opportunity to reconstruct their financing to our level, at which point they would stop. We were being made a stalking horse for the management cabal and we strongly felt that, the way things were going, at the end of the day the board would throw the company in that direction. But we were not going to be denied.

I was extremely upset by the manner in which this auction was being handled. I felt our efforts were being sabotaged by the special committee and I wanted to make myself perfectly clear about what would happen if the committee got in our way. I wanted the committee and the board to know I was ready to take action.

"Don't do it," Ken Miller said. "Who knows what the result will be?"

"You'll get them upset at us," Philippe told me. "It will make things harder, it'll make things worse."

With all due respect to Ken and Philippe, both of whom, to repeat, I hold in very high regard, that was not the way I saw it. There comes a time when you draw a line and say, "Enough is enough." I was putting the accumulated savings of a lifetime as well as a lifetime of work on the line, and I was being mistreated and humiliated. Underestimated and denigrated. It enraged me.

We were pushing the limits of my financial capacity. The next bidding increase would put me over that margin of safety. We looked at the company's debt capacity. The businesses of Viacom would have to do extraordinarily well in order to support the increased weight of debt. This was not a judgment about which I could be wrong. It was a huge gamble. If Viacom went under, I could lose as much as $400 million. My ownership of National Amusements was not at risk but the tangible results of my entire life's work could be lost, not to mention the reputation I had built up over a lifetime.

I agonized over it. I met with Philippe and Ken Miller and some of Ken's Merrill Lynch associates every day. "We think this is a good deal," they told me, "but it's your decision." I knew that, but I wanted them to be more than investment bankers and lawyers. I wanted them on the line with me. I like to discuss serious issues with people who know how I think and whom I can trust, people who will tell me, "This is screwy," if they think I'm heading over the falls. "Forget what your roles are," I said to Ken and Philippe. "I trust you as individuals. Step away from Merrill Lynch and Shearman & Sterling and tell me exactly what you think."

That's what advisors are for. Sometimes they might say, "Wait a minute. You can't put your entire fortune at risk. You need $50 million to support your lavish Palm Beach lifestyle." But Philippe and Ken knew me well. They knew my material needs were minimal. And they knew that I enjoyed risk and challenge as long as it wasn't irrational risk and challenge.

We had all listened to the same presentations, the same investment bankers and the same projections. I wanted them to say, "This is not crazy. You are not a man doing something that is objectively bound to fail." I wanted to hear that, given my capacity for risk, this was a rational decision, that Viacom had the potential to be an extraordinary success. I was already convinced of that but I was looking for confirmation.

I knew Ken and Philippe understood what I was asking. Both men said, "Yes."

We upped our offer to $3.4 billion, while at the same time raising the rate of interest we would pay the stockholders to 9 percent if our regulatory clearances did not come through on time. It was our third raise in a week. In the offer letter to Allan Johnson I wrote:

> There is something inherently wrong in a process which involves delaying a third party bidder, particularly a major stockholder of the Company, in order to give the Company's management the opportunity to learn the contents of the offer and to respond by making not a superior offer, but rather an inferior offer. Were it not for our perseverance in the face of almost every management entrenchment device devised to date, the members of manage-

ment would have bought the Company for themselves at a significantly lower price than that currently offered.

After expressly representing that it was making its "final" offer on February 26, the management increased its offer after being given sufficient time to learn the contents of our offer. Even then, the management made a competing offer that had a lower value than ours. The management must have the sense that it need not have the best offer in order to win. Neither we nor, we believe, the shareholders will stand for such a result.

It was a shot across the bow. In fact, I had toned down my wording a little. I thought I had been entirely too guarded in my language in that letter, so I called Johnson on the phone.

"You think you guys can get away with anything?" I said angrily. "*I don't know what insurance you have, but take my word for it, you don't have enough to protect you from the kind of lawsuit I'm going to file against the whole bunch of you!*"

The next day Johnson called and asked, "What do you want us to do?"

What I wanted was a meeting at which everything would be concluded. If they were going to be auctioneers, be fair auctioneers. I wanted Viacom's board of directors to go into a room with its special committee and its Goldman Sachs advisors, review all the offers and not come out until a decision had been reached. No more bids would be considered and the company's future would be decided once and for all.

Johnson accepted the terms and said he would set up the meeting.

While I had no trust in the board or its special committee, I had great confidence in Goldman Sachs. Previous banker-to-banker conversations had revealed that its people knew that ours was the better offer. They were also well aware that management was putting in so little equity that it would have to liquidate the company to repay the debt. Goldman Sachs's business ethics were also on the line and I knew they would not be compromised.

The Viacom board met to review all final offers on March 4. We were not at all certain which way they would go. On the positive side, we felt if the board went with us, the outside bidder, the members could certainly not be accused of breaching their fiduciary duty or acting to favor someone they knew. But if they went the other way, they had better make damn sure the management bid was clearly superior to ours or else face a long time in court. The board members were operating under some degree of pressure because they knew I was fully prepared to sue everyone in sight. However, the control of a major entertainment corporation was at stake and who knew how far management was prepared to go to get hold of it.

I have no knowledge of what went on behind those closed doors but I would speculate that management argued long and hard to protect their position, that the special committee searched for good reasons to accept that position, and that Goldman Sachs told the board members, "You guys have no choice; the Redstone offer is better for the stockholders of Viacom." If they hadn't until then, I suspect most of them also started thinking about their own personal liability.

The meeting began at nine in the morning at the financial district offices of Hughes Hubbard & Reed, the law firm representing the special committee. We were parked in one conference room and I presume the management group was installed in another, although we never crossed paths. I was accompanied by Philippe and his associates from Shearman & Sterling, and Ken Miller and his people from Merrill Lynch.

The deliberations ran all day. We didn't expect an answer in the first few hours, but there was nowhere else for us to be and no other work that could hold our attention. Ours was a room full of men used to taking action and there was none to take, nothing any of us could do but pace and wait. Ken Miller had brought a novel and he sat quietly in a chair, reading. "What else am I going to do?" he said. "We could be in for a long night." Later, as it got toward evening, I went back to my apartment to wait for the word.

I called our team every hour or so. "What's going on?" But they didn't know; they were just sitting there. So was I. I certainly wasn't going to the movies. I needed to be in touch in case decisions had to be made.

Every few hours a board representative came into our conference room and was bombarded with questions. "What's going on?" We wanted to be absolutely certain we weren't getting screwed. "You're not negotiating with the other side, are you?"

"No, no, we're deliberating. Don't worry."

"Don't do anything without letting us know," we demanded.

The building staff went home and no decision had been made. Dinner was ordered in. Still no word, just the occasional visit from a board member with nothing to report.

Well into the night, a Goldman Sachs investment banker for the special committee walked in. It had been a long day and the guys looked at him. He brought some jarring news. The management group had come into the meeting and attempted to add a dollar per share to their bid.

Our team hit the roof. "That's a violation of the agreement!" Philippe said. "Bidding rules, which we all agreed on, stipulated that the final offers had been made. This was a condition that Sumner exacted."

The banker tried to calm them down. "You're right," he said. "That's not going to affect the decision. Have no fears. Don't worry."

Of course that made them worry. Philippe and Ken called me immediately.

My response? *"It's a goddamn outrage!"*

But both Ken and Philippe saw this apparent betrayal by management as a good sign. They took comfort from the banker's saying, "Don't worry." The protocol among investment bankers would not have allowed him to soothe us on the one hand and then ignore the rules of engagement on the other. To entertain a new bid at this time would be a serious breach of conduct, which would affect Goldman Sachs's ability to interact with us, and more importantly with Merrill Lynch, on any deal in the future.

"What does it mean?" I asked.

"We think the board is leaning toward us," Philippe told me. "Why else would Elkes come in with a desperation dollar, unless he thought they were losing? The board is not accepting their bid. We'll stay on it and call you as soon as we know something."

About four in the morning, representatives of the special committee walked into our conference room. I don't think anyone stood to greet them.

"The board has decided to go with your deal. Congratulations."

There was no great explosion of emotion. Everyone in that room had been far too anxious for that. They were all totally exhausted, but when Ken and Philippe called me I was wide awake.

"Sumner, you got it!"

I didn't carry on either. There was still work to be done. Philippe, Ken and I were worried that something unforeseen would happen. After all, Elkes and his people had Drexel Burnham and DLJ massed on their side, and even though the board had voted in our favor, until we signed a binding document we had no deal. Ken and Philippe said, "Let's get it done right away." I agreed completely.

The special committee wanted some drafting points on the contract agreed to, so at four in the morning Philippe sat down with the committee's lawyer and resolved them. His attitude was, "Fine, if it's not significant, you've got it." After all the haggling, the final touches took about ten minutes. We just wanted a signed piece of paper.

We had a car waiting and Philippe shot up the deserted streets to the Carlyle. I met him at the door of my apartment in my bathrobe. Neither of us was of a mind to celebrate. We didn't have an agreement until we exchanged signature pages.

"Where do I sign?" I asked.

He showed me, flipping through the contract pages, paper rustling, explaining the changes written in longhand because there had been no time to type them. I initialed them all as fast as I could. We were in a race against anything that could go wrong.

"I'll call you when it's a deal," Philippe said. He left my apartment, jumped back in the car and headed downtown.

The next time I heard from Philippe he said, "It's done. We've got it."

"That's great!" I told him. We congratulated each other. Then I went to bed. I felt as if I'd been in a war zone—and I had won the battle.

SEVEN

VIACOM—RUNNING THE SHOW

E*veryone said I overpaid.* The newspapers and financial analysts were giving me grudging respect for having worn management down, winning a "war of attrition." Actually, it was more like a shooting war; they didn't know about the roadblocks that had been put in our way or the threatened firefight between us and the board. But paying $3.4 billion for Viacom, when management's original offer had been $2.7 billion, seemed to strike the press and the Street as excessive.

I had bet my life on Viacom and I was looking forward to making the company a huge success. Everything I had was now locked into it. I had a new passion, a passion for Viacom. But there was still one more roadblock ahead. We were gathering our regulatory approvals and preparing to finalize the purchase of the company when Bank of America, which was providing the financing, told us it couldn't come through. The bank's representatives apologized profusely but they could not come up with the money required to complete the deal. After we had won the battle, our supply lines were cut.

We had gone with Bank of America because its financial covenants and other provisions in the loan agreement were more attractive and less onerous than those of competing institutions. BOA had given us a "highly confident" letter, a banking term of art in which a bank states that it is "highly confident" that it can arrange the financing. Well, the bank may have been highly confident then, but when it came time to do the deal, the money was not forthcoming.

Bank of America is a California bank and the amount required to complete the deal was beyond its legal lending limit. The people at BOA had planned to raise the balance by organizing a syndicate involving other institutions, but when they made their approach they found they were being boycotted by the New York banks. These banks had not been given the original assignment, they didn't like losing the business, and they weren't about to lend a hand to some out-of-state interloper. We were in the middle of a banking turf war. The New York banks sat on their hands and refused to participate. They were going to show these Californians: You want to deal in the big leagues, you've got to come to us.

We had a serious problem. But my approach to all problems is quite simple: Let's find a solution.

We held a frantic round of meetings. "How can this be?" we demanded of Bank of America. "You promised to raise the money. We went with you, we put our faith in you, we chose you over Citibank. You said you would deliver and now you are unable to deliver." Market conditions have changed, BOA told us. But the reality was the bank's judgment had not been accurate. "Look," we said, "we cannot let this acquisition fall apart because you are unable to get the money." BOA would not admit defeat, but no funds were in evidence. We told them, "You've got to bring in Citibank."

In our initial financing explorations, we had had many discussions with Citibank, which was far more established than BOA in the areas of financing and syndication. But the people at Citibank had offered less favorable terms. Now we quickly went back to them. We were in a tight spot and they knew it. Did they try to take advantage of our lack of leverage? Of course they did. But even though I'd had little experience in such high-level financial dealings, I understood the world of negotiating.

We faced the same objections concerning the sale of specific assets to pay down our debt from Citibank that we had faced from BOA. Once again I refused to commit to selling MTV. I told this different bunch of bankers the same thing I'd told their industry colleagues months before: "I am not buying this company to break it up. If it seems like the proper move I will make it, but I will not be locked into sales that will weaken the company's future."

Ken Miller didn't think I could get the money without making that concession. As we were about to leave for one meeting with the bankers, he told me, "You're not really going to take that position, are you? If you do, I'm not going."

"Then stay home!" I said. To his surprise and delight, I won the point.

The people at Citibank also demanded a concession to my age. I was sixty-three and in fine health, but they wanted a condition that the loan could be called if I passed away. I told them, "I will give you my best-efforts representation that I will not let that occur!"

Citibank ultimately did us a big favor by agreeing to be the co-manager of the financing and itself lend us as much as $600 million. Citibank got it done. The deal was restructured to make it more attractive to the New York banks. Of course Citibank received large fees, so we did have to pay up, and perhaps its portion of the financing cost a few dollars more than if we had gone with Citibank in the first place. But we remained in a better position overall because the original loan agreements from Bank of America, which stayed in the deal and was still able to provide a large part of the financing, were more favorable. Nevertheless, don't think for a minute that the New York banks were going to let some non–New York institution run away with this kind of deal. Without Citibank we would not have been able to acquire Viacom.

———————

My mother and father had moved from Boston to Florida. My father was in his eighties and had a prostate problem. He had had it for years.

The cancer was progressing slowly. The doctors in New England had decided to let him live out his life, but for some reason the doctors in Florida decided to operate. It was a last-minute decision and I did not even know that the operation was going to take place.

It did not go well. I got a call: "He's in deep trouble."

I flew to Florida immediately, rushed from the airport to the hospital and hurried down the linoleum corridors directly into his room. I believe he had been waiting for me. My father put his arms around me, hugged me, kissed me and died.

My mother had heart trouble and before they moved to Florida I had visited her often. Three months after my father died, my mother also passed away. She had pushed and pushed to make me a success. I miss them both very much. One of the great regrets in my life is that neither my mother nor my father lived to see what I finally accomplished.

On June 3, 1987, Viacom shareholders approved the sale. We owned Viacom.

I was excited. And while there was some feeling of exhaustion, I was invigorated by the thought of what lay ahead. I have always loved my businesses. I loved scouting locations and coming home with signed contracts for Northeast. I loved negotiating favorable picture deals for National, and building state-of-the-art theaters and expanding our scope and influence. Now I had a company whose influence was everywhere. Television production, cable TV, pay-TV, radio—we played to a lot of people and I was going to see to it that we played to many more.

I'm not one given to great displays of power, but I was the corporation's new owner and Terry Elkes stuck me in an office the size of a closet. Then he had the effrontery to tell me I was not welcome at his staff meetings. While he did not express it, it was apparent that I was still, in his mind, a peasant from Boston, probably incapable of running Viacom. One should never underestimate one's adversary. He did. He should have learned something from the intensity and adroitness with which we had conducted the battle to acquire the company. For Elkes to suggest that I get out of his way was insulting and absurd. He just didn't get it.

Of course I took this insult personally, but I was still determined to do what was best for Viacom. Elkes was clearly upset at having lost the company to me, but he had made several smart acquisitions during his tenure and he had run Viacom well—so well, in fact, that I had wanted to buy it. If he was willing to bury the hatchet, I was more than willing to have him continue as CEO.

Elkes called Philippe and asked him to come to Viacom headquarters to act as an intermediary between us. Philippe knew the purpose of this meeting would be to discuss what Elkes was looking for in the way of compensation and assumed he wanted an employment agreement with a nice option package. Philippe was prepared to hear the request and report it back to me.

Over lunch in one of the conference rooms, Elkes told Philippe that because of the value of his stock options and the bidding war that had driven up the price of Viacom stock, he had made approximately $30 million and really didn't need to work. However, he and his management team were willing to stay on one condition. He demanded that I give him personally 20 percent of the equity in Viacom.

Philippe thought, This is huge! After all, Elkes had lost! Trying to find out whether he really meant it, Philippe said, "Well, I think Sumner is going to be a little surprised by this request." Elkes told him I had no choice. "Sumner needs me to run this company," he said. "It's in a very tight financial situation and he needs me and the rest of my management team, and this is what I need to stay." Philippe thanked him, left the conference room and reported directly to me.

I do not like to make changes unless it becomes absolutely clear that there is no alternative. I prefer to work with whoever and whatever is in place, and if things are going smoothly, I am very comfortable with leaving things the way they are. I had been prepared to give Terry Elkes a great deal, one of the best compensation packages offered to any entertainment executive. But his greed had taken a quantum leap. Now he was going to get nothing.

I was furious. "It's an outrage!" I roared. (Philippe thinks one of the reasons I am so healthy is that it is not in my nature to hold anything in.) After all the tricks he had pulled during the takeover battle, Elkes had the gall to try to hold me up for 20 percent of the company. "This is blackmail!"

Of course it wasn't really blackmail because Elkes was free to do whatever he wanted. But he obviously felt his bargaining position was strong enough to ask for almost as much as he would have gotten had he won. Maybe more. I had taken all the financial risk, he was the loser, and he was sticking me up. After a few expletives I was calm again.

"Terry thinks he is indispensable," Philippe said. And at that moment he became dispensable—immediately dispensable.

Now we needed a CEO. In a hurry.

I was not yet qualified for the job. I knew how to run a company and I had all the necessary entrepreneurial instincts, but I did not at that time have the breadth of knowledge about the various businesses of Viacom, which even then was a highly diversified corporation. I knew exhibition, I knew negotiation, but I didn't know cable or production or television or radio. Whoever the new CEO was, he would have to be well versed in the entire entertainment industry because the scope of Viacom was already extensive and I intended to expand it even further.

That afternoon we drafted a short list of people who I thought could do the job. I considered Bob Pittman, who had impressed me. Richard Frank of Disney was a possibility. William Schwartz of Cox Communications. Winston "Tony" Cox at HBO. I got on the phone and started making calls to several people in the entertainment industry whose opinions I respected, asking for recommendations. I called Lew Wasserman and Sidney Sheinberg at MCA, I called Barry Diller at Fox. For input from within Viacom, I ran it by MTV's Tom Freston.

The name that kept coming up was Frank Biondi.

Biondi had graduated from Princeton and received an MBA from

Harvard Business School in 1968. He had worked at brokerage firms on Wall Street, then in the nascent cable television industry and as assistant treasurer and assistant director of business affairs at Children's Television Workshop. He had joined HBO to direct the program-planning department and had eventually risen to the position of CEO in 1983. All on the ascendance. But along with HBO successes came several losses, and in 1984 Biondi had been fired. Michael Fuchs, who replaced him, said, "I made no secret of the fact that I didn't like the way the company was being run."

The next year Biondi was hired by Fay Vincent as executive vice president of Coca-Cola's Entertainment Business Sector, which included Columbia Pictures and Columbia Television. He and Coca-Cola had prospered, and while I was negotiating to win Viacom, Biondi was promoted to chairman and CEO of Coca-Cola Television.

Interestingly, while Terry Elkes was threatening to leave Viacom unless he got what he wanted, even he had brought Biondi's name into play. His point being that he himself was the only man for the job of CEO, Elkes tried to make me choose between himself and the impossible. "Look," he told me, "I can understand your making a change in management if you can get someone like Frank Biondi—whom you could never get." He as much as dared me.

Elkes wasn't the only person who said Biondi was an impossible hire. Everyone told me the same thing: Biondi had just been promoted, he had sold his house in Riverdale and was planning to relocate to Beverly Hills, he was unattainable. His friends had already arranged and scheduled going-away parties for him. But based on the merits, Biondi seemed an excellent choice, and maybe the very fact that everyone said he couldn't be hired added an extra stimulus to at least try.

I needed Coca-Cola's consent to talk to Biondi so I called Fay Vincent and asked for permission. As a former major shareholder in Columbia Pictures before it was bought out by Coke, I had a relationship with these people and I didn't get too much resistance. In fact, when I spoke to some of the people at Columbia, it wasn't clear to me that they really wanted to keep Biondi. A particular story from his HBO tenure was following him.

The rate which premium television services usually pay for individual pictures is derived by a formula based upon the picture's gross in theatrical exhibition. The rate is set before the film is released and there is almost always a cap negotiated on that gross. That way, if a movie becomes a *Titanic*, the network doesn't end up paying hundreds of millions of dollars for the license of that one picture. It had been suggested that Biondi, for one reason or another, did not negotiate a cap on *Ghostbusters*, and that when the film became a breakout box-office hit the cost to HBO was astronomical and basically destroyed its profits for that year—and perhaps longer. I have never sought to confirm that, but it was supposed to be the reason HBO had said goodbye to Biondi.

For my purposes, however, he was the perfect candidate. Biondi had experience in the fundamental businesses of Viacom that I did not. I called him on a Friday evening. He arrived at my apartment for breakfast the next morning.

My immediate impression was that he was a man who would tell it as it was. Biondi was articulate and not flamboyant in any way, which I considered an asset. He was not at all a "Hollywood type." He had no aura of dynamism or charisma; rather, he presented himself as a knowledgeable, rather quiet-spoken person of intelligence.

Our conversation was easy. He came so well recommended that I was interviewing him not with an eye to his qualifications, which were apparent, but to his character. We discussed compensation, but it was clear that compensation was not the issue; we would pay him well. The issue was his getting this job. He wanted the job—and he should have wanted it. CEO of a major media company—there aren't a lot of those positions around. It was a bigger job than he had ever held, more powerful than the one he was moving to the West Coast to accept, and it offered him great opportunities.

For a man who had sold his house and was about to move to the coast, Biondi had to be more than interested to be talking with me. And he was. His enthusiasm was clear. I wanted a man to whom it was important to do well. I wanted someone who was stimulated by the opportunities for the company—a man who was totally motivated. Biondi appeared to be that man. I was extremely impressed with him. I offered him the job and he accepted.

From my apartment, with Biondi sitting in the room, I called Philippe to put our agreement on record. In spite of the fact that it was Saturday, Philippe was at his desk at Shearman & Sterling. I dictated ten points—title, salary, etc.—Philippe put them into legal language and had the document typed up, and on Monday Biondi had a two-page terms sheet on his desk. That was his employment agreement. We didn't get around to putting a long-form employment agreement in place until about a year and a half later. I remember calling his wife, Carol—a woman whom I have always liked but who may understandably have misgivings about me—and saying to her, "Carol, congratulations. Now get ready to unpack."

Four days had passed since Philippe had had lunch with Terry Elkes. I called Elkes on the phone. He probably thought he had me over a barrel: Either I was going to accede to his demand for equity in the company and make a counteroffer at a lower figure or I would try to mollify him with a major compensation package.

"Terry," I said, "you know, actually your thinking was right. The guy for us, all things considered, was and is Frank Biondi." I paused. "I have him."

Elkes had underestimated me from the very beginning and had miscalculated every step of the way. This was his ultimate miscalculation. As CEO of Viacom, he would have had the opportunity to bring our company into the future and reap the benefits I was convinced would come with it. But he blew it and now he was gone. I could hear the shock, incredulity and dismay on the other end of the phone, but he had it coming.

It didn't take long for the executive exodus to begin. Out the door went the rest of the upper echelon of Viacom executive talent. They had been my adversaries, and once we were all on the same side, they seemed to continue their adversarial roles. I knew I couldn't count on them. If they didn't support me, they couldn't support the company. There were really only two people I had wanted to keep: Jules Haimovitz of Viacom Entertainment and Ralph Baruch, the co-chairman of the board. I liked them both. Haimovitz was very smart, and Baruch and I had formed a relationship, in part because he couldn't stand the rest of the management team. Why? One of the reasons was that, despite having had a lot to do with Elkes becoming CEO of Viacom, Baruch had been left out of the planning for the LBO. He'd read about it in the newspapers. But they both departed, well provided for with golden parachutes. I was not in the least dismayed.

I was pleased that we had good people within the company to take their place: Tom Dooley, treasurer; Tom Freston, whom we promoted to president and CEO of MTV (there had previously been two presidents); Geraldine Laybourne, president of Nickelodeon. Freston, who was quite young, impressed me from the first day I met him. He was smart, and smart I can spot right away. Moreover, he had committed his loyalty to me and was entitled to mine. To this day Tom and I have remained more than business associates; we are simply good friends. And then, of course, we were bringing in Frank Biondi. We also brought in Tony Cox, who had worked with Biondi at HBO, to run Showtime.

I was walking into a large organization, having spent most of my life running a small one. I had no idea where the bodies were buried or which of the live ones were more competent than others. I would learn pretty fast, but the main thing was to find the people I could trust.

Trust, of course, cuts both ways. I earned people's trust by the way I dealt with them. And I don't mean just in terms of compensation. I made it clear very early that the people at Viacom could depend on me. National Amusements had been run out of a small building in Dedham, Massachusetts, with guys I'd known and been friends with for decades popping in and out of my office all day long. I encouraged the people at Viacom to do the same. I had been a part of the lives of the people at National and they had been part of mine. And since very little was more important than the work we were doing, we were all in it together.

You can't overestimate the importance of personal involvement and personal relationships in the context of running a business. People appreciate being treated like friends and colleagues rather than employees. As I've said, I'm not at all comfortable with even the word "employee." I much prefer cultivating the friendships of the people around me, making it clear that as I count on them, they can count on me, now and forever. There is nothing feigned about my interest in the people who work with me. As a result they are more committed than ever and more able to share my passion for Viacom.

There are some who have suggested that I am excessively hands-on. If that means going after every problem and solving it, trying to take advantage of every opportunity and creating opportunities where none exist, then I plead guilty. I am hands-on.

It may sound strange, but I also invite confrontation. Confrontation leads to truth. People know better than to agree with what I say simply because I say it. I don't want that. I don't respect it. I like issues to be thoroughly debated to take advantage of the best our minds have to offer. If there's a problem, it is a company problem that will be solved by the management team.

I created a good management core in those first months at Viacom. And when projections for the future financial health of the company came out in May, they were considerably better than expected. No question about it, people in the old management had totally low-balled their projections. If you listened to them, Viacom was going to sink unless they, with some mandate from God, saved the company. Tom Freston had told me, "Don't believe it, Sumner. It's all horseshit. The company is going to do fine." He was right.

Biondi went to work and I went to work next to him. Frank was every bit as knowledgeable as he had been touted to be. For the next several years, I learned the breadth and nuances of the entertainment business at his side. We had a very close relationship. Although I owned

Viacom, we operated the company as partners. We were back and forth in each other's offices every day. He'd walk in, I'd walk in. He introduced me to pieces of the company with which I had no experience. Fortunately, I'm a fast learner.

Frank was CEO, it was his job to run the company. But it is in my nature to be intimately involved in every corporate activity, and I was. While I gave him wide latitude, there were no important decisions which he made by himself. I participated in every staff meeting and he would often ask me for whatever thoughts I could contribute. I, in turn, would praise him to the investment community. But when it came to long-term vision and strategic planning, that was my domain. From day one I was trying to create in Viacom the premier software-driven media company in the world.

Frank was a very hands-off executive. As he put it, "I'm a big believer in [the concept] that the most important thing you can do is hire good, smart, motivated people and let them run their businesses." As I've said, I am a bit more hands-on. One of the first strategies we put in place was to bring the top executives of all the Viacom companies together. Viacom was a broadly diversified corporation with several businesses that up to that point had had nothing to do with one another. I wanted to make our people understand the interrelationships between their businesses and foster a sense of Viacom identity. Too often one business, or even one division, can develop tunnel vision and lose sight of the greater goal, which is the development and growth of the entire corporation. MTV, meet Showtime. Showtime, meet radio. Radio, meet television production. Only good could come from those introductions. I wanted all these CEOs to understand that each of them was, first and foremost, an executive of Viacom. It was a theme that I have had occasion to reiterate throughout my entire life at Viacom—the necessity for everyone to make divisional agendas subservient to the entire company's objectives.

I also wanted to get a better sense of the executives as people. I'll say it again: You can't overestimate the beneficial effect of personal involvement and personal relationships in a business context, both within and outside the company. Viacom had been a place of low morale, of suspicion and distrust. I wanted to make a major change in the way people thought of their jobs. At National Amusements we were free to be gruff with each other, free to kid each other. And we were all passionately involved in the company. I wanted Viacom to work the same way. I love what I do and I wanted the people around me to love what they were doing as well. I wanted to like the people at Viacom, and the fact is, I wanted them to like me, too.

———

Largely as a result of my purchase of Viacom, I was beginning to become a public figure. The national media, which had rarely had cause to mention my name, were all of a sudden quite interested in finding out who this guy was who had just bought Viacom. It came as a surprise to some to find that I was lecturing at Harvard Law School and Brandeis University and had been on the faculty of Boston University Law School, where I had lectured and taught courses in entertainment law since 1982. It was assumed that I was just another smart investor, but in fact, teaching was and is to this day among my greatest pleasures.

I was called a media mogul and it made me uncomfortable. One can be excited about one's business, one can feel a legitimate sense of accomplishment, without being a mogul. "I would hate to view myself as any type of tycoon," I told the Associated Press. "Words like 'tycoon' and 'mogul' and 'magnate' turn me and my children off." Those are money words and I have never been motivated by a personal need for money. I didn't intend to take a salary at Viacom. I was not giving up anything I wanted. I simply didn't care about it. I put the money back into the business because, as I've said, growing the business to its ultimate potential was my all-encompassing goal. My material aspirations have always been minimal. Winning was the goal. Achievement was the goal—proving my competence, trying to be better than other people at what I did. That was what counted.

"[My children and I] have a sense of maybe we can make it mean more than money," I told the AP. "Any time you are involved in communications networks there are opportunities to play a small role [in improving society] without being pretentious about it." In the blush of newfound media attention I might have overstated myself, but I do believe that power involves social responsibility. The word "mogul," on the other hand, brings with it the implication of excessive power used selfishly, which I would find offensive.

When I began working in a small concession stand in a drive-in theater, I fell in love with motion pictures. I was in awe of the magic of stories on film and the powerful craft of storytelling. To think that a simple human idea, molded by the imagination, could reach out and engage the minds and hearts of people around the world—that's the power of the creative mind. It's a power that kindles a passion for what I do that transcends the responsibilities of the bottom line. Transcends—not neglects. To Wall Street that may sound sacrilegious, but it's neither sacrilegious nor noble, simply essential. To my way of thinking, corporate interests and social interests can be mutually reinforcing. At Viacom we had the opportunity to do some good and also satisfy our stockholders. The two were not incompatible.

The banks were not yet clamoring for us to pay down our debt, but we did hold preliminary meetings with Coca-Cola, Gulf & Western and MCA about the possibility of each buying a stake in Viacom. I might have persuaded myself rationally, considering the high leverage of the company, that it would be a good idea to investigate that possibility, but ultimately those talks went nowhere because in my heart I never wanted to sell what Viacom owned.

We did hold more prolonged talks with Disney about Disney becoming an equity partner in Showtime/The Movie Channel. Disney's president, Frank Wells, was very interested. So was I. Showtime, in 1987, was having difficulties. It was being creamed by HBO. For a major studio to have an equity interest in Showtime would have been very significant because it would have ensured a pipeline for its product directly to our channel. The talks went back and forth. We fixed a value on the network of $700 million and were discussing selling half. It would have begun to pay down our debt. But ultimately we decided not to sell. In addition to being a movie outlet, Showtime had the potential to be a source of original programming and I was hell-bent on software.

However, we did find ways to pay down the debt.

In the normal course of our buying media stocks, National had acquired a big piece of Orion Pictures Corporation. Viacom had also held an interest in the studio and had representatives on the Orion board of directors. When Viacom became mine, my combined position at Orion rose to upwards of 26 percent. The press assumed, probably because we had just acquired Viacom, that I had empire aspirations and would continue purchasing more Orion stock and make a play for control. I had no particular interest in owning Orion; at that time it was simply a good investment, but with a questionable future. We had sold the stock in every media company we had ever bought—except, of course, for Viacom.

John Kluge, who was reportedly friendly with Orion CEO Arthur Krim and held a seat on the company's board, was the second-largest shareholder. Kluge, perhaps as a "white knight" against the possibility of a hostile takeover, began to increase his position, which very quickly outstripped my own. I did not want to be a minority shareholder in a public company, and in order to protect my investment, I bought more stock. We very quickly appeared to be in a bidding war—for a company in which I, to repeat, had no interest.

Did I want to run a studio? Not that one. As an exhibitor I understood the complexities of the movie business. I had no intention of getting involved at that time or with that company. To keep the fever high, however, I did not want to appear anxious to unload my stock and therefore intimate that a lower buyout price might be acceptable. When Ace Greenberg of Bear Stearns called and basically said, "I talked to Kluge. I can arrange a trade here," we responded, "Let's resolve this."

Kluge is notoriously reclusive and he and I didn't need to meet. Philippe handled the deal, fielding the offers and relaying them to me. It was done on the phone. Kluge offered a subprice, I came back with a higher one, and the deal was settled like a stock trade. Kluge came away with the company, we came away with a nice profit to put toward the removal of our debt, and everyone was happy. Every deal should be so easy.

We sold our cable operations on Long Island and in Cleveland to Chuck Dolan of Cablevision. Chuck is a smart guy; he had come to me early on and offered to "help us" lower our debt, low-balling us, naturally. We respectfully turned down his initial offer but we understood that both Cleveland and Long Island were very important to him; he was trying to become the premier cable player in the New York metropolitan area and these systems would be a tremendous plus. We simply refused to sell below a certain price. We met many times in our conference room, and during one session someone on our side suggested a willingness to listen to a lower offer. I immediately got very angry and made it clear that no flexibility had been indicated. In fact, I called Dolan later and said, "Chuck, I don't want you to get the wrong message. There is no sale under the price we discussed."

Ultimately, we agreed on a figure of $550 million, or $2,750 per subscriber, an unheard-of price at that time. However, it made more sense for Dolan to pay my high price for the cable systems than for him to live without them. And it worked out for him in the long run. This is the best kind of deal, one in which you get everything you want, and even though it may take a little longer to reach its goal, the other side makes out as well. As a result, we developed a warm and friendly relationship with Dolan—a relationship which I treasure to this day—and he was able to fulfill his strategic objectives.

The old management pronounced the company name "*Vee*-a-com."
Vee-a-com. To me that sounded weak, like newborn birds clamoring for
worms. The word almost tweeted. During the takeover battle I kept re-
ferring to the company I was after as "*Vi*-a-com." That sounded strong,
something worth fighting for. "*Vi*-a-com." Struggle and accommodation. It included both conflict and resolution in the same word. So at
our first board meeting in 1987, I announced to the world that we were
no longer "*Vee*-a-com," we were "*Vi*-a-com." No market research, no advertising campaign to reposition the company in the public eye and
ear. No rational, logical reason whatsoever. Viacom. That was us from
now on.

Two years after the takeover, we were running a lean operation. We had
reduced our debt substantially, we were taking in hundreds of millions
of dollars from our syndication of *The Cosby Show*, and MTV was beginning to take off. Things were going very well.

In May 1989, however, Viacom faced a barrier we could not afford to
ignore. Showtime and The Movie Channel, our premium movie channels, were getting pulverized by HBO and Cinemax, which were owned
by Time Inc. Time also owned New York City's Manhattan Cable and
was one of the two largest cable operators in the country. Time was pro-
tecting its movie channels by refusing to allow Showtime/TMC access
to its systems and, therefore, to its subscribers.

It was the gatekeeper syndrome. In New York, Denver, Memphis and
other cities, Time was not only favoring its own product, it was exclud-
ing us entirely. Time controlled 65 percent of the pay television market.
We were competing against HBO for movies and had to pay the same
amount in licensing fees to the studios, but we were denied millions of
potential viewers by Time's refusal to give us access to its cable systems.
Among other consequences, it cost Time a lot less per subscriber to ac-

quire films than it cost us. One entertainment lawyer likened it to "a supermarket that only sells its own label goods." Actually, it was worse than that. At least a supermarket has competitors, and a consumer can drive over to the next store and comparison-shop. Cable franchises were a monopoly and the cable consumer had nowhere else to go to see Showtime.

It was perfectly obvious that Time was violating antitrust law, but its position simply was "Tough luck." This was completely ill-advised. Here was a natural cable monopoly—there was no competition in the cable industry, there was only one system per designated area—and apparently the management at Time thought it was a smart move to exclude a competitor from access. In this case, absolute power was corrupting Time. In fact, it was corrupting the industry. The people running Time had powerful brands, they had channels which could certainly stand up to legitimate competition and a system which could easily accept several premium channels. Shouldn't they have known intuitively that their actions involved the potential for serious legal liability?

We warned them, "This is just intolerable. It is a violation of antitrust law," but apparently they didn't believe we would follow through on our threats and sue. After all, these were the same cable systems that carried our programming for MTV, Nickelodeon, VH1 and Nick at Nite. We depended on them for our livelihood. Surely, they must have thought, we would not be so foolish as to jeopardize our main sources of income. None of the other suppliers were lining up to sue the people on whom they relied for viewers. No one else would dare.

There was significant trepidation inside our company about the possibility of suing Time. Tom Freston asked for a meeting to discuss what could be an extremely perilous course of action. Gerry Laybourne was involved, as were Frank Biondi and all of our top people, including, of course, Philippe Dauman and Tom Dooley. I would make the final decision, but I wanted to know the full range of Viacom thinking. At Viacom, everyone had a right to state his or her view and fight for it; this was critical to the environment which I fostered, an openness to ideas. I was not looking to dictate a consensus; that would have been about as bad management as you can bring to a company. These were intelligent people and I needed to hear their concerns. And they were concerned. "Sumner," I was told, "I hope you know what you're doing suing the biggest customer we have."

If you are going to take critical action that involves the life of the company and includes a high element of risk, your job is to try to make everyone understand the importance of the issues and the necessity to preserve the integrity and long-term strategic objectives of the company—the ultimate need to proceed with an admittedly risky lawsuit. I appreciated the risks. If we did sue and Time won the case and decided to throw MTV and Nickelodeon off its systems in a fit of retribution, it would be difficult to recover. Some might say that we would face ruin. With that, of course, I disagreed. In the final analysis, the consumer always prevails.

In the end, I made the decision to file a lawsuit. It was not unlike my decision in 1956 at National Amusements to file suit against the major film distributors. Again my corporate life was on the line; we were facing a risk that went to the very core of the long-term viability of Viacom. If allowed to continue, this boycott could kill Showtime. But one thing you cannot tolerate is someone using raw power to disenfranchise your company. You cannot tolerate it, either in terms of the immediate economic consequences or your long-range ability to do business in that world. Threaten me and I will enforce my rights. We have to be able to stand up and protect the integrity of the company. People have to know that if they attack Viacom, they are not going to get away with it. It's not personal, it's critical business. We will make their lives more miserable than they make ours.

The risks were high, the nuances complicated. There were other elements to be considered as well. Time Inc. was in the middle of negotiations to merge with Warner Communications. We were in a position to request a restraining order to enjoin that merger, which could have been disastrous for the potential Time Warner corporation and gave us unusual leverage. This fact was not lost on the people at Time.

While that course of action was open to us, we ultimately decided not to follow it. We thought the lawsuit itself would accomplish our purposes and we did not want to inflict any more harm on Warner than we had to in order to protect our interests. Warner, thus far, was an innocent bystander. I was not an intimate friend of Warner chairman Steve Ross, but I had respect and admiration for the role he played, and I thought that the degree of damage and injury we might cause would be excessive. I know this seems odd to say in the context of a lawsuit, but I think one ought to use one's power with some consideration for the other side. I was confident that we were right and would prevail, either in court or via a settlement, and I just didn't want to hurt either Time or Warner excessively. Besides, sometimes the mere fact of leverage, like a big stick tapped but not swung, serves its full purpose.

Candidly speaking, another reason we didn't seek to restrain the merger was that we were doubtful of our ability to prevail. We had enough going for us. Plus sooner or later, I felt, we would be doing business with these companies again. Why poison the atmosphere forever? To end up bitter enemies with all the people involved in this dispute was not in my personal interest or in the interest of Viacom.

But I wasn't going to be a patsy and endure predatory and abusive conduct. I filed suit very reluctantly; I had no other recourse. You didn't have to be an antitrust lawyer to understand that if people had the power to control access to a market and totally excluded a competitive product from that market, they were hurting their customer, they were hurting the consumer, and they were violating the antitrust laws. Furthermore, there was a First Amendment issue; they were refusing to allow the consumer—the public—to see and hear the speech we were presenting.

Viacom brought charges against Time Inc. under the Sherman Antitrust Act, which had originally been signed into law to stop robber barons from controlling huge sections of American industry. We charged Time with predatory behavior, conspiracy to monopolize the pay television industry in the United States, monopoly and abuse of the monopoly power in certain local markets for cable television, restraint of trade, and coercion. We alleged that its merger plan would lessen competition and tend to create a monopoly in pay television. We asked for $2.4 billion. From the moment that I made the decision to file this lawsuit, I had the full support of the entire management team at Viacom.

The cable industry was not pleased. Our suit focused the attention of Congress on the cable monopolies. Congress was already holding hearings on the subject, looking into a system that was fraught with the potential for abuse and that had disenfranchised not only programmers but also consumers, as was indicated by the treatment of Showtime. We spoke with Senators Howard Metzenbaum, Ernest Hollings, John Kerry, Tim Wirth and everyone else who played a role in this arena. But we had to be extremely cautious to focus on the individual inappropriate behavior by Time and not on the industry as a whole. Cable *is* a monopoly—but it is a natural monopoly. We were not taking the position that it was wrong for Time to own a vast number of cable systems, or for Time to own pay television channels. We were attacking only its abuse of power against us. Frank Biondi told the press, "This is a private action between members of the same industry, and we think the laws under which this action was brought are sufficient to remedy the claims we made. We don't think there's a crying need for re-regulation. . . . This is not an attack on cable and monopolies. It is an attack on abusive behavior and predatory practices by a monopoly."

We won that lawsuit in discovery. Time was an arrogant company with a monopolistic attitude, and in the process of our massive discovery, we found ample proof of its corporate intention to exclude competitors and, thus, to violate the antitrust laws.

Time executives had considerable problems and weaknesses in their position. They knew the facts, they knew we had the facts.

Finally Time caved. And while the process took several years to complete, ultimately a very favorable settlement was reached. We hadn't expected, and of course did not receive, $2.4 billion. However, had we tried the case, it could have taken several more years to conclude, with uncertain results.

In the settlement we received a wide list of attractive benefits that related to all parts of our business: favorable operational issues including joint marketing campaigns by Showtime and HBO, increased advertising purchases by Time Warner on MTV Networks, and, most important, wider distribution of Showtime/TMC on Time Warner's cable systems, plus a significant cash settlement to Viacom. Showtime has gone on to prosper and is now the country's largest producer of original programming on premium cable. Without this lawsuit the network would not exist today. Today, our relationship with Time Warner is constructive and friendly. I consider Gerry Levin one of the great leaders and visionaries in our industry. And from my perspective, I also consider him a very close friend.

EIGHT

I WANT MY MTV

The people at MTV Networks thought of themselves, not surprisingly, as kids. Despite the fact that they were as much a part of corporate Viacom as Showtime or Lifetime or any of our cable systems, broadcast TV or radio stations, they were very uncorporate. They didn't have a dress code, they didn't work standard hours, they didn't look or talk like the rest of the Viacom family. In fact, I liked the anarchic environment and the offbeat-looking people I found there. What they did have was a great idea. I am aware that I have a reputation as something of a micromanager, but I never had the slightest intention of attempting to influence the programming of MTV; that was the job of Tom Freston and his team.

Even though advertisers, the record industry and cable operators were not immediately tuned in at its inception, at its heart MTV was a great idea. From its launch in 1981, MTV was an extremely consumer-focused company which paid close attention to its own consumer research. MTV's creative people and businesspeople were trying to create a new type of television business, almost a cross between a specialized magazine and a TV network. MTV, Nickelodeon and VH1 all had the same philosophy: It's our world. For teenagers and people in their early twenties, in the case of MTV in particular, this idea had been irresistible. The music video was a new form and, surrounded by offbeat promotional elements and funny graphics, MTV had developed a personality and style that was transforming America. It was the place where new superstars were born, discovered and made.

The concept was electric but it needed a continuing flow of money to broaden its scope and appeal. We soon began to get involved in the global expansion of MTV. In 1987, in a joint venture with the Robert Maxwell Group and British Telecommunications, we went into Europe. We arrived in Asia and Australia in 1990 and expanded into Latin America in 1994.

But by 1987 the music video format had lost its novelty. It was no longer enough to play band after band and expect the kids to be satisfied. Keeping music at its core, Tom Freston and his team began to introduce more substantive programming involving many of the underpinnings of popular culture: music news, fashion, movies, comedy. The vagaries of the music business are legendary; what would MTV do in a down period? A music magazine would begin to put people like David Letterman or Mel Gibson on its cover; MTV did the same thing.

We also recognized that, unlike the traditional concept of generations that evolve in approximately twenty-year intervals, the MTV audience seemed to change every four or five years, much like a class of kids working its way through high school or college. The kiss of death would be to follow one group of viewers to graduation. They would move on and the network would die. The baby-boom generation, Generation X—sooner or later everyone grows up. It was the unique strength of MTV that, like incoming freshmen, hordes of new viewers would insistently tumble our way. This was a blessing. The challenge was for MTV to stay focused on the late-teen/early-twenties audience and continually reinvent itself to remain cool and relevant.

This cost money, and in the beginning, saddled as we were with the need to pay down our debt, there was little leeway for investment. Our byword: Cash is king. As a result, MTV was forced to grow its business internally, to develop its own programming and create its own product. That business, like the rest of Viacom, had to generate profit to help pay down the debt. The fact that the banks wanted to sell MTV to service this debt only amplified the pressure.

The real problem for this youth-culture network was how to maintain relevance and make money without seeming to be part of the corporate beast. The cost constraints that forced us to work in-house had the fortuitous result of giving MTV's reigning geniuses close control of the programming content. Make fun of yourself, don't take anything too seriously, focus on what the kids want now—these were all part of the MTV credo. Success depended on quality, and Freston and his crew always put a new face on cutting-edge concepts. MTV was no longer a string of videos or one program or one series; it was an entire way of looking at the world. That ever-changing face, that attitude, was MTV.

MTV Networks reinvented brand entertainment. "Before us," Freston said, "Disney was the only television network with a brand; every other network was just a place where a bunch of shows ran. MTV was a brand! We thought we could put a lot of value into that brand, grow it and charge advertisers more to be associated with it." We had cachet. We would tell advertisers, "If you advertise on our network, part of what we have will rub off on your product." The fact that our audience was young and just beginning to establish buying habits that would last a lifetime was also an important sales tool. "Our audiences are early adopters" was an MTV sales mantra.

Biondi and I drove the MTV executives. We insisted that they grow the company, and they did. Each year we set the bar higher and each year they succeeded. They reorganized their staff, hiring more aggressive ad sales people, and revenue rose 25 percent per annum with profits rising approximately 24 percent. Incredibly, that growth continued every year.

In 1989, fueled by proceeds from *Cosby* syndication sales—on which we worked damned hard and for which we got $4 million per episode for 125 episodes, a total of $500 million, more than anyone else had ever received for syndication of a single show—and a boom in the cable industry on which we capitalized significantly by selling a cable franchise for the highest price in cable history, Viacom began to succeed beyond Wall Street's wildest expectations. Many trends were with us: the growth of cable and satellite television in the United States, increased penetration of cable and satellite TV into foreign markets, the deregulation of the media. All brought increased money into television advertising, and we were able to ride the technological changes to our advantage.

We relocated MTV from its digs at 1775 Broadway to our corporate headquarters in Times Square and there were those inside the operation who thought, Oh, no, we're moving back in with our parents. But they maintained their style and independence, which was all to the good. Where only two years earlier we had had to budget MTV production tightly, in 1990 we spent over $110 million enhancing our programming with new and acquired productions. We hired directors and writers and reinvented TV animation for kids with *Nicktoons*. Freston said, "Nickelodeon needs its own mouse," so we began the investment that ultimately produced the wildly popular series *Rugrats* and many other big hits.

Promoted and positioned to maximum exposure, MTV was creating its own culture. I was certainly no expert on the younger generation's music, but what I did understand was that MTV was creating a new kind of business and I trusted Tom Freston to drive it forward. Although I didn't discuss which videos to play or what shows to run, Tom would bring his programming and business plans to Frank Biondi and me. Frank was somewhat reluctant to gamble too much on MTV. I made the decision to give MTV Networks maximum support. Tom laughed with me appreciatively, knowing this was alien to my usual way of doing business, but I believed in him and trusted his judgment. Tom's credibility with me was enormous. Like a trusting parent, I essentially gave MTV the keys to the car.

The insular in-house programming that had begun as a necessity became a signature generational point of view at MTV and played a large role in sustaining viewer interest and growing the company. There was, however, some resistance from the music industry, the people who were supplying the videos. Every hour of our own shows was an hour when their music wasn't being played, and they resented the intrusion. No matter that we needed long-form programming to sustain ratings and bring them their audience, what had been a pure showcase for their products was now less music-focused, more diverse, and a serious tension did arise.

VH1 was a hodgepodge and VH1 president John Sykes basically reinvented the company. He came up with the concept of differentiating VH1 from MTV as an all-music channel in which even the programming that was not solely videos would be based entirely on the music industry. Concentrating only on the music solved two problems: the lack of identity for the channel and the complaints of the music business. We created *Behind the Music, Legends, Storytellers, Where Are They Now?, Before They Were Rock Stars, Pop-Up Video, The List* and *Rock & Roll Jeopardy*. We produced a pre-show before the Grammys and televised the Rock and Roll Hall of Fame induction ceremonies. The music industry loved VH1 and the channel took off. Now we are producing a wide variety of new shows, including a music awards show and the very successful fashion awards.

Our international expansion came in stages. Early on, satellite transponders (the machines that receive and redistribute satellite transmissions) were very expensive, and because our initial strategy was to obtain distribution for MTV in any way we could, we opted for the panregional broadcast. At one point there was a single MTV feed serving thirty-five countries. The economics of that arrangement were excellent and for a time we found success because the notion of MTV and satellite television in general were novelties. English was the lingua franca of rock and roll. However, we knew the best broadcasts would be culturally specific—an Asian outlook for Asia, German music for Germany—and it was clear to us that one-feed programming left much to be desired.

With the advent of digital technology and the ability to compress signals on satellites and produce them more cheaply, we were able to put six or seven feeds on one transponder and customize specific programming for the United Kingdom, Germany, Spain and wherever else we wanted to reach. Not only was the audience more targeted and therefore more satisfied, we could offer that audience more directly to local advertisers. Where we had previously had no answer for the sponsors who said, "I don't want to advertise in Lithuania. I just want the German market," now we could give it to them. Our approach became much more flexible.

As cable grew, our European programming improved. In the early '80s, with a small viewership and a small budget, MTV had had to make do with the available on-air talent: German or Danish video jockeys, whom MTV dubbed "veejays" (after DJs, the short form for disc jockeys), who spoke English as a second language. The programs had an aura of international coolness and they worked. But when local competitors came on the scene and began to take away viewership, Freston recognized the necessity to regionalize. This took money. He came to us and we gave it to him. He had our complete trust.

There came a time when the controlling interest in MTV Europe came up for sale. In January 1991 we had bought British Telecommunications' 25 percent and in August of that year Robert Maxwell was in trouble. Maxwell owned 50 percent of the franchise and was under a great deal of pressure, the details of which we were not privy to. All we knew was that he needed money.

Maxwell had not been the greatest of partners. To begin with, there was his usual attitude of superiority. The first time I met him was over dinner at his office in London. We were ushered into his extremely pretentious dining room but Maxwell wasn't there; he had to stage his ceremonious arrival. At the dinner table during the course of the meal he displayed his somewhat flamboyant personality. "How does it feel to operate that little company that you've just acquired?" he asked me. That little company was Viacom. To which I replied, "Well, I'm enjoying it." And added, "Actually, I wasn't aware of how small it was."

The man was insufferable. "You know the difference between you and me, Sumner? I just thought about it," he said. "If I walked down the streets of Japan with a beautiful woman, all the media in the world would say, 'Who is that woman with Robert Maxwell?' If you did it, no one would notice." This is not strength, I thought to myself. This is weakness.

Not long afterwards, Maxwell sat in my office in New York and I negotiated to purchase his 50 percent of MTV Europe. I paid $62 million, which some of my associates thought was too much. A few months later Maxwell disappeared from his yacht and was never found, his corporations approximately $720 million in debt. Today MTV is worth billions and is the world's foremost international television network.

Nickelodeon was on the verge of success. When I acquired Viacom, the financial world and others said that Nickelodeon would never make it. Who, they asked, would be interested in a kid's channel? Gerry Laybourne, a former schoolteacher, was running Nickelodeon and running it well. Gerry understood what Nickelodeon was all about. She understood what kids were all about. This was a channel, Gerry thought, that was not for parents; it was a channel for kids. The kids owned Nickelodeon. Gerry and I became extremely close friends.

In February 1992 we brought all the MTV Networks managers down to Key West for a retreat to celebrate our past successes and plan our future strategies. The mood was festive, and after listening to the staff's ideas in an afternoon symposium, I addressed them the following day. "I learned a lot yesterday," I began, "so listen to me, you turkeys! . . . Only a short four and a half years ago there were still some in the world who considered that MTV was a fad. MTV is now entrenched as part of the culture of America and fast becoming entrenched in the culture of the world." I proudly noted the successes of each of the MTV Networks individually and collectively and called 1991 a "year of triumph."

I looked out at the audience and saw many women. MTV Networks had a large percentage of female managers and executives, beginning at the top with Vice Chairman Gerry Laybourne and Senior Vice President, Creative Director Judy McGrath. "There is no way I can convey to you the full sense of my excitement about what you have become and about what all of you are," I told the crowd. "I must say that I am particularly turned on by the enormous presence of women in the MTV Networks group, for it is in many ways the manifestation of what MTV stands for and what I believe in." The cheering came from both the MTV women and the men. If the only thing you care about is competence, as we do at Viacom, then you're going to have a lot of women filling important positions in your company.

There is much to be said for listening to the people around you. I had been told that the people at all levels of MTV wanted a cafeteria. They didn't like having to leave their exciting yet insular world every lunchtime to fight for a sandwich or a slice of pizza in Times Square. Many were kids and I suspect they didn't eat that well to begin with. They wanted a place of their own, and of all people who deserved it, the MTV staff topped the list. They were creating their own culture; they wanted their own clubhouse. I gave it to them.

"We need more time together," I told them. "A place where we can talk more to each other and listen more to each other. I, for one, hate the solitude of private dining rooms. So let me tell you that I am committed to that cafeteria of our own. That's where I will be eating—as long as they serve oat bran flakes." A roar went up from the crowd.

Tom Freston came to me afterwards and said, "Do you realize how many millions of dollars that is going to cost us?" He didn't oppose the idea; he was just being budget-conscious. "Tom," I told him, "it's going to be all right."

More than all right, it would be a fine cafeteria. And later at a giant party at Key West's Viva Zapata club, the MTV crowd was tossing back shots of tequila—myself included—and dancing on tabletops—myself not included—singing "Redstone for President!" I really loved these people.

I still wasn't a big fan of their music. I was more likely to listen to Tommy Dorsey than Tom Petty or Tommy Lee. I used to tell Tom Freston, "Everybody loves this new music—call it rock, call it whatever you want to call it—that MTV symbolizes. But don't think for a minute that these same people have such narrow tastes that they still wouldn't love the music I grew up with. Big band music. The greats. It's time to play Benny Goodman, it's time to play Tommy Dorsey."

"They're all dead, Sumner."

MTV was constantly faced with the need to do something radically different. That was its mandate, that was the way it got attention. Danny Bennett had come out of the rock world, where he had been an artists' manager, and now represented his father, Tony. Tony Bennett. Danny wanted to get his father on MTV to, as Tom told me, "hip Tony up." I was a fan of Tony Bennett and pushed Tom hard. I knew it would work on MTV.

So in the early '90s there was Tony Bennett onstage as a presenter at the MTV Video Music Awards with Flea and Anthony Kiedis from the Red Hot Chili Peppers. They did a funny, relatively off-color bit that went over well. Tony carried himself with grace, looked great, sounded great, didn't embarrass himself in front of an audience that could have been his grandkids. He had a nice way about him.

Building on that momentary success, Tony made a video, which was unusual for a man singing his kind of material in his subtle and urbane style. When I heard about it, I told Tom, "Tony Bennett. Now you're talking my kind of music." The song was classic Tony Bennett, smooth and tuneful and sophisticated, and the programmers at MTV aired it for a lark. Some lark!

Imagine everyone's surprise when the video did well. His album sales moved up and MTV got credit for having put Tony Bennett, this icon of a past generation, on the air. His transgenerational appeal received wide attention in the press and, most important, attracted the MTV audience, which, as I had suspected, found his music beautiful.

On the strength of that video and my continued pressure on Tom Freston, MTV decided to include Tony in its series of intimate acoustic concerts called *Unplugged*. I attended the rehearsal at the Sony studios on Tenth Avenue and was enthralled. It was the perfect venue for the perfect singer. All the hot young stars looked to Tony as their mentor, asking him how they should phrase their songs, where they should stand, how he had remained so cool. The show was a success; the resulting album was a smash hit and won Tony a Grammy. His career was rejuvenated, all because of MTV—and a little help from me. As I've said, I have never been a stargazer but Tony has long been one of my idols, and now he is my friend. Imagine my shock when my Viacom associates threw me a surprise birthday party and Tony Bennett stepped out of the crowd—having traveled some two thousand miles to get there—and sang a song for me.

If MTV could breathe new life into music careers, it also had the power to electrify political careers. I am a great believer in participating in the political process, in voting and encouraging other people to vote. From the '30s when I was growing up, through the tumultuous '60s, the McGovern '70s and the Reagan '80s, young people had traditionally been active political participants. As we headed into the '90s, however, this activism had slowed to what seemed like a standstill and the generation of so-called slackers was known not for its youthful zeal but for its disengagement. MTV was in a position to change that.

Early in the 1992 presidential campaign Tom Freston and his team developed the concept they called "Choose or Lose." The idea was that young people, who under normal circumstances feel as if they do not have adequate power or a voice that is heard in the making of their world and have become understandably cynical, should become involved in the political process. The "Choose or Lose" campaign combined election reports, on- and off-air voter registration activities, and special programming all designed to inform, educate and motivate young people to take an active interest in politics. MTV's election reports ran up to twice as long as typical network news stories and covered topics from voter apathy to political buzz words, from the history of the two major political parties to profiles of each of the major candidates. This campaign developed into a voter registration drive called "Rock the Vote," which used on-air promotions and the power of the MTV word to put over 750,000 young people on the voter rolls. This was not only a good thing for America, it was also a great way to extend the MTV news franchise, to bring the network closer to its audience and to establish MTV even further as a generational force to be reckoned with.

"They hold elections and no one ever asks the young people what they want," Freston said. "Let's see if we can get the candidates to actually talk to young people and answer their questions. Let's do our version of campaign coverage." He hired consultants to bring MTV entry into the political world and they canvassed all the primary candidates in both major parties. Would they talk to the kids?

Bill Clinton was the first to say yes. Younger and more youth-oriented than his fellow Democratic candidates, the Arkansas governor was canny enough to be making the rounds not only of the Sunday morning news shows but also of the Johnny Carson show. He put on sunglasses and played the saxophone on Arsenio Hall, and he was not at all averse to talking to kids. All the Democrats followed his lead and were interviewed by MTV, but Clinton was the first to agree to appear at a town-hall-style forum. It suited his style perfectly, and he appeared engaged and casual and inviting. (Perhaps too inviting; this was the moment in political history when a candidate for major office was first asked, "Boxers or briefs?") Clinton received extensive media attention for his MTV appearance and made a connection with young people that significantly enhanced his chances for election. When he became the Democratic candidate, he continued to recognize the network's power.

President George Bush wanted nothing to do with MTV, despite the fact that our research showed that a majority of the MTV viewers who had voted in 1988 had voted for him. "We tried and tried to sell them," Freston said, but the Republican White House apparently thought an appearance before our audience would be beneath the dignity of the president. Only in the final days of the campaign, when he was trailing in the polls, did Bush finally consent to be interviewed. Tabitha Soren spoke with him on the rear platform of a train as the world went whizzing by. The appearance was indeed disdainful.

Clinton exploited the opportunity to, as Tom said, "image himself up with MTV," connect with young people and get them excited about the possibility of a generational political change. MTV appeared to be almost a pro-Clinton network, and through working together our staff did establish many friendly ties to his. But MTV is neither a Democratic nor a Republican network; it appeared one-sided only because the Republicans seemed to feel we were some kind of sinful outlet that ought to be avoided. As a result, Clinton had a clear run.

When Clinton was elected, the MTV brain trust decided, "Let's throw an inauguration party." There were many formal black-tie affairs scheduled around Washington, D.C., for the night of the inauguration, but our unofficial Rock and Roll Inaugural Ball would be something completely different. The distance between ceremonial Washington and unceremonious MTV would be delicious for the rock and roll audience that lives on such irony, plus it would garner the network tremendous attention. We also hoped such a media event might heighten our claims of political influence and establish the network as something of a king-maker.

Many musicians are politically active, and Don Henley, Sheryl Crow, R.E.M. and several members of U2 were to perform in a huge concert production that MTV would air live. But there were parties galore that night and Freston was worried. "Man, I don't know if anyone is going to show up for this," he said. But when the doors were opened, in walked Jack Nicholson, Warren Beatty and Robert De Niro. We had the hottest party in town. Wall-to-wall supercelebrities. Not that I was there to see it. Neither Frank Biondi nor I attended. Who knew?

President and Mrs. Clinton arrived, danced and said, "MTV had a lot to do with the Clinton/Gore victory. . . . Thank you, MTV! Thank you, MTV viewers!" Hillary told Tom Freston, "Give my regards to Sumner and tell him how much I appreciate him." "I had chills down my spine thinking that this was actually happening," Tom recalled. "Some people thought we were a little nickel-dime network, and this legitimized us in the eyes of the bigger companies and took MTV to a whole new level."

That was the night MTV became an important voice in America.

While I am not an intimate friend—unlike DreamWorks' principal partner, David Geffen, I have never slept in the Lincoln Bedroom; it's not my style—I have come to know and like the Clintons. I have often visited the White House and frequently have sat with the president trading thoughts on everything from education to the unrelenting press. The last time I was invited to the White House, I was Hillary's dinner partner and was afforded the unusual opportunity to speak at length with her. She was well aware of Viacom's global expansion and told me how, as she traveled, she ran into MTV all over the world. I liked that.

Their daughter was about to leave for college at Stanford University and Mrs. Clinton was worried that the Secret Service guard around Chelsea would separate her from the rest of the student body and interfere with her life as a normal teenager. I found Hillary very down-to-earth and was touched by her concern for her child.

"Chelsea!" She brought her daughter over to our table. "I want you to meet the man who owns MTV!" Chelsea beamed.

I do count President and Mrs. Clinton among my friends. I admire the former president for all that he has done for the country. He is a smart, personable, well-educated man with the country's best interests at heart. His accomplishments are manifold and I feel sorry about the fact that, because of one mistake not totally relevant to his performance as president, his legacy has been tarnished.

Recently, at a dinner given by Michael King, who with his brother Roger is part of King World, and thus part of Viacom, I sat next to President Clinton. When the president spoke, he spoke with the same passion and compassion about this country's achievements and its aspirations. I can only say that it is too bad that he has disappointed his supporters and that his wonderful legacy as a great president has been tarnished.

———————

During the '90s, with the creation of such highly successful generational programming as *The Real World, Road Rules* and *Beavis and Butt-Head*, MTV's distribution increased dramatically. As a result, the fees we received from cable operators similarly increased. Advertising became a significant factor and MTV ended the decade as a powerhouse, providing more than 50 percent of Viacom's cash flow. As eager as I was to purchase MTV, and as determined as I was to hang on to it, even I did not dream it would become such a fabulous success.

MTV Networks has now lived long enough to have taken its viewers from childhood into middle age. We start with children watching Nickelodeon, enjoying the programs and learning the lessons. They become MTV viewers, rocking in their teens and twenties, and then graduate to VH1, where they are a solid mid-age audience. And now we have CBS for older audiences, although that demographic, fortunately, is getting younger. We never have to lose people who have grown up with us. It's a great advantage. And sooner or later these kids will have kids of their own and the continuum will start all over again. MTV Networks: We grow our own.

NINE

THE PARAMOUNT DEAL

W*hen I acquired Viacom* I had a vision of creating the number-one software-driven media company in the world. We had cable networks, television production and TV and radio stations. I needed a movie studio to fill out the picture. Almost from the beginning I had my eye on Paramount Pictures.

It was clear to me, even when MTV Networks was in its infancy, that we would grow that franchise not only domestically but all over the world. I had to be confident, I had to be optimistic; that is my nature. And by 1993, I had been proved correct. My original stake in Viacom, $400 million plus a later purchase of $100 million in stock, was now worth $5.5 billion. All those who said I had overpaid for the company, or that it would fail, had been proved wrong. We were thriving. The marriage of Viacom and Paramount's parent company, Paramount Communications, would create exactly the company I had originally envisioned. I had the same confidence in Viacom's ability to grow Paramount that I'd had in my own ability to grow Viacom.

It would have taken several lifetimes to accumulate the assets of Paramount Communications and it would have been impossible to put the company together from scratch. Paramount Communications included the Paramount Pictures studio (motion picture production), the Paramount television production operation (*Frasier, Cheers, Taxi,*

Wings, MacGyver, Laverne and Shirley, Star Trek: The Next Generation, Entertainment Tonight) and a library of 890 films which was one of the best in the world, including the *Godfather* series, *Star Trek, Beverly Hills Cop* and *Indiana Jones.* The company also included Paramount Parks, five regional theme parks (you couldn't build parks like that; the cost of the real estate alone would have been staggering); more than a thousand movie screens, which of course attracted me, including Famous Players, one of the two leading circuits in Canada; Famous Music, a venerated music publisher which controlled the rights to many multiple-platinum Paramount Pictures and Paramount television sound-track albums and had just begun to sign such talent as Paula Cole, Björk and Boyz II Men. Also part of the Paramount Communications empire were Simon & Schuster, the leading American publisher, which included the number-one educational publisher in the world as well as Prentice-Hall, Macmillan, Scribner and Pocket Books; Madison Square Garden, "the world's most famous arena," as well as ownership of the New York Rangers and the New York Knicks and cable's MSG Network; co-ownership of USA Networks; and seven television stations across America.

Paramount Communications was a gourmet media meal. To order it à la carte would have been prohibitive. I was hungry for the challenge, but there was no certainty that the entire feast was even available. Paramount was run by its CEO, Martin Davis, who was clearly having a very good time doing his job. Martin and I went pretty far back.

In 1964, Herb Siegel and a partner had taken a run at Paramount Pictures. In response, the studio set up a three-man committee to fend off the attack. The three men were Martin Davis, who at the time was in the Paramount publicity department, the eminent attorney Louis Nizer and me. I held maybe fifty shares of Paramount stock and was there to represent the stockholders. "You'd better buy a hundred shares, Sumner," Davis had told me. I did.

In those days Martin Davis was a mere publicity guy and a somewhat abused one at that. As an exhibitor I had seen him get kicked around fairly often. His boss, Paramount general sales manager Charlie

Boasberg, used to beat him up over some campaign that wasn't up to par or some job he hadn't done, and I was around to hear the shouting. It made me very uncomfortable.

Even so, our triumvirate went to war against Herb Siegel's hostile takeover, fought off the attack and won. Gulf & Western, in the person of Charles Bluhdorn, stepped in as a white knight, and when Bluhdorn took over Paramount, he brought Martin Davis with him to the parent company. When Bluhdorn died in 1984, Davis was elevated to become Gulf & Western's chairman and CEO. Having been in the trenches together, Martin and I had developed a mutual respect and fond friendship.

Martin Davis has never received sufficient credit for his shaping of Paramount. He took Gulf & Western, which was essentially a holding company, a conglomeration of wildly different businesses from sugar to auto parts to zinc, and by shedding its non-entertainment and non-publishing assets, pared it down to create the company he renamed Paramount Communications. Of course, he had the greatest management team in the world working for him: Michael Eisner, Jeffrey Katzenberg and Barry Diller. But in many ways, Martin resented those three. They were Hollywood and he was a mere CEO, a businessman. And for the most part, they made more money than he did. He ultimately drove them away from Paramount—a great loss to the company.

Davis was the CEO of Paramount, he was the boss, but he was not a giant stockholder. As a result, he was always vulnerable to the possibility of a takeover. Rumblings of change would occasionally break out, and in this atmosphere, Herb Allen of the entertainment investment-banking firm of Allen & Company tried to broker a friendly deal. Herb put me and Martin together for a series of talks and for a while we seemed to be moving forward.

I was interested in Paramount, of course, but I was interested only if I could assume control of the company. Viacom would be the buyer. It would be a merger between equals, but I had no intention of owning a media empire and not running it. Davis, on the other hand, while recognizing the need to protect the company from invaders, insisted that Paramount be the buyer, and he was completely invested in running the company himself. We negotiated. The fact that we were friends smoothed many difficulties, and several times we approached an agreement.

One night Martin and I were at a charitable function when he turned to me and said, "Sumner, one good thing about a merger is we won't both have to go to these things. You'll go to one, I'll go to the other." Despite our reputations as men who "wouldn't last together one second," we enjoyed each other's company and were developing a close working rapport. At one point Martin insisted, "When we merge you've got to stop taking taxicabs and get a driver." That was the level of his involvement. He was that close to accepting.

And then he would back off. He came to the brink and then retreated a number of times over the course of several years. *Years!* Under the terms of one proposal, Paramount would have acquired National Amusements and Viacom in exchange for my receiving 30 percent of the company. Time and again we thought we had a done deal, then it was undone. The first few times this happened I thought perhaps Martin's reticence was in some way related to the terms of the deal, but I was wrong. It wasn't Herb Allen's fault that we couldn't consummate a deal, and it wasn't mine. Finally it became clear that Martin simply could not bear to let go of the reins of Paramount. He had built and shaped and focused this company, he was having a wonderful time running it, and he was not emotionally prepared to part with it. I'm a control freak too, and I understood his feelings. However, we had spent thousands of hours over the course of months and years in serious negotiations about that company and I was furious that, bottom line, Martin's emotional problems had wasted huge amounts of our time. We all admitted defeat and went our separate ways.

By 1993, Paramount Communications had more than a billion dollars in cash but had taken a downturn. The studio had released a series of flops and was losing market share. The clouds of change were gathering and there was talk in the industry that several possible buyers, including Davis's former employee Barry Diller, now chairman of QVC Network, Inc., and Tele-Communications, Inc.'s John Malone, were increasingly interested in wresting control. In April 1993, Bob Greenhill of Morgan Stanley called and said, "Sumner, I want to get together with you and Martin Davis. Let's have dinner."

"I don't know where you're going with this," I told Greenhill. "Certainly, I'll be happy to have dinner with you. I'll be happy to have dinner with Martin Davis. But if you think this is the beginning of a negotiation, forget it. I've been through this with Martin for years. He just can't do the deal."

I prepared for that dinner with Philippe Dauman, who was now at Viacom. As I've said, Philippe was a man in whom I placed tremendous trust and faith. He was young and smart and during the Viacom takeover battle we had spent a lot of time together, talking about real-life issues. Ordinarily after such a battle, the client goes about running the company he has acquired and the lawyer, like a wartime consigliere, moves on to the next confrontation. In the following years Philippe had made partner at Shearman & Sterling and become a successful takeover attorney. After the acquisition, however, I had placed him on the Viacom board of directors and continued to bounce ideas off him informally. We socialized and went out to dinner together with our wives. I entrusted him with my estate planning and designated him a trustee and executor of my will. Then in 1992, while he was on vacation, I called and said, "The first day you're back I want you to come over for lunch and talk about life." When Philippe arrived I offered him the job of senior vice president and general counsel of Viacom. "I know you love the company," I told him. "We're great friends and I would like you to come and spend all your time here." He accepted my offer. "Can you start tomorrow?" I asked.

"Sumner, I've got clients!" Philippe went on a whirlwind tour, found them all proper representation and began work at Viacom in February 1993. From that time forward, he was in and out of my office constantly.

Philippe and I developed a strategy for our first meeting with Davis. We decided not even to discuss price with him. Price, in fact, was hardly the issue. We would discuss the "cultural" issues, the perfect fit of Viacom and Paramount and the determination of who would have control of the resulting company. Davis didn't have to be negotiated so much as he had to be seduced. Price would come later. We would suggest that Martin become CEO of the combined Viacom/Paramount. Viacom and Paramount would have equal representation on the board of directors with an additional seat for me as chairman. That meant we would control the board.

Still, as I approached the meeting that night at dinner, I had no great hopes. Was Martin willing to talk about merging Paramount and Viacom again because of the threat of outside forces or because he saw that the remarkable fit of the two companies would bring tremendous value to Paramount's stockholders?

The fit was indeed extraordinary. Viacom possessed a vast array of outlets for Paramount products. We also possessed the growth engine of the entertainment industry, MTV Networks, while Paramount had a vast potential for crossover production of Viacom products. Talk about shared opportunities! The acquisition of Paramount and the marriage of the Paramount studio, television operations and library to MTV Networks would allow me to realize my dream of creating the premier software-driven media company in the world.

Martin Davis did not exude warmth. He had a reputation as a screamer and there were people who had worked for him who did not view the experience as particularly pleasurable. But I had never seen that side of Martin and we had a great affection for each other.

Davis, Greenhill and I ate in a private dining room at Morgan Stanley, a very long, casual dinner. Martin and I reminisced about our working together successfully in the past, which I felt would make it easier for us to live together in the future. It didn't take very long before the conversation turned to a possible transaction between Viacom and Paramount. He seemed to indicate that he was interested.

I was thunderstruck but I was determined not to wade through any more of Davis's uncertainty. "Martin," I said, "I understand how you might feel. But I'm telling you in advance, so we don't waste time, that unless you accept the principle that Viacom will control the company, there's no sense in trying to go further. I'm not saying you should or you shouldn't, but unless we have absolute control, I'm not interested."

I was astonished when he answered, "I know you, Sumner. I'm reconciled to your control." I then laid out our position regarding the makeup of the board. "We will not have Viacom control the corporation on paper but not for real," I said. "Viacom will control the board." Davis agreed. "But we'll still be partners in the operation of the company, won't we?" he asked.

Why was he being so accommodating? There is a body of opinion that says what finally drove Martin was not his belief that a combination of Paramount and Viacom would be in the best interest of his stockholders, but that he was worried about losing his job and his company to Diller and Malone. Davis would certainly deny that—he denied it to me—but if he was worried about Diller and Malone, he was concerned about formidable people. And in all fairness to him, while Davis was controversial, he had always been a man who focused on delivery of value to his stockholders. I prefer to think that he had a genuine affection for me, that he trusted me and preferred to do business with me rather than with Diller and Malone, and more important, that he saw the powerful company we could create between us. I suspect that all those factors were at play that night.

Partners in the operation of the company? "Absolutely," I said. "We'll put two desks in the same office if you want it that way." Two desks were fine. Wherever we put the desks, I was going to have control of the company.

We discussed the new company's name. Viacom Paramount? Paramount Viacom? And we discussed the other possible suitors. Davis had disdain for both Diller and Malone. Diller had worked for him and there was a history of bad feeling between them. One of the problems, as I previously noted, was that despite the fact that Diller had reported to Davis, he made more money than Davis did and that seemed to rankle Martin. Diller also received far more media attention and accolades than his boss. He had the "Diller Sizzle," that ability to look good in public and get credit for everything. Davis had fired Diller, who got a job at Fox. "Don't trust him," Davis told me. "He's got too big an ego. He thinks he's better than he is."

I disagreed. Barry Diller and I were extremely friendly. When I was a motion picture exhibitor and he was a Paramount executive, we had met regularly in California and shared ideas about the industry. We had both respect and affection for each other. After he had been booted by Fox and was trying to figure out what to do with his life, Barry had come to my office to ask my advice. Should he go into the network business? What about certain cable operators with whom he was considering working? I told him, "Watch your back."

After he landed the job as chairman of QVC Network, Inc., a home shopping network best known for purveying cubic zirconia, Barry had called me. We were launching an MTV shopping network and he was screaming. "What kind of a friend are you? You're killing me!"

"Barry, I don't know what you're talking about," I said. "Stop already."

"You made a deal with Malone to do a shopping channel with Home Shopping Network. What about me? I have QVC!"

"But Barry," I said, "they're both Malone operations. Why don't you just call him?"

"I'll never call him!" Diller shouted. "He's a predatory monopolist. Everyone lives in fear of him. He's going to do only what's good for him!" He was carrying on as if I'd stuck a knife in his back.

"All right," I said, "slow down. I don't know if it'll have any effect, but I'll talk to him on your behalf."

I called John Malone. What did I have to lose? "Have you considered the possibility," I asked him, "that maybe MTV should do the shopping network with QVC? It doesn't make any difference to us and Barry is quite upset." Malone agreed and threw the deal to QVC.

I told Davis I thought Diller was an extremely smart and able man. "Diller's got more sizzle than substance," he said. He also said that John Malone was not to be trusted. He didn't want any part of the man and seemed to fear him. "The guy is a genius," he later told *Vanity Fair*, "—but then so was Al Capone. He's the smartest guy you'll ever meet. He's brilliant. But he stands for nothing, believes in nothing, and has contempt for anyone that walks and talks." Davis's method of handling this potential adversary at the time, however, was to sweet-talk him. He told *The New Yorker* that Malone was "one of the great visionaries of our time." Though Davis would have been the last to admit it, Diller and Malone together undoubtedly caused him a lot of anxiety.

I respected Malone for having started with nothing and rising to become chairman of the very successful Tele-Communications, Inc. During one of the off-again periods of the on-again/off-again negotiations we conducted over the years with Davis for Paramount, I had met Malone at Herb Allen's conference in Sun Valley, Idaho. Hearing of the potential deal, he had said something to the effect of, "Why don't we do this together?" I parried the suggestion because that was not my vision of what we wanted to accomplish at Viacom. If we were going to go at Paramount again, we wanted to do it alone. Nevertheless, I had great respect for Malone and felt he was one of the smartest men in the media industry.

I came back from dinner with Davis and Greenhill thinking, You know, it's just possible that it's for real this time.

Much of the ensuing negotiation was done by proxy. Philippe would sit down with Paramount's Executive Vice President and General Counsel Donald Oresman and work out the details of a merger. We felt this was the least emotional means of dealing with Martin Davis. He had agreed in principle to cede control of Paramount to Viacom, and therefore to me. This had not been an easy thing for him to do and we wanted to maintain both the deal and his composure.

Martin would be CEO of the merged companies. The real issue was who was going to succeed him. He said he was planning to retire within a few years and just wanted to run the company until then. His natural successor would be Stanley Jaffe, his second-in-command. That was not my preference. At our next meeting I said, "I have to be absolutely clear with you, Martin. Your successor is not going to be Stanley Jaffe. It's going to be Frank Biondi."

We were calling this deal a merger between equals, but Viacom was the acquiring company and our CEO was Frank. He had been with me almost from the day we acquired the company. He knew Viacom's operations inside out, and had had motion picture studio experience at Columbia Pictures.

Frank Biondi was not without his problems, however. He was not a negotiator. The fact is that if you were in a negotiation, you would want him on the other side. Frank's transactional inclination was to figure out what the other side wanted and give it to them. He was not interested in the intricacies of negotiation, nor was he all that interested in the price we would pay. If he decided he wanted something, price was hardly a major consideration. "Let's make the most aggressive offer we can," he would say to me. Worse than that, he would tell the other side the same thing. If we had had internal discussions, he might blurt them out, too.

"Frank, why?" I complained. "*Why?*" I never got a good answer to that question. "Let's make the best deal we can," I would tell him, "not give it away." I, of course, felt that if there was one last penny left in a negotiation, we should take it. "Shouldn't we draw them out?" I said. "Why not make a more rational and somewhat conservative offer? We can always raise our bid. We can't lower it." Frank never seemed to grasp that point. Fortunately, Viacom was possessed of good negotiators. I had a lifetime of such experience and Philippe was impressive in his own right.

Nevertheless, Frank had extensive knowledge of the entertainment industry and how the parts of Viacom and Paramount would relate to each other. The analysts on Wall Street and the press loved him because he was knowledgeable, straightforward, likable, very honest, and he communicated well. He had extraordinary strengths. Even in the worst of times, I thought him highly competent and considered him my friend. And I hold those views today.

But with all of his strengths, Frank's manner of doing business was also causing me concern. He was a hands-off guy. He would leave the office early, while the rest of us were still pounding through deals, and often seemed to be at the gym or playing tennis. He took a lot of vacation time every year. When we were going crazy with details, trying to plan our next move, it became easy to leave him out of such important Viacom business because he was so laid-back that he sometimes seemed oblivious. But I repeat, Frank had remarkable skills. He had made a great contribution to Viacom, and I felt that he would be a suitable CEO of a combined Viacom and Paramount.

From my earliest days at Viacom, I came to know Tom Dooley as a brilliant young executive, totally trustworthy, totally loyal—loyal to Viacom and loyal to me. He played a major role in my early education at Viacom and continued to play a major role throughout all the years he was with the company. Both Tom Dooley and Philippe Dauman were among those who I considered would someday be competent and experienced enough to run Viacom.

Stanley Jaffe had a different reputation as a manager. He had been a successful movie producer and had been partners with Sherry Lansing in a production team at Paramount. He was extremely intemperate, however, and he shouted at people. We heard stories that he would be yelling and screaming and all of a sudden blood would start gushing out of his nose. He also had a reputation for not always being there. Paramount owned Madison Square Garden and he would leave work to go to Knicks games. Who the hell was running the studio, I wondered. The people around him in the organization made their displeasure clear.

Martin Davis stood by Jaffe as his successor. Jaffe had been hired after a long search process to bring Paramount credibility in the movie community. He was president of Paramount once before and had been in place at this new job for a relatively short time. It appeared to be a matter of personal loyalty for Davis. It was also my impression that Davis did not like Frank Biondi. I told Martin I was not going to back off and he told me the same. Ultimately the issue was resolved by agreeing to make both Jaffe and Biondi co–chief operating officers. I told Frank, "Don't worry about it. I'll see to it."

The issues we negotiated were price, breakup fees in case the deal didn't go through, lockup options for Paramount shares—meaning we were entitled to buy up to 20 percent of Paramount's outstanding shares at market price—the name of the company and the exploration of possible future joint ventures. In June, Paramount brought in Felix Rohatyn of Lazard Frères to represent the company. Bob Greenhill had by this time moved from Morgan Stanley to become president of Smith Barney Shearson and was representing us. I was so convinced we had a deal that I said, "This has nothing to do with money, this has nothing to do with glory. This is an act of destiny!" I didn't think it was foreordained, but I sensed we were nearing a momentous accomplishment.

But every time we thought we were within a dollar of a deal, Davis upped the ante. Finally, on July 6, 1993, we met at the Mark Hotel for what I thought would be a final negotiating session. Our offer for Paramount stock, after months of negotiation, was $63 a share. Martin came into the meeting and said, "It better begin with a seven."

"Begin with a seven?" I exploded. "Seven and what? Seven dollars? Seventy and a quarter? Seventy-nine?" Davis had done it again. He had no intention of selling. After years of flirtation, followed by months of intensive seduction on both sides, this romance had turned instantly frigid. I told Greenhill, "I've had it. If Martin wants to talk to you about this deal, talk. But you've seen that every time we thought we had a deal, we didn't have a deal. The price that we thought was realistic keeps going up. I'm through."

I faxed Greenhill a memo the next morning:

Dear Bob:

As you know, I have the highest regard and affection for you and will always have; however, lest there be the slightest misunderstanding, I want to repeat what I stated this afternoon when you visited me. The deal that you have been working on is off! There is no deal! I have other things to do. I appreciate all your past efforts on our behalf.

Warmest regards.
Sincerely,
Sumner M. Redstone

Of course, instructing an investment banker who wants to make a deal not to proceed is semi-futile. Greenhill would get his fee only if the deal went through. He listened to me and he didn't listen to me. He tried to keep the deal alive.

On August 16, I faxed him the following:

Re: A suggested transaction

With respect to the request that I meet with the other side this week, I have concluded that it would serve no purpose to do that; and, barring some circumstance with which I am not familiar, such a meeting in my view would have no value. . . .

While April has not yet become September, it is on the verge of becoming so and I find that this theoretical transaction is more fantasy than reality. Had it been based on reality—realistic desires and commitments—it would have been done.

I understand discussions were also going on between General Electric and Paramount at the time, and I later heard that GE had thought it had successfully closed a deal in which NBC Television, owned by General Electric, would be acquired by Paramount. GE went to bed thinking it had a deal with Davis and woke up the following morning to find it didn't. That would not surprise me.

Arthur Liman of Paul Weiss Rifkind Wharton & Garrison brought me and Martin together for another dinner. While he did represent Smith Barney, Liman had a personal relationship with Davis and the purpose of the meeting was not so much to indulge in negotiation as to express his opinion that the deal ought to be done and to cajole Martin into making a realistic one. At the same time, Bob Greenhill would not be sidetracked and continued to involve us. Even though I was still very uncertain about Davis's intentions, as I had come closer to taking control of Paramount it was crystal clear in my mind that it was an astonishing property. I could not resist one last attempt at acquisition. We had already put so much time and effort into this deal, ultimately I had to see it through. So we made another offer, and as we saw the deal slipping away, we kept raising the price.

Back to negotiating again, we worked each item hard. We paid particular attention to the so-called lockup provisions. Thorough research of the issue brought us and Davis to an agreement that if another bidder entered the arena, Paramount would issue Viacom 24 million shares which we had the option to purchase at the deal price. We priced these extra shares in the most conservative way possible in order to avoid even the appearance that we were being given an inappropriate edge. As a result of this lockup provision, any new bidder would have to pay at least $165 million more to acquire Paramount. I thought that between the high price we were already paying for stock and the additional provisions of the agreement, third parties would be discouraged from attacking the deal.

Still Davis insisted on $70 a share. I finally called Philippe in exasperation and gave him my bottom line: I would go up to $67.50 per Paramount share, I would take an option at the deal price and a $150 million termination fee, including (not plus) expenses. I told him to get it done on that basis or I would walk away.

On September 7, Philippe, Oresman, Greenhill, Rohatyn and their supporting casts met all day in Greenhill's conference room, each stepping out from time to time to consult by phone with me or Davis. Both sides seemed determined to make it work; both sides sensed this was our last chance. We went up on our price, after gut-wrenching conversations in which Philippe and Bob urged me not to exceed the $67.50 limit I had set. For all Davis's disclaimers, money *was* an issue. We ultimately arrived at $69.14 a share, consisting of $9.10 in cash and the balance in Viacom stock. It was not something beginning with a seven, but it was very close. We reduced the termination fee to $100 million. The day was grueling, but at last the deal was done.

It was concluded. Agreed upon. We were paying $8.2 billion, and at the end of the day I would own 69.8 percent of the voting stock and 38.5 percent of the equity of what we were calling Paramount Viacom International, Inc. (In previous years we had created the non-voting Viacom B stock, which accounted for the differences.) The new company would have $3.5 billion in debt, annual revenues of close to $6 billion and a stock market value of approximately $15 billion. Creative, forward-looking, we would be a powerhouse in the industry. With the strength of our balance sheet, we would have unlimited opportunities, and we were only beginning. All we needed were the signatures.

Late that afternoon, I got a call from Donald Oresman. "Sumner," he said, "Martin would like to visit you at your apartment this evening without any advisors." I was happy to invite Davis to join me and my wife for dinner at the Carlyle. "I believe," Philippe warned me, "he'll be looking for an extra dollar on the deal."

So I had been tipped off.

Martin arrived in good spirits. I, while wary, was more than pleased. Finally, Paramount would be mine.

We were both able to enjoy the evening after such a long and draining negotiating process. But Davis was nothing if not relentless. "Sumner," he told me after we had eaten, "I've got to have a dollar more."

Under normal circumstances this might have disturbed me. We had, after all, been negotiating this deal for four years and now, well past the final hour, Davis was trying to hold me up for more money. I have been known to respond with some verbal force. But I was prepared. "No, Martin," I said calmly.

"How about a half-dollar?"

"No."

"How about a quarter?"

"Martin," I said, "we already have an agreement." The issue at that moment was not the price I was paying for Paramount, which was considerably higher than I had anticipated. There was absolutely no way I was going to allow Davis any avenue of exit by reopening the negotiations, which as far as I was concerned had been concluded.

He looked at me. At that moment I knew he was really going to go for this deal.

"Okay," he said finally, "you win." He looked out the window at the beautiful view of the city at night. "You know, Sumner," he said, "when this deal gets done, they'll build a big statue of you in the middle of Central Park and I'll be forgotten."

"No, Martin," I replied, "they'll build statues of both of us and I will be looking up to you in admiration." He laughed. It was just the right touch. We had merger for dessert.

Over the next few days, the lawyers and bankers conducted due diligence and negotiated the agreements. On Sunday, September 12, 1993, we triumphantly announced Viacom's acquisition of Paramount and the creation of Paramount Viacom International. Paramount was a great brand, much better known by consumers than Viacom, and we decided to lead with it. There was no ego involved for me; it was the company that counted, not the name.

I was feeling terrific. We had truly put together a monster media company and I believed that I was well on the way to succeeding in my ambition to create the number-one software-driven media company in the world. From day one the company was running just as we had planned. "Two weeks ago," I told *The New York Times*, "Paramount agreed to pay Viacom $800,000 for book rights to 'Beavis and Butt-Head.' It was scheduled to be a Warner Bros. movie. Now Paramount will make it." I was exultant. My dream would be realized. I said, "This is a deal only a nuclear war will tear asunder."

TEN

THE DEAL FROM HELL

There was considerable discussion in the press about the value of Viacom stock and its place in the purchase of Paramount. Some analysts said the price of the company should have been closer to Paramount's $77-per-share asset value, but Ed Hatch at UBS Securities correctly noted that by taking Viacom stock at the given price, Paramount shareholders would not only avoid taxes, they would also participate in the combined company's upside potential.

If I had been convinced that we had priced Paramount sufficiently high to discourage other bidders, I was wrong. Almost from the day we announced the deal financial birds of prey began to circle, ready to feast on me and Paramount. The names which arose consistently in the press accounts were AT&T, Ted Turner, and the combination of Diller and Malone. It made me uncomfortable. Every time another name surfaced—Bertelsmann A.G., Blockbuster—I said, "One more beast that thinks—inaccurately—that he is going to eat us up."

Did I welcome the possibility of facing AT&T? Hardly. It would make a very formidable opponent but I was confident we could prevail. Ted Turner worried me less. I didn't think he could swing it financially. Because of his relationship with Time Warner, which owned 19 percent of Turner Broadcasting System, there were regulatory issues which would militate against him. And basically, while he was one of the greatest entrepreneurs in our industry, I didn't think he possessed the killer instinct that was so clearly present in John Malone. (That's a compliment to Turner.) I didn't see him as the enemy.

In the flush of victory, I had sent Herb Allen a check for a million dollars. He had first put me and Martin Davis together, and although he had been given a full opportunity and that deal had not come to fruition, I felt Herb deserved both recognition and recompense for his efforts. In retrospect, it was abundantly clear that I should have continued to involve him more actively in our negotiations with Paramount. I should have called Bob Greenhill and suggested, "Why don't we bring Herb into this and make him a partner, too?" *The New York Times* described Allen & Company as "the boutique bank of choice for the entertainment industry," and Herb felt he should be a part of all big deals in his domain. The acquisition of Paramount was not only a big deal, it was a *giant* deal.

Herb returned my million dollars. Four days after we announced our purchase, *The Wall Street Journal* reported that Allen was helping Barry Diller weigh a bid for Paramount.

I contacted Herb quickly. I liked and respected him and did not want to hurt or offend him. "Herb," I said, "I know you're upset because Bob Greenhill represented us." In fact, he seemed almost beside himself. "That was not my choice. You and I did everything we could do, we worked together and it wasn't your fault; you simply weren't able to make the deal. I don't see that as a failure. It wasn't as if we dumped you. It wasn't like we said, 'We're not satisfied with your work.' Martin wouldn't move. The deal was dead. Greenhill comes in, I don't think he's got a chance, and he ends up getting it done. But, Herb, I must tell you, I think you have a conflict of interest if you're working with Diller to acquire Paramount. You got a lot of information from us."

Herb Allen was not the only one displeased with the situation. I was extremely upset that a man who had represented me, who had been given a vast amount of confidential information about our company, our finances and our state of mind, was now representing a competitor.

I could not be sure that Allen would keep that information to himself. I had no right to trust him and he wouldn't expect me to trust him. He was representing a competitor and would do everything in his power to see that his client won.

I was hoping that Herb would back off. I thought he *should* back off. I had serious reservations about his right to oppose us. Herb saw it differently and there was a potential area of some significant conflict. Ultimately, after discussing the matter with my colleagues, I chose not to take a legal position. I had too much respect for Herb. We were not going to litigate the matter but I was sorely displeased.

On September 20, a package arrived for me by messenger at the Carlyle. In a handwritten note, Barry Diller expressed the hope that the enclosed copy of a letter being delivered simultaneously to Paramount's board of directors wouldn't affect our friendship. The letter contained QVC's offer to acquire Paramount.

I was more than a little upset with Diller. Shortly after I had closed the deal with Davis, Barry and I sat in my office and I had told him, "This is not a case where you and I are competing. Davis and I have a deal. It's a done deal and I can't see you coming at it."

Barry and I had been friends for a long time, we had consulted each other on various matters, I had intervened on his behalf with Malone. But sitting in my office that day, he had been very careful about what he said. His face gave away nothing, but when he left I was convinced he would come after us. Had I been in his position, I would not have done the same. If Paramount had been available, if there were no deal in place, then I would have felt his offer was totally justified. But we had a signed deal and he was basically trying to break up a contract. He clearly had a different point of view and I questioned the honor, or lack thereof, of his position. Barry was supposed to be my friend.

John Malone I knew only by reputation—not a man you wanted to tangle with. *The Hollywood Reporter* called him the "godfather . . . of the cable TV industry." Now here was my former investment banker aligned with both Diller and Malone, two of the fiercest businessmen on earth, about to do battle against me.

On September 21, QVC Network, Inc., backed by as-yet unwritten commitments from its two principal shareholders, Malone's Liberty Media Corporation (a spin-off from TCI) and Brian Roberts's Comcast Corporation, laid on the table its bid of $80 a share—or $9.5 billion—for Paramount. Their per-share offer consisted of $30 cash and 0.893 share of QVC stock. The offer also stated that QVC's financial advisors, Allen & Company, had assured QVC that additional capital would be readily available to complete the transaction. Our offer had put Paramount "in play." As noted fund manager Mario Gabelli said, "Let the auction begin!"

I was incensed. This was a betrayal of the highest order. The acquisition of Paramount was critical to the fulfillment of my original vision for Viacom; there was no other way for us to get there. And I was confident we would get there.

But my confidence notwithstanding, Viacom stock had been in decline and shares that nine days earlier had been worth $69.10 were now at $63.175; our $8.2 billion offer was now worth $7.5 billion. Diller and Malone were outbidding us by $2 billion.

Fund managers Mario Gabelli and Larry Haverty, who held large stakes in Paramount, Viacom, QVC, Comcast and TCI, were loyal to the bottom line. "I'm neutral as to whether Redstone or Diller is better for the long-term interests of shareholders," Haverty said, "though Diller does have the advantage of being twenty years younger." I sputtered when I read that. Was that a reason to favor one company over another in a gigantic merger? Because its leader was younger? And not necessarily healthier or smarter. "As a shareholder, though," Haverty added, "in the near term I have to maximize the wealth of my clients." A lot of the Wall Street people had affection for me, they had seen the battle we had waged to win Viacom and the successful job we were doing to grow it, but they, too, were only interested in the last dollar. To say I was concerned would be something of an understatement. But not for the first time I said, "We are not going to be diverted by the press."

How could any investor, particularly one in the entertainment industry, prefer QVC to Viacom? QVC is a shopping channel. Paramount and Viacom would be a true merger of equals; Paramount and QVC would be a travesty. Which was in the better position to grow the company, maximize its opportunities and make it prosper: Viacom, with the most valuable and dominant networks in the world plus cable systems and media outlets, or QVC, with its twenty-four-hour rummage sale? Cubic zirconia and stainless steel cookware, or Nickelodeon and MTV? You choose.

Apparently the Street was going with the dollars. "There's no way the Viacom deal can get done with such a significant difference in the QVC bid," *The Wall Street Journal* wrote, quoting someone close to QVC. "What counts today is money."

QVC's stock had been "hyperinflated," said the *Journal*, "since Diller came onboard."

We were getting burned by the Diller Sizzle.

No one in our industry is better at self-promotion than Barry Diller—not to diminish in any way his considerable ability. He had success heading both the Paramount and Fox studios and creating the Fox television network, and he is the best manager of the press I have ever known, giving reporters access and asides and personality in the service of whatever project he is involved with. Diller encourages the press to invest in his dreams. Now he was clearly working overtime.

Based on nothing but speculation the *Journal* wrote, "He could start a fifth network to rival the fourth one he launched at Fox." Speaking of a possible QVC-Paramount merger, *Daily Variety* said, "This is the opportunity to lock up programming for whatever distribution channel he dreams up down the road."

"If QVC created new programming services using Paramount's films and television series," *The New York Times* added, "it would have an easy time distributing those programs to the nation's cable systems because of its two financial backers that are already prominent in the business."

It was all sizzle; there was no substance. QVC had nothing in place—except Diller. And the only thing Diller was bringing to the table, his greatest asset, was himself.

We needed to respond, but what was that response to be? The melding of Paramount and Viacom was so obviously in the stockholders' best interest, the potential for growth so staggering, that I didn't feel the need to jump in and raise our bid immediately. We were prepared to meet just about any bid within the limits of reason, but we thought that anything we could do along the way to weaken Diller's status would pay off in the long run.

Nevertheless, money was a problem. While QVC stock was skyrocketing and the Diller-Malone bid was now worth $9.9 billion total and $83.58 a share, ours rebounded slightly but remained at only $7.5 billion and $63.375. To counter, we pointed out that QVC's offer was as yet unfinanced, and that an offer without a financing commitment was really not an offer at all, certainly not one you could depend on. Therefore, we told the press, we didn't feel the need to raise our bid.

Frank Biondi had not been aware of the early negotiations with Martin Davis, and had only been informed of the pending deal with Paramount the previous fortnight. Frank was doing a terrific job of running Viacom, but as I've said, he was not a negotiator. Frank was well liked by the press, he had a lot of connections, was in constant touch and had a tendency to talk to reporters about whatever was going on at the time. He was kept out of some of our strategy meetings because we could not be certain that what we were doing would remain confidential. Now, when asked by the *Journal* to comment on the possibility of a sweetened bid for Paramount, he did not rule it out, saying, "That is not the only option. . . . It's not in our interest today to signal what we will do precisely."

But that is precisely what he had done, which was totally inconsistent with the agreed-upon—and best—strategy for Viacom. If you are trying to make the best deal possible, you do not say you might increase a bid before you find it necessary to do so. There was nothing to be gained from tipping our hand—what do you gain by indicating hunger?—and a great deal to be lost.

I was caught by surprise later that day when the *Journal* called for comment, and I did not react well. "Maybe Frank is not as precise or as articulate as I am," I told the reporter forcefully, "but there has absolutely not been any discussion or contemplation of increasing our bid. We have not had a word of discussion with Paramount about increasing our bid."

I then held a meeting with the executives of the company—Philippe, Tom and Frank—and said I did not see that it would serve our interests to reveal our negotiating strategy. I understood that it was typical of Frank and his impulse to make a very aggressive offer, a manifestation of a basic difference in negotiating philosophy between Frank and me. Unfortunately, that divergence of approach hit the newspapers. There was no blood shed between us—I truly admired and had great affection for Frank—but I was upset.

If Barry Diller was point man in the battle against us, John Malone controlled the artillery. We wanted them both out of the way. But we had a specially good reason to rid ourselves of Malone; he was trying to destroy us.

Through his companies TCI and Liberty Media, John Malone controlled access to more than 10 million of the nation's approximately 60 million cable-TV homes and had more cable subscribers than anyone else in the United States. If he didn't want your programming on the air, he was in a position to prevent it. Malone had the power to cause ruin and recently he had been using that power to try to crush Showtime/The Movie Channel.

The Showtime/TMC contract with TCI had lapsed earlier in the year, and rather than negotiate to renew, Malone had stalled and attempted to force a merger between Showtime and the Encore channel, which he owned, on particularly unfavorable terms. We, of course, had resisted. We were completely unwilling to essentially hand him Showtime. Malone, however, was completely willing to squeeze us, and he set about replacing our channel with Encore on his systems. There was no subtlety to his actions. If he persisted, if we were prevented access to TCI's subscribers, Showtime would be largely without viewers and would soon die. Knowing that, he hardened his bargaining position. It was the essence of monopoly.

Malone had been very effective in expanding his monopoly power. He had used the same tactics time and again throughout the industry. And there was no end in sight. If a man like Malone, who had exceptionally keen predatory instincts, could get control of enormous software and programming capabilities at the same time he controlled access, that power would grow wildly. If he owned Paramount and set his sights on Columbia, who knows if that studio or others in his way would have continued to see the light of day.

Many programmers felt the way I did—that Malone's behavior was unconscionable—but not one of them would ever dare to file a lawsuit against him. The reason was obvious. The very power he wielded instilled fear. What if he knocked them off the system? He had a grip on the throat of every cable programmer. But we were going to lose Showtime unless we acted.

As often as I have been accused of doing the contrary, I never get involved in litigation unless the issue is extremely important and unless we are right. Acquiring Paramount was extremely important, and there was no question in my mind that Malone's behavior violated basic antitrust laws and was prototypically monopolistic. We had been studying the legal aspects of a potential case against him. Was the timing of this lawsuit accelerated by the Paramount acquisition? Yes. I brought in Philippe's old firm, Shearman & Sterling, along with Simpson Thatcher

& Bartlett, and aided by Philippe we drew up a complaint. I do not normally write complaints myself, but I participated in the crafting of this one because of the strength of my feelings. To a large extent the words were mine.

The complaint began, "In the American cable industry, one man has, over the last several years, seized monopoly power. Using bully-boy tactics and strong-arming of competitors, suppliers and customers, that man has inflicted antitrust injury on Viacom and virtually every American consumer of cable services and technologies. That man is John C. Malone."

The writing was flowery for a law document. We planned to disseminate it to the press and I wanted to get my point across.

When word got out among the Viacom managers that we were planning to file a lawsuit against Malone, they asked for the opportunity to express their concerns to me before we took such drastic action. We called a meeting and assembled in a conference room near my office. The divisional executives were uniformly opposed to suing Malone. I understood. Their businesses—MTV, VH1, Nickelodeon, Nick at Nite—were doing well. In fact, because our networks were so strong, these businesses were the building blocks on which TCI constructed its programming, and they were being positioned respectfully by Malone, not torn down. Furthermore, cable operators ran the cable world like a tight-knit club and that club did not like being involved in litigation; it put all of them under scrutiny. Our executives were afraid of retaliation. One by one they lined up to ask, "How can you file a lawsuit against our biggest customer?" Even Tony Cox, who as CEO of Showtime was being severely victimized, was thinking about the greater good of the company and was nervous about the effect such a suit would have on the rest of Viacom. "We are worried that they are going to kill us," I was told.

I cut them off quickly. "Look, I understand your concerns, but let me give you the reasons we have to do this. The future of our business depends on it." If Viacom's most powerful executives were reluctant to oppose Malone, other less successful programmers had to be living in fear. I laid out the facts. "We have a deal with Paramount and Barry Diller comes after it. I would never try to bust up somebody else's deal. I've been his friend, and now he's coming after our deal and John Malone is coming with him. Malone controls cable. We had a contract with TCI and now he won't give us distribution. He wants to do a joint venture and steal Showtime. If he can do that with one channel, he can do it with all of them. He's trying to kill Showtime, and if we remain complacent, if we permit him to destroy one part of our business, we will not only invite him to do with us what he wants, he will destroy the integrity of Viacom."

Viacom's executives looked at me, stunned.

"You guys don't get it! Your company's future is at stake! Your integrity is at stake. Your life is at stake, the future of Viacom is at stake, and *you're afraid?!* I'm aware of the downside of suing our customer but I'm also aware of the downside of letting our company be subject to every kind of abuse. And in my opinion, the latter is more dangerous." I was getting heated.

"If we don't stop it here, if we don't fight back now, what you're all afraid of is truly going to happen. It is going to happen! The only way it's *not* going to happen is by filing the lawsuit that you fear! We can't *not* file a lawsuit!"

I explained to my executives that it seriously troubled me not to go with the consensus—particularly because I respected them so much. But I also explained that when I was absolutely convinced that my way was the right way to preserve Viacom, then it was my job to make that decision. I had made a similar decision in 1958 when I sued the movie studios, and again when I sued Time Warner. When your life depends on it, you must wage war.

We filed suit in federal court charging John Malone and TCI, along with several related companies, with antitrust violations in an attempt to monopolize the cable television market.

"Malone seeks to exert monopoly power over key stages of the delivery of cable programming to the American consumer," the complaint alleged: "Control over the creation of programming in studios; control over cable programming services; control over the mechanics of transmitting programming by cable and satellite; and control over delivery of programming to the home. At every stage in this process, the consumer has paid—and will continue to pay—a monopoly tax to John Malone. . . .

"Through his strategy of ceaseless acquisition, Malone has created a formidable base upon which to expand his control over every aspect of cable television, and inflict antitrust injury on his customers, suppliers and competitors.

"[Malone and TCI's] monopoly power as cable operators, together with their expanding interests in all other aspects of the cable industry, gives them unparalleled power to dictate terms to cable television programmers, such as Viacom. Without access to Malone's cable systems, cable network programmers cannot achieve the 'critical mass' of viewers needed to attract national advertising or a sufficient number of subscribers required to make the network viable.

"As a result of Malone's unique control over this lifeline, he can—and does—extract unfair and anticompetitive terms and conditions from cable programmers, including Viacom. . . .

"Malone and TCI and its affiliates, both among themselves and with others, have devised a strategy to use proprietary technology to create and to tie up narrow bottlenecks in the distribution of programming [and] intend to take control of the cable television and home satellite distribution makers, and will eliminate competition and raise prices in the national market for non-broadcast television programming services and submarkets thereof. . . .

"Malone and his controlled companies have also sought to use their monopoly power over access to approximately one in four American cable homes, in TCI's words, to 'crucify' Viacom's The Movie Channel service as a viable competitor and, thereby, coerce extortionate concessions from Viacom. . . .

"QVC's acquisition of Paramount . . . would allow defendants and their co-conspirators to take their anticompetitive plan to the next level."

The New York Times called our suit a "legal ploy." The Wall Street Journal said it was a "tactic [that] failed to impress the stock market." TCI called the suit "frivolous." The Diller Sizzle was on the griddle.

I got several calls of support from programmers, who congratulated me for bringing suit. Would they join me? No.

Because this was a very substantive lawsuit with important national issues at stake, we began a concerted campaign in support of it in Washington. I made calls at the Justice Department. I testified before Senator Howard Metzenbaum's antitrust committee and met with several members of the Federal Communications Commission and every member of the Federal Trade Commission. I also met with leading senators and representatives, particularly those concerned with telecommunications and antitrust law, from the chairman of the Judiciary Committee to Massachusetts congressman Edward Markey. I met with Vice President Al Gore. He was sympathetic, not surprising given the fact that he had previously called Malone "the Ringleader of the Cable Cosa Nostra."

Finally, and most importantly, I met with Anne Bingaman, the head of the Justice Department's antitrust division. When I asked her for ten minutes, she said, "Plan to spend three hours." Our meeting included the government's top antitrust lawyers and I was encouraged when they asked me, "What relief do you want?"

———————

It was at this point that the struggle for Paramount turned into open warfare. In our army we had lawyers, investment bankers, public relations advisors and all the people who were doing the day-to-day work on the guts of the deal. We began each day with a briefing. We all knew where this was going: Ultimately we would have to compete with QVC's cash offer. We would have to come up with an additional $2 billion. Under normal circumstances that might have been a problem. But not with Paramount in play.

The acquisition of Paramount was the glamour deal of the day. With software and cable and entertainment as its primary elements, everyone thought this deal held the key to the future of the entertainment world. The fact that both Diller and I were actively in pursuit added to the excitement. It was an ideal situation in which to encourage others to invest their money with us. Instead of pleading for money, it was as if we were interviewing people about why they should be allowed to invest. Everyone was paying attention. Everyone wanted in.

Over the next two weeks, we engaged in a frenetic series of meetings and negotiations with potential sources of cash, and we had complete control of the bidding process. We started a bidding war. We met with cable companies, virtually every regional phone company, publishing companies and media entrepreneurs. The King brothers of King World were interested in investing. Everybody wanted a piece of the action. In fact, the hard part of these negotiations was scheduling meetings with each of the prospective investors. We literally had them sitting in conference rooms on separate floors of Smith Barney and Shearman & Sterling. We didn't mind their knowing that their competition was somewhere in the building. Word was out. Philippe and Greenhill primed them and then I would walk in and make our presentation. We talked to one group, then moved down the line and talked to another. We scheduled meetings late at night just to fit everyone in. We had meetings at midnight.

We could have as much equity money as we wanted, and we certainly wanted it on favorable terms to allow us to compete with QVC. But critical to us was not the money these companies were throwing at us, but choosing the right strategic partners.

One of the first companies we talked to was Wayne Huizenga's

Blockbuster Entertainment Corporation. Blockbuster had been trying to create its own Paramount. Concerned that pay-per-view and video-on-demand TV might damage its core video rental business, in the preceding year Blockbuster had acquired Spelling Entertainment, a stake in Virgin Interactive, Republic Pictures' library (including all of NBC's rights in television shows before 1972), Music Plus and Sound Warehouse, as well as cut a deal to jointly own and operate Virgin Megastores in the United States, Europe and Australia with Richard Branson. We had noticed all this activity, and in conversations among ourselves commented that Blockbuster could be an attractive company for us to acquire.

I had met Wayne Huizenga several years earlier at an Allen & Company conference where we had had some very general discussions about working together on joint ventures. My first impression was that he was smart, aggressive, tough. But something in his eyes warned me that I should be careful. That didn't detract from the admiration I had for his business skills, however. He was one of the world's great entrepreneurs and had built his multi-billion-dollar business from a $5,000 loan to buy a truck. His job had always been to negotiate the best deal he could for himself. If I ever had occasion to deal with him, my job would be to watch my back.

Huizenga was terrifically interested in getting in on the Paramount deal. Blockbuster had excellent cash flow, exactly the kind of income stream we would need to service what was certainly going to be a very large debt in the early days of our acquisition of Paramount, should we win. What Huizenga wanted in return was some of our assets, for starters our theme parks. The fact that Paramount owned Madison Square Garden, the Rangers and the Knicks must also have been a factor in his thinking; Huizenga owned hockey's Florida Panthers and baseball's Florida Marlins and appreciated the power of all those sports franchises. I would have been surprised if he wasn't thinking, Is there any way I can get my hands on all or any part of MSG?

"Look," we told him, "make the investment. We are not interested in selling anything, but we can develop a strategic relationship. It will make sense; we'll be your partner." Blockbuster agreed to buy $600 million of a new class of Viacom preferred stock, convertible into Viacom B (common, non-voting) stock at $70 per share. The Viacom B stock was trading at $55 at the time (since split). I have a particular yen for voting control and was not anxious to dilute it. So from my standpoint it was a pretty good deal.

The phone companies were also dying to get in. They were talking about entering the entertainment business and thought they should be able to provide not only the means of communication but the content as well. Having a piece of Paramount would theoretically give them increased access to important software.

Philippe and Bob Greenhill were in my office daily, listening as I called various phone companies and fed the frenzy. "All the other phone companies are coming in," I told them. "We just want to give you the opportunity. We're not telling you you should do this, and we don't need the money, but we just thought in fairness you ought to know about it." That, of course, whetted their appetites. They were worried about their competition; none of them wanted to be left out, not because they had thought it through, but because "if the other guy wants it, then I *must* want it."

We created a marketplace for a commodity which might not otherwise have been valued so highly. NYNEX, for example, saw involvement in Paramount as an opportunity to acquire some pizzazz. NYNEX was a typical phone company, rather staid and predictable. (Bell Atlantic/NYNEX ultimately merged with GTE to form Verizon, and today is operated by my good friend and Viacom board member Ivan Seidenberg.) While we never made a commitment of exclusivity or preference in price to NYNEX, we did offer the implicit opportunity to participate in the exciting and alluring world of entertainment. In our negotiations, we said, "We only want $600 million from you." NYNEX told us, "Six hundred million is not enough to move the needle for a company of our size. We need to double that. We must have a billion two."

"Well, we really don't want you to give us more than $600 million, but okay, we'll take the billion two." We used the Blockbuster deal as a template and NYNEX bought Viacom preferred stock, convertible to common stock at $70 at a time when the market price was less than $50 a share. Again, a good deal.

Not all companies approached investing with us in the same way. John Clendenin, CEO of BellSouth Corporation, in conjunction with Bruce Wasserstein of the investment banking firm Wasserstein, Perella & Company, seemed prepared to invest billions. After a few pleasantries Clendenin told me that in return for his investment he wanted 50 percent of the deal. Fifty percent of Paramount? No, 50 percent of Viacom! And if we didn't give it to him, he threatened to go to the other side and get it from Diller.

Was this guy joking? Nobody threatens me. I must have been speechless.

"Do you have anything to say?" he asked.

"Yes," I told him. "Goodbye." And I walked out of the room.

As a condition to their investing, the people at Cox Enterprises, a major cable company, asked for a series of unacceptable commitments obligating Viacom to Cox. We were unwilling to make that deal. We would let them invest in preferred stock and said, "This will give you a strategic relationship with us. You will be our partner and on that basis will be able to negotiate agreements with us, but we will not tie our hands." They demanded concessions and when we refused they walked away.

The same week we got our infusion of cash from Blockbuster and NYNEX, Malone's Encore Media bought the ten-year rights to 350 films in the Disney Company's library and the rights to all new films that were released. Showtime owned those rights for films released through 1997 and we were hoping to renew the contract. Because of the diminishment of Showtime's value, Viacom's stock fell slightly, decreasing the value of our Paramount bid. Malone was playing hardball.

This wasn't the first time Malone had crossed us. Several months earlier, Encore had bought pay rights to Universal Pictures films while we were negotiating a contract for the same rights. We had included that maneuver in our antitrust suit.

While we were amassing a war chest, Paramount was dragging its heels in responding to the QVC offer. Diller had not produced the paperwork necessary for Paramount to evaluate his offer so the Paramount board simply declined to consider it. For the next week a great part of the press coverage and industry conversation concerning Paramount focused on these delays. Herb Allen went so far as to personally hand-deliver documents to Felix Rohatyn at Lazard Frères. Allen doesn't usually run papers over and this was an extraordinary gesture of friendship, but later in the day Paramount rebuffed him and issued a press release saying that it "has received financing documents with respect to QVC's proposal today and will review them." According to *The New York Times*, someone close to QVC said, "I wouldn't want to face their liabilities as directors" if they didn't approve the QVC offer.

The people at Paramount were entitled to ask legitimate questions about financing and regulatory problems, but for them to allow to linger and fester the perception that Diller was not being given sufficient consideration was a wrong strategic move. "This is clearly a stall tactic," Mario Gabelli said. Gabelli had been an investor with me for a long time and he was a smart guy. He has said many times that he always wanted to be my partner. I saw it the way he saw it. "Give Diller and Malone all the attention in the world—they are entitled to it," I kept saying, "and then make the right decision." A week after Allen's personal delivery, the board authorized "informational discussions" to evaluate the QVC bid.

In an effort to move things along, Frank Biondi had been talking to people at Goldman Sachs as if they were consultants. No one told him to, we never retained them, but all of a sudden we read about it in the newspapers. Bob Greenhill wasn't very happy to hear the news.

Word running around the industry on October 11 had it that John Malone was no longer a player in this drama. TCI was about to announce that it would be bought by the Bell Atlantic Corporation in a deal valued at $33 billion. I couldn't have been happier. We had been working hard to neutralize Malone and we had succeeded. While most people in the industry felt that he had kissed off Diller in pursuit of a larger deal, in fact Malone had been forced to move on. The Federal Trade Commission was seriously considering a consent decree which would prohibit TCI from acquiring any equity or ownership in QVC.

Malone tried to put the best face on it. "We totally support Diller . . . and will honor our commitment," he said, but then immediately added, "If in the final analysis our ownership interferes with Barry's ability to complete the deal, we would make whatever modifications . . . up to divesting." The Paramount deal, which had been so important to Malone only a few days before, was "really very peripheral to [the TCI–Bell Atlantic sale]." He wished Diller "a lot of luck" but said that winning Paramount wasn't "central to or a core part of the Bell Atlantic and TCI strategy." It was "relatively small in the scheme of things."

We had forced Malone out! It had been one of our primary goals and we had achieved it. We had won that battle. However, it proved to be a hollow victory. If Malone had simply stepped away that would have been ideal, but within days Diller announced that both Cox Enterprises and Si Newhouse's publishing and cable company, Advance Publications, Inc., had invested $500 million in QVC. A cool billion between them. The concentration of the power of the cable industry— the so-called natural monopolists—behind QVC's proposal was increasing.

I knew the Cox people pretty well and we at Viacom had had friendly relations with them. But apparently they thought that cutting my throat would help them. They had demanded monumental programming concessions from us and we had turned them down. I can only speculate on the terms of Cox's deal with Diller, who all of a sudden needed them.

As it was becoming increasingly apparent that the battle for Paramount would not be decided by the corporation's board but by its shareholders, Diller began meeting with the Wall Street investment community. The Diller Sizzle was not to be taken lightly. If he could persuade the analysts, he could convince the shareholders, so we felt it necessary to arrange meetings of our own. I told the analysts that a merger with Viacom offered a significantly better future for Paramount stockholders than a merger with what I properly characterized as a shopping channel. QVC would have to grow Paramount on Paramount's assets, not its own. It was obvious to us, although admittedly we were not objective, that Viacom could grow Paramount not only on its own assets but also on the strength of our networks and our businesses. The issue, as far as we were concerned, was not how much money one or the other of the suitors was willing to put on the table, but how much Paramount would be worth in the years to come under the respective companies.

The perception that Paramount was stalling would not go away. QVC complained about it to the media constantly. But Paramount, which was being very careful in its due diligence and didn't feel it was stalling, had waited seven days for QVC to produce the important financial documents that had been requested and found the accusations of foot-dragging disingenuous. Nevertheless, on Wall Street perception is often reality, and had I been in Paramount's shoes, I would have rushed to give proper consideration to Diller's bid.

One day after submitting the documents that Paramount had requested and stating its willingness to meet and negotiate a transaction—and before Paramount had a chance to respond—QVC decided to bypass the board entirely. Who knew what was in Diller's mind? Did he think Paramount was going to embrace him? It was common knowledge that Martin Davis had a tremendous dislike for Diller. Paramount also truly believed that a merger with us rather than him made more sense. Davis, I think legitimately, did not want to do a deal with Diller. Still, Diller desperately wanted Paramount.

QVC came out with guns blazing. Diller and his backers took the battle directly to the stockholders and made a two-tier tender offer, a hostile bid to take over Paramount. They would offer Paramount's stockholders $80 per share, all cash, for 51 percent of the company. If successful, that offer would be followed by a merger in which the remaining 49 percent of outstanding shares would be converted into QVC stock. The overall value of the deal was the same $9.5 billion the board had been considering.

We complained loudly that this was an old-fashioned, front-loaded, two-tier, coercive tender offer—a public relations stunt, a grandstand play. QVC was not, in fact, offering all Paramount shareholders $80 cash for their stock; they were extending that offer only to the first takers up to 51 percent of the outstanding stock. What stockholders would receive for the remaining 49 percent, after control was obtained, was of uncertain value and would not be in cash. Stockholders therefore faced a difficult decision: Sell at a coerced price or hold and quite possibly receive even less.

In a coerced tender offer, shareholders want to make sure they get in on the first part of the deal. Even if they do not believe the offered price is sufficient, the one thing they do not want to do is hold their shares, not tender them for sale, and then find themselves with no choice but to sell for a reduced price on the back end. *That* is the coercion.

Over the next weekend, in round-the-clock negotiations with Paramount, we agreed to amend our original merger agreement to provide for a two-step transaction. In the first step, Viacom would match QVC's cash component, a tender offer for 51 percent of Paramount's outstanding shares at $80 a share. In the second step, however, Paramount shareholders would receive Viacom securities valued at $80 a share, consisting of Viacom A (voting) common stock, Viacom B (non-voting) common stock, and a portion of Viacom preferred stock similar to that which recently had been purchased by Blockbuster and NYNEX, and which arbitrageurs would be more likely to treat as cash equivalents. While the value of the back end of QVC's offer was on its face approximately equivalent to the value of ours, the inherent value of Viacom's common stock and the more clearly monetizable value of Viacom's preferred stock made our back end superior.

In addition, the Viacom-Paramount merger agreement was amended to make it clear that there would be no impediment to superior offers. The poison pill lockup provisions would be waived when there was a significantly superior offer outstanding from someone else.

This tender offer involved a timetable for a whole series of governmental approvals, and we calculated and set in motion a series of timing advantages aimed at winning us the company. It worked this way.

Upon making a tender offer, the purchaser is required to keep his pitch available for twenty business days. During those twenty days a seller is permitted to tender his stock for sale and then withdraw and tender them to someone who has made another tender offer, a competing buyer. People can switch back and forth the same day—until the close of that twenty-day period when the offer ends. If at that time a sufficient number of shares have been tendered, in this case 51 percent, the purchaser can say, "Sale!," buy them, and the deal is complete—game over. If you are competing against that purchaser, you want to dissuade the shareholders from tendering into your competitor's offer and encourage them to tender into your own. The twenty-day period begins with the initial offer. If you amend the offer in any important way, that second offer stays open ten business days from the time of amendment. Each time you change your offer, you restart the ten-business-day clock.

Once you announce a tender offer, you are legally required to start it within five business days. Diller announced, but he didn't have his papers in order. That was a huge tactical mistake. He should not have said a word until the instant he was about to file. We had an opening and we made a decision: "All right, we're going in. We're going to match them."

We had already lined up the funding, we had our papers ready, we filed our documents with the Securities and Exchange Commission and then announced our tender offer to the press. Essentially, we slapped our money on the table and beat QVC to the opening bid by two days.

This was a tremendous advantage. The Viacom and QVC bids were not very far apart in terms of dollars, and one could make an argument one way or another as to whether to believe in the Diller Sizzle or the Viacom substance. There was a subjective judgment to be made about whose offer was superior. We were trying to convince stockholders that we were offering the same amount of cash plus the long-term value of Viacom. QVC was arguing the reverse: Cash plus Diller. And Diller was working the public relations angle overtime to sell himself as a manager and a visionary. But even if these longer-term issues canceled out and stockholders considered only cash on the barrelhead, with our two-day head start they could legitimately think, If I tender my shares to Viacom, it's a sure thing. If I wait for QVC, in two days the dynamic could change. Maybe some problems will arise, maybe they'll lower their price, maybe their deal won't go through. And if Viacom wins I'll be left out and have to wait a number of weeks for Viacom's merger. I'd better take my $80 now. Small shareholders were apt simply to pick one side and stay with it. Money managers controlling large holdings of shares were more likely to go with the offer that ended earliest. If there was a $5 difference in price they might wait; if the bids were only a dollar apart they might say, "What the heck, take the money now."

In addition, if QVC were to raise its offer, we would be in a position to counter that bid and always stay ahead. We were basically leapfrogging each other, and if you've got the high bid and a couple of days' head start, you have a significant time advantage.

Diller spun it the other way. He was orchestrating the press and *The Hollywood Reporter* wrote, "A number of analysts believe Diller outmaneuvered Redstone and Davis as in a high-stakes game of poker. By setting the commencement date of QVC's offer out a few days, Diller forced the Viacom and Paramount chieftains to lay down their cards, giving Diller the luxury of watching their reaction without ever having to act." That was all spin. QVC had made a mistake and was trying to cover it up. We were working the press ourselves, but we weren't doing nearly as well as Diller was.

At the same time its coercive bid was announced, QVC also announced that it was suing Viacom, Paramount and various Paramount directors to invalidate our breakup fees and lockup provisions. Because Paramount was incorporated in the state of Delaware, QVC sued in Delaware Chancery Court, asking for a preliminary injunction to stop our offer. In essence, QVC was alleging that Paramount was not responding to its offer with appropriate consideration and was favoring Viacom and therefore violating its fiduciary responsibility to its stockholders. We'd see them in court.

While QVC was negotiating with BellSouth to amass a larger war chest, we received commitments from Morgan Guaranty Trust, Citibank and Bank of New York for a $3.5 billion senior, unsecured revolving credit line and a $1 billion bridge loan. There was some concern that regulatory matters might delay NYNEX's $1.2 billion and we needed to be prepared for the next step. QVC had not bid in eleven days and was no doubt preparing the next assault wave. There were rumblings that Malone would sell Liberty Media, which held 22 percent of QVC's common stock, to BellSouth and therefore appease regulators worried about his monopolistic tendencies. *Daily Variety* described Wall Street as "getting antsy."

Where could QVC go in the bidding? At this stage we felt that to distinguish oneself one had to go up in $5 increments. A buck or two wasn't going to get the job done. Eighty-five dollars a share. To make that bid Diller would have to canvass a large number of partners. He had Newhouse, Comcast and Cox with whom to discuss the deal, and BellSouth to come. This was a vulnerability: First of all, it would take time, and when rapid response was necessary, he would be hamstrung.

Secondly, if any one of his partners said, "I've had too much of this, it's too high," Diller was done. We, on the other hand, could make quick, unilateral decisions. We preempted him.

On Saturday, November 6, we raised our amended bid to $85 a share. Our offer was now $10.1 billion. It seemed like an audacious step forward. But another of the beauties of this bid was that, even with the amended timetable, our newly presented tender offer still expired two days before QVC's original one. We were still two days ahead. *Daily Variety* called it a "weekend sneak attack" and "a brilliant move. Not only did it force Diller back to the negotiating table with his would-be partners, it also weakened QVC's lawsuit in Delaware Chancery Court."

At about the same time, we amended the complaint in our antitrust suit against TCI and added Comcast to the list of defendants, accusing that company and other QVC backers of conduct that had forced Viacom to raise the amount of our offer by $2 billion. We also alleged that the Bell Atlantic–TCI acquisition was a part of the anti-competitive conduct. We were alleging a conspiracy by Malone to monopolize the cable and cable programming business, and therefore, to the extent that he forced us to raise our price, he cost us $2 billion in damages. We again debated the wisdom of suing a large customer but thought the litigation might disenchant Comcast with the entire Paramount battle.

Two days later BellSouth, the same people who had tried to strong-arm and threaten me, did indeed join Diller's army. They invested $1.5 billion. In return they extracted the agreement to form a joint venture with QVC to develop an "interactive gateway" and to use the new technology to deliver goods, services and information into the country's homes. "Interactivity" was the great buzzword of the time, particularly for the phone companies, which had visions not only of running the wires and signals to their customers but also of controlling the programming that went over them. With the proposed Bell Atlantic–TCI deal funneling production even further, the phone companies might have been concerned about the scarcity of programming. Marion

Boucher of Donaldson, Lufkin & Jenrette said, "Down the road, that [content] could be what makes your product better than somebody else's." Jack Grubman of PaineWebber saw it differently. "How is Bell-South going to help Paramount make better movies?" he asked. "They're not. And what can Paramount do for BellSouth? Nothing. . . . There are deals that are being done that should not be done. I think this is one of them."

I don't know what ever became of this joint venture, but it was clear that BellSouth got from QVC what we never agreed to give to it or NYNEX.

But just as Diller was raising substantial funds and gaining an ally, he was losing the same. The Federal Trade Commission's consent decree was finally signed. In a document which virtually adopted word for word the antitrust arguments I had made, TCI agreed to divest "absolutely and in good faith" all ownership interest in QVC and terminate all existing agreements concerning the voting of shares or stocks of QVC. TCI and Liberty Media Corporation (which was QVC's largest shareholder and had been repurchased by TCI in the intervening months) were prohibited from "entering into any agreements with QVC or Paramount that grant TCI or LMC exclusive exhibition rights to recently released theatrical motion pictures after Paramount's current contract with certain other parties terminates." No more little Encore-Universal maneuvers.

TCI was also prohibited from acquiring, "directly or indirectly," any equity or ownership interest in QVC, Paramount or USA Networks without the consent of the FTC. Any TCI board members who were presently on the boards of QVC or Paramount had to resign, and no others could serve. And finally, TCI and its affiliates were prohibited from acquiring any equity in QVC, Paramount or USA Networks for a period of three years.

"By accepting the consent order . . . the Commission anticipates that the competitive problems alleged in the complaint will be resolved." With that, Malone gave up the fight.

I was meeting in my office several times a day with Philippe, Tom Dooley and Frank Biondi to map out strategy. There was no moment for relief. The entire company was a war room. I am fiercely competitive, Barry Diller is no slouch when it comes to competition, the men and women around us are all competitive. Each side knew the other was working in overdrive. Everybody wanted to win. The adrenaline was pumping, no one was getting much sleep because we were all on an incredible ride. Every day was unsettling, nerve-racking, tension-ridden because we had to respond to every fresh attack.

Six days after our amended bid was announced, QVC raised its hostile bid to $90 a share, $10.8 billion for the company. The next day the Paramount board, supported by a fairness opinion from its investment banker, Lazard Frères, refused to meet with QVC and unanimously rejected the offer, citing the better fit of Viacom and questioning the offer's "highly conditional nature" (BellSouth's "memorandum of understanding" with QVC was non-binding) and "numerous legal and financial contingencies." The day after that, we were in Wilmington, Delaware, in court to respond to the lawsuit that Diller and his cohorts had filed against us.

All Americans have a right to expect consistency, predictability and fairness from the rule of law. Businesspeople, in particular, need to know that corporate law is consistent and will be applied honestly, impersonally and without regard for results. The fiduciary principles of the state of Delaware, certainly, rest on the principles of fairness. However, and this is a major point, the law has to be fair not only to the shareholders of an acquired company but also to the acquiring company. We were entitled to judicial respect as well.

As far as I was concerned, going into this trial we had a done deal. Paramount and Viacom were engaging not in a sale of one company to the other but in a strategic merger that would yield significant long-term value to the stockholders of Paramount. Almost 50 percent of the fruits of the deal were going to Paramount shareholders, who would have a big stake in the future of the company. Our original price, $69.14

per Paramount share, was 30 percent over market price one month before the deal was finalized, when rumors about a merger had already begun to intensify. The price was entirely legitimate. We had bargained hard for it. In fact, Viacom was paying a premium for control.

However, there was a line of Delaware cases that treated a change-of-control transaction as a key event that triggered special duties on the part of the target company's directors, requiring them to concentrate principally, if not exclusively, on maximizing realizable value for their shareholders. These were known as Revlon duties, after the cosmetics company whose future had been decided by the Delaware courts in this manner.

The basic questions I saw in Diller and his cohorts' lawsuit were:

Did the change of control from Paramount to Viacom automatically trigger Revlon duties? Or, conversely, could the Paramount board enter into a strategic stock-for-stock merger with Viacom with the mission of growing the combined business and realizing long-term value? Were the lockup provisions and termination, or so-called bust-up fees, legitimate? Basically, on September 12, 1993, when the Viacom-Paramount merger was entered into, did everyone live up to his fiduciary responsibilities? Unless QVC could discredit that action, it had no case.

The Delaware cases being cited by QVC were *Revlon, Macmillan* and *Barkan*.

In 1985, Pantry Pride, a company led by a then relatively unknown businessman named Ronald Perelman, made an unsolicited tender offer for Revlon. Revlon promptly installed a poison pill takeover defense, threatening to issue tons of stock to dilute control and make an unfriendly takeover prohibitively expensive. And in order to compete with the Pantry Pride offer, Revlon made its own counteroffer to its shareholders, agreeing to purchase most of the company's shares for a note instrument (essentially, "We owe you this money") as well as convertible preferred stock. Pantry Pride matched the offer with all cash.

Revlon then sought out and found a white knight, which included Revlon's management. Revlon had found a third party but management was going to be part of the acquiring company. After several rounds of competitive bidding, Pantry Pride publicly announced that it would better any white knight offer. Nevertheless, Revlon accepted the white knight bid and granted an asset lockup, which is to say, the right to purchase one of Revlon's subsidiaries at an extremely low price. Here was the board declaring, "We're going to support this third-party bid in which management is participating, and we're going so far as to say that if somehow or other they don't get it and Pantry Pride succeeds, we will allow this group, *including management*, to buy one of Revlon's most valuable assets at a deeply discounted price." A pretty big inhibitor.

The Delaware Supreme Court invalidated the transaction. It concluded that by agreeing to the asset lockup the Revlon board had authorized either the bust-up or sale of the company; therefore the breakup of the company was inevitable and, the court wrote, "the duty of the Board had thus changed from the preservation of Revlon as a corporate entity to the maximization of the company's value at a sale for the stockholders' benefit." An auction, the court was saying, was appropriate. The asset lockup was invalidated as improperly terminating the bidding contest between the white knight and Pantry Pride. Who was going to bid for Revlon when even if they won they were going to lose a valuable subsidiary?

We found support in *Revlon*. The court recognized that a board may protect other interests if it provides "rationally related benefit[s]" to the shareholders. To us, *Revlon* appeared to support the view that so long as Paramount's stockholders would receive "rationally related benefit[s]" from the merger of Viacom and Paramount, that company's board could take those benefits into account in planning for the future. Doesn't it make sense for the law to permit Paramount's directors—or any directors who are considering a merger in which shareholders would retain a material ongoing economic interest—to worry about, plan for and govern for that future; to weigh all the factors, including the element of control, the quality of management and, most of all, the relative value of the proposed merger partner compared with other contenders?

The merger was a corporate event which would create Paramount Viacom International, a powerhouse company in which Paramount shareholders certainly gained a strategic advantage and maintained a continuing future interest. We were not breaking up the company; in fact, we were keeping it together with the result that half the benefits would accrue to current Paramount shareholders.

We and Revlon were totally distinguishable.

Macmillan, three years after *Revlon,* was a case which involved blatant management self-dealing. Macmillan's board authorized a restructuring transaction by which management would achieve absolute majority control not by investing new capital at prevailing market prices, but by being granted several hundred thousand restricted Macmillan shares and stock options. Management was not investing any money, it was just taking the company for free. The Bass Group made a competing offer to buy Macmillan for cash. Macmillan's board then restructured the restructuring so that management would ultimately own 39 percent of Macmillan's most valuable subsidiary, instead of a majority. The court concluded that this would confer upon Macmillan management "effective control."

Robert Maxwell then emerged and offered a very rich all-cash offer for the company. The board turned to Kohlberg Kravis & Roberts as a white knight, with which the management was to participate prominently. Several rounds of bidding in a formal auction followed. On the day when the final bids were due, management tipped off KKR about Maxwell's bid. As a consequence KKR, joined by management, made a higher bid. KKR's bid was accepted by the board and KKR also received a substantial asset lockup whereby, as in *Revlon,* it could purchase valuable Macmillan subsidiaries at a considerable discount if Maxwell raised his bid and won.

Focusing especially on the tip to KKR, the Delaware Supreme Court construed these events as an egregious case of self-dealing and invalidated the KKR transaction, including the asset lockup. As in *Revlon*, the court found that Macmillan was going to be either dismembered or sold for cash under either competitive bid and, as a consequence, the board's obligation was to maximize the sale price.

But *Macmillan* did not apply to us. We were transferring control of Paramount to Viacom, not dismembering it, and we were creating a company in which Paramount shareholders continued to have significant interest. Our asset lockup, 19.9 percent of Paramount's stock, would not be used to dismantle the company but to grow it.

In *Barkan* the court actually discussed the change-of-control issue in only one sentence, which was dicta, or aside. There was no question that the target company was for sale for cash; the only issue, therefore, was not *whether* there was a *Revlon* transaction but *how* an auction or sale transaction should be carried out. In all three cases, it was clear that the companies were going to be sold for cash. If you're going to sell for cash *anyhow,* the court found—forget about egregious circumstances—why not hold an auction and sell for the highest price?

Revlon and *Macmillan* had certain features in common. Both were self-dealing transactions. In both cases, the target company was either to be sold outright for cash or restructured in such a way as essentially to be torn into pieces. In both cases, as a consequence, the shareholders were to be left with no value or a greatly reduced value. Both cases involved an asset lockup, initiated in the middle of the auction, which bartered away the company's most valuable businesses at a substantial discount and which, if implemented, by itself would result in the dismembering of the companies.

Anyone reading those three decisions would fairly conclude that a transaction that culminates in a change of control is an important event for shareholders, particularly if the transaction results in management or board self-dealing and extinguishes the shareholders' interest in the ongoing business. But those cases did not address the issue which was presented in Viacom-Paramount. Nobody, including Viacom, doubted that a change of control represents an important event in the life of the corporation's shareholders. That's why we gave Paramount shareholders a 30 percent premium. The proper issue was whether a change of control should be the be-all and end-all of analysis.

When a corporation is broken up and sold for cash, the departing shareholders cease to have an interest in what happens thereafter. But the Viacom-Paramount transaction was principally stock-for-stock, totally different from the Delaware cases being cited. Even though the Paramount shareholders were transferring control, they still owned 50 percent of the new company's equity. They had a vast economic stake in its future success, which was not true in those other cases.

The second issue involved the matter of both the 19.9 percent stock lockup provisions and so-called bust-up fees, payment for our expenses and trouble if another bidder were to materialize and prevail. The termination fee of $100 million may have sounded like a lot of money, but in the context of an $8.2 billion deal, it represented only 1.2 percent of the value of the company. Our lawyers demonstrated in affidavits that fees of 1.2 percent and even much higher have been standard in transactions of this kind. Similarly, a 19.9 percent stock option had also become standard. We found 227 prior transactions involving stock options exercisable for 19 or 20 percent of the issuance of stock. Our option, in fact, was somewhat less generous than at least 172 prior transactions. We argued strongly that we had negotiated and bargained for both over the course of many months and that they fell well within industry standards.

We relied on another case decided by the Delaware courts, in which Paramount, led by Martin Davis, had contested an announced stock-for-stock merger transaction between Time Inc. and Warner Communications. Time and Warner had then restructured the proposal by having Time make a tender offer for Warner, keeping its own defensive tools, such as the poison pill, in place to repel Paramount's offer. Paramount sued and argued, as QVC was arguing now, that the original Time-Warner merger represented a sale of both companies and that therefore Time was in play and subject to *Revlon* duties.

Delaware's respected Chancellor William T. Allen rejected Paramount's position. He said it was crucial that no change of control would result from the Time-Warner merger because, before and after the merger, control of Time would be held by a "large, fluid, changeable and changing market"—the stock market as a whole.

The Delaware Supreme Court went out of its way to state that it was *not* premising its decision on the same grounds, saying, "We premise our rejection of [Paramount's] *Revlon* claim on different grounds, namely the absence of any substantial evidence to conclude that Time's Board, in negotiating with Warner, made the dissolution or breakup of the corporate entity inevitable, as was the case in *Revlon*."

Since the "dissolution or breakup" of Paramount was not contemplated in the Viacom merger, we not only considered that language helpful to our case, we viewed it as decisive.

I was disturbed, however, by the course of the argument. Paramount's attorneys did about as bad a job of lawyering as I had ever seen. They did not answer questions put to them by the court, they failed to bring out relevant responses and facts when confronted with questions, they answered other questions, they floundered. We were staggered by their bad performance. QVC's lawyers, on the other hand, were terrific. Lawyers are not supposed to make a difference, the law is supposed to manifest itself, but in this case I was deeply concerned that our view of the law was not being presented to its best advantage. *The New York Times* wrote, "The sentiment on Wall Street seemed to be that QVC would have a better chance of winning by raising its bid once more, rather than hoping the court will strike down the merger agreement." Wall Street must have been following the law, not the trial. I couldn't have disagreed more.

While the trial was proceeding, QVC announced it had obtained the financing commitments for what was reported as a $10.6 billion offer. At the same time, tendered shares were running about 58–1 in our favor. We were doing well in the market, if not in court.

Vice Chancellor Jacobs, who was hearing the case, delayed his ruling for several days. This disturbed us further. We thought the case was so obvious that even bad lawyering couldn't lose it for us, but as time passed we became more and more concerned. In addition, the close of our tender offer was about to arrive and the judge asked both sides to extend our deadlines by two days. Despite our sizable lead, we had no choice but to accept.

Finally, the judge ruled.

We got clobbered.

In a sixty-one-page opinion Mr. Jacobs ruled that *Revlon* duties did apply, that because I owned about 70 percent of Viacom a change of control had taken place and therefore Paramount had put itself up for sale. He rejected our arguments concerning strategic advantage to Paramount shareholders and held that the issues in the case had previously been well settled by Delaware law, in particular the *Revlon* rulings. He struck down the stock option lockup provisions but left standing the bust-up fees. He particularly took the Paramount board to task for their rapid rejection of QVC's most recent bid, which had topped ours. "Meeting with QVC was the last thing management wanted to do," he wrote, "and by skillful advocacy, management persuaded the Board that no exploration was required. Those are not the actions of a Board motivated to inform itself of all available material information."

Vice Chancellor Jacobs expressly noted that Viacom was not being accused of any wrongdoing or fault. If we were "accused" of anything, it was of being very aggressive negotiators. "Viacom," the court wrote, "a sophisticated party with experienced legal and financial advisors, knew of (and in fact demanded) the unreasonable features of the stock option agreement." This was maddening. We bargained hard for those provisions, and I would have thought that negotiating the best deal possible was what we were supposed to do on behalf of our own shareholders. Indeed, we might have been criticized for breaching our own fiduciary responsibilities if we negotiated *less* than the best deal possible. The court said it was enough that we knew (or so the court surmised) that Paramount's directors were breaching their duties and that we were able to negotiate a contract with them that provided us with the fruits of that breach.

It didn't stand to reason. Why should we assume Paramount's directors were breaching their duties even though they were advised by lawyers and bankers, when the court said we did nothing wrong? We felt the discussion went against a long line of Delaware cases that have held that a corporation cannot be accused of aiding and abetting another's breach of fiduciary duty if it negotiated an agreement like Paramount's.

There never was any contention that Paramount's directors were disloyal or engaged in self-dealing. In judging that they breached their duties, the court pointed principally to their purported failure to satisfy the duty of care and investigation in entering into and proceeding with the Viacom transaction. But the truth is that a bidder like Viacom seldom knows what investigation or inquiry the other company's directors have undertaken before agreeing to a deal. We certainly did not know. Viacom never attended or asked to attend any Paramount board meeting. Viacom never saw or asked to see the board's books or hear the advice given to the directors by their bankers or lawyers. For all we knew, Paramount's directors privately might have actively solicited a sale of the company or performed an extensive market check through its bankers before agreeing to the transaction with us. We simply did not know, and in many, if not most, deals the bidder *would not* know. For in sharing that information with the bidder, the potential merger partner would be giving up important leverage in bargaining for the best possible merger transaction.

I was furious! It was hard to believe that a court would adopt a principle that had as its basis the right to abridge a contract, particularly with respect to a party that the court said hadn't done anything wrong except negotiate hard. I think the court would have done better simply to admit that it didn't like the fee and stock option, and to openly apply some variant of an "unconscionability" test in order to invalidate them.

Our legal team, many top outside lawyers and mergers-and-acquisition people and a large segment of the business community were shocked by this decision. As for me, it's hard to describe the combination of dismay and rage I felt. Not only did I disagree with the court, I was extremely incensed at Barry Diller for the role he played—something I would never forget!

Within a fortnight I was all but being accused of manipulating stocks to further my acquisition of Paramount. Geraldine Fabrikant reported in *The New York Times* that WMS Industries, a company that manufactures pinball machines and video games and in which I was the largest individual shareholder, had been buying Viacom stock "when the market value of Viacom stock was an important issue in the debate over the relative merits" of the Viacom and QVC bids. The implication was that I was influencing a third party—masterminding a plot—for the purpose of raising the value of Viacom stock to make it more valuable in the Paramount transaction.

What was my connection to WMS Industries? Video games are played in movie theater arcades across the country and I knew this business. WMS was a smart investment for National Amusements. However, while I had been involved with this company for over a decade as a passive investor (and I remain a passive investor today), I had never been on its board and I doubt I had met WMS's chairman and CEO, Lou Nicastro, more than a couple of times in my life. Had his picture not appeared in the papers, I would not have recognized him. I certainly was not encouraging him to buy Viacom so that our price would rise.

On its surface WMS's purchases of Viacom stock might have

seemed a legitimate source of concern. However, the implied accusations were pursued much more fully than our denials. Critical comments by several analysts without firm knowledge of our history were published in the following days by the *Times* and other publications. However, few journalists apparently bothered to explore the reason for the WMS purchases. I was implicitly being accused of stock manipulation and I was extremely upset that my ethics were being questioned.

What the press did not bother to report was that when we were raising money to purchase Paramount, WMS had expressed interest in investing in Viacom and had been turned down. Philippe had told Nicastro that his relatively small investment would not be of sufficient size for our purposes. Unable to purchase stock directly from us at a premium, WMS went out on the open market and bought 500,000 shares. We didn't know anything about those purchases—"Nobody touted it to me," said Nicastro, "I made the call"—and they didn't move the price of our stock in the slightest. So much for manipulation. The real issue went deeper. We released a statement saying, "Rather than inflating the price of Viacom securities, the more legitimate inquiry is whether the repeated inaccurate and misinformed publication of rumors and innuendo has served the agenda of QVC by damaging the reputation of Viacom's management and by artificially damaging the market price of Viacom's stock."

QVC filed in Delaware Chancery Court to have me deposed concerning WMS's activities. QVC representatives encouraged the Securities and Exchange Commission and our investor NYNEX to do the same. We had assiduously resisted criticizing Diller or making this battle personal, but apparently the other side wasn't operating under the same set of stipulations. They worked the press like wranglers, roping in slights against me and herding them into print. It got to the point where I simply didn't want to see the newspapers before I went to work each morning. They were so partisan, so one-sided and unfair, that the coverage felt orchestrated. The media never quite made accusations—they were very careful about that, knowing the legal consequences—but they constantly cast aspersions on my character.

In the world in which I live, if you don't have character or credibility you have nothing. I was being flayed. "Sumner's stock-buying behavior has disgusted people," a "prominent banker outside the deal" told *Business Week.* Unfortunately, this person did not have the courage to put his name to the quote. The *Times'* Ms. Fabrikant quoted another anonymous source "involved in the messy takeover battle" as saying, "In knife fights, there are no rules." I don't agree. There ought to be rules. It seemed that Diller could do anything and get away with it.

Diller had known me for decades. Now, he and his people were trying to capitalize on scurrilous material which they should have known was unfounded. The fact that Barry Diller would be a party to both unfounded business allegations and the besmirching of my character was unconscionable. No amount of money, no merger would ever have led me to conduct myself in that way.

Ultimately I appeared voluntarily before the Securities and Exchange Commission, testified in detail, and that was the end of it. But while the headlines were flying, the WMS affair was exactly the distraction it had been created to be.

We immediately appealed the chancery court's decision to the Delaware Supreme Court, and although I didn't hold out much hope for victory—the supreme court rarely overruled—the appeal was heated. We felt we had been put upon by Diller and that the court's decision was wrong. A certain amount of bitterness on my part was only natural. Had I not been bitter, I would have been irrational. But was I about to give up? Never. That was not to be considered.

We lost in Delaware Supreme Court as well. The three-judge panel ruled that Paramount was in play and that it was to be auctioned off to the highest bidder. Not only that, the judges rejected our termination fee.

I don't think we lost on the merits. I believe the Delaware court felt it had gone too far in the Time-Warner case and was concerned about that decision's application. The judges were cutting back that decision, establishing change of control as the all-important element in a merger agreement. Speaking as both a lawyer and a businessman, I believe this will have a chilling effect on future strategic mergers involving companies like Viacom that have controlling shareholders. The vast majority of American businesspeople, lawyers and economists believe that merger activity is generally desirable in the business world and generates efficiencies and economies of scale. The future Paramounts of this world will be reluctant in many instances to make strategic deals with shareholder-controlled businesses such as Comcast and Cox as well as other high-growth companies such as Microsoft and Times Mirror. Why? Because the very announcement of the transaction will be a change-of-control event that effectively puts the merger partner in play. Boards may well forgo highly desirable transactions in a world where change of control is everything. Why negotiate if the end result will only be that you've started an auction for somebody else?

I also believe that the Delaware decision will place enormous strain on, and no doubt produce a wave of litigation about, the definition of "control." Control can mean different things in different contexts. If a group of shareholders owns 30 to 40 percent of a company, that's effective control; can they not enter into a strategic merger? Effective control, outright control, the ability to control, the claim of control—all might kick in at different levels. What is control? The courts will have to grapple with these issues as they arise.

Meanwhile, Paramount was now up for auction. QVC raised its bid by $100 million to $92 a share, or $10.5 billion, about $500 million more than we were offering. Wall Street once again focused on the ego angle. "The winner will really be the loser in the eyes of the stock market," said analyst Jessica Reif. "This is in the late stages of seminuttiness," said investment banker Emanuel Gerard, "and the question is, are things just ego-driven for this deal at this point?" *The Wall Street Journal* called me "an irascible billionaire" and Diller "a college dropout who made his name as a young ABC programming whiz."

While I will admit that I don't like losing one bit, it wasn't ego that was driving me. How frustrating would it have been to lose Paramount, the key to the ultimate success of Viacom, to Barry Diller? Enormously frustrating. However, I will not make an investment which I do not believe can succeed. Paramount was the gateway to the expansion of Viacom and the fulfillment of my dream. Sound business judgment pushed me forward, but what *was* sound business judgment?

Napoleon Bonaparte said, "An army travels on its stomach." He understood that to win a war you need a steady supply of resources. We were in an all-out war for Paramount and we were running a wartime operation. The price had gotten so steep that both sides were now scrambling for cash. The other side had begun with Comcast and TCI, and when Malone was forced out, they'd brought in Cox and Advance and the very deep pockets of BellSouth. We had begun with our own resources and brought in NYNEX and Blockbuster. Diller had his troops in order, he had ample supplies and a solid pipeline. We were about tapped out. If we could raise no more money to make another bid by January 7, 1994, we were dead. Unlike a few months earlier when we had simply opened the doors and allowed investors to run in with their funds, the battle had left other potential investors wary. Diller and QVC had also aligned themselves with many of the most likely candidates. I think they were celebrating. They thought they had us.

I convened a meeting at my apartment which included Blockbuster's Wayne Huizenga and Steve Berrard, NYNEX's Fred Salerno and CEO and Chairman Bill Ferguson, Frank Biondi and Philippe. I told our investors, "The future course of this battle is up to you. I am asking for your further investment and your advice." We needed another $600 million.

Bill Ferguson said he would support whatever we decided to do but that NYNEX's board could not invest more cash in our bid. This was a surprise; they were the ones with deep pockets. Huizenga, who had been sitting and listening quietly, was considerably more impassioned. He stood up to speak.

"We're on the brink of greatness here," he said heatedly. "Viacom can be one of the great companies of the world. We have gone this far and we should do everything we can do to prevail. These opportunities come rarely in this life and we cannot let it slip away. We must dare to be great!"

I just about cheered.

ELEVEN

TO HELL AND BACK

The day after QVC raised its bid, *The Wall Street Journal* reported that my wife had sued me for divorce and then withdrawn the suit. In bold-faced type in a box inside the first column of a Viacom-Paramount news story it said, "Her action raises questions about whether Mr. Redstone could ultimately lose control of the company in a divorce proceeding."

I was livid. My marital status was not an issue in the war for Paramount. First, my trusts and will were specifically designed to prevent control of Viacom from passing to anyone during my lifetime. Second, while I did have strong feelings about the timing of my wife's actions, I found the entire topic inappropriate for public discussion and extremely offensive. I also suspected the timing of this news flash.

Diller was facing no such distraction. He met with Martin Davis and assured him, he told the *Journal,* "my behavior [toward Davis] would be impeccable." With the price at $10.5 billion, the Paramount board voted to approve the merger of Paramount and QVC.

If we did not respond, Paramount was gone.

When we were negotiating for his original $600 million investment, Wayne Huizenga had been eager to buy some of our assets. This late in the game, when we needed another $600 million, he was even more relentless. From December 17 until just before Christmas, there were many meetings between the Huizenga camp and ourselves. While we were daring to be great, he was looking for options on our theme parks. We continued to turn him down. We were not parting with assets. We discussed a joint bid; we discussed a merger.

Huizenga was a brutal negotiator. Blockbuster had made hundreds of small acquisitions and he had engaged in continuous deal-making as he crisscrossed the country buying up video store operations. Along the way Huizenga developed a specific theatrical routine. He and his Blockbuster associates would swoop in on some video guy who saw money for his store dangling from Huizenga's pockets. When negotiations came to an impasse, rather than say, "We have a problem with the proposal," and make a counteroffer, he would say, "Sorry we couldn't do a deal. Good luck to you," shake the guy's hand, pull on the leather coat and head for the elevator.

Seeing the deal about to fall apart, the video operator, who only moments before was seeing dollar signs, would run after him. "Wait, don't go. Come back. Let's talk about it." Huizenga hadn't hit the down button. He had been waiting. That's how he got his concessions.

The first time you see this in operation, it's quite impressive. But it works only once. The second time he walks out and hangs by the elevator door, you figure it out.

Huizenga tried to get you where you could taste the deal, and then whisk it away. At two in the morning in a conference room we would make a proposal, Huizenga and his cohorts would go talk about it privately, come back and tell us, "We're at an impasse. Sorry we couldn't work this out. Best of luck." We let them go. Huizenga would get to the elevator and no one would run after him. One time he waited there for fifteen minutes before it dawned on him that we weren't going to chase him. He got to his car. Nothing.

He would soon find some excuse to call—he left papers in our office—waiting for us to say, "Why don't you come back." Still nothing. Once he was literally on his plane, perhaps even circling the neighborhood, when he phoned and said he had to be back in New York for a Merrill Lynch dinner anyway and maybe we could get together.

Huizenga had a bag of six or seven negotiating ploys that he used over and over. My personal favorite was one we called the "belly drop." In a belly drop negotiation, you would spend significant man-hours working out and coming to agreement upon all the individual points down to the fine print, and just when you could taste the deal, Huizenga would hit you in the belly with some huge new ask. "Here's the thing: I need"—and he would name a substantial figure or significant element that had not previously been mentioned—"to get the deal done." Your belly would drop. You had worked so long, you had invested so much time and energy and money, and now it all seemed to be going for naught. Why not make one last concession and get the thing finished? The temptation was tremendous and many people would simply give in. As we got to know him, there always came a moment when we would wonder, what's the belly drop this time?

As our negotiations continued, we were fully prepared to dare to be great. We were not prepared to pay Huizenga his exorbitant price. Our negotiations fell apart. The deal was dead and we said goodbye right before Christmas.

I was upset; we were so close to my goal yet so far from an agreement. I wanted Paramount with all my soul but I refused to mortgage our future to get it. We would have to find the money someplace else.

But in the meantime, there was some mutual posturing going on. Discussions between Viacom and Blockbuster actually continued, principally through investment bankers, each one saying, "I have an idea we can rekindle this thing." It's a time-honored game, each banker acting as if he wasn't getting instructions from his principal, each disowning his client's involvement or even interest. We would never take at face value a statement from an investment banker that started, "Well, I haven't discussed this with my client, but . . ." They're always trying to make a buck, so there's some believability to their disclaimers, but I wouldn't bank on it. One way or another we continued negotiating.

Huizenga's leverage came from the fact that we could not do the Paramount deal without him. This was significant. He knew we needed his money. He was our last hope. He also knew that we would pass on the deal rather than go beyond the line of rationality. He continued to look for an option on some of our valuable properties—at a price that was well discounted from our view of their value. We continued to say no, we wouldn't do that. Ultimately, the decision came down to whether Viacom would buy Blockbuster, and at what price.

We had no problem accepting the idea of acquiring Blockbuster. We felt the merger was good on its merits. Of course, we needed the $600 million to pursue our bid for Paramount, but we did not feel that in acquiring Blockbuster we were making a great sacrifice to obtain it because Blockbuster itself was a growing company with a bright future. Its cash flow was terrific, which would put to rest concerns about our being able to service the debt involved in obtaining Paramount and would also enable us to grow. The acquisition was not without its downside and its risk—investors asked, "Is it really value-added?"—but it was our opinion that Blockbuster by itself would fit just fine into Viacom. We were prepared to live with the company in the very likely possibility that we would not end up with Paramount.

Huizenga, however, was being tremendously difficult, particularly around the money issues related to how many shares we would offer for each share of Blockbuster. At the same time, he was walking a thin line. He knew we would have considerably less interest in merging Blockbuster with Viacom if January 7 came and went and we didn't have the money to bid on Paramount. We might still negotiate with him, but the edge would be off. As the deadline for our bid approached, we were both under considerable pressure.

There was a view in the business community and the media that because of my ego I wasn't going to lose Paramount at any price. Frankly, that wasn't a bad view to let circulate in the marketplace; and it wasn't a bad view for Barry Diller to carry in the back of his head, the certainty that we were not going to let him beat us.

Meanwhile, more than enough Machiavellian analysis was circulating in the press. *The New York Times* reported on January 5, two days before the deadline, that I was "leaning against going forward." "Skeptics cautioned," said the *Times,* "that Viacom might want to be seen as dropping out of the bid. Throwing in the towel would cause Viacom's stock to rise, since shares of losing bidders generally rise with the news they are not assuming debt in a merger. If Viacom's stock recovers, Viacom could raise its bid more easily."

That would be pretty good strategy. It wasn't ours. We were not being manipulative but we were certainly aware of the possibility of that happening.

Philippe, Tom Dooley, Frank Biondi, our attorneys and I were negotiating with Huizenga and his advisors, including Steve Berrard, round the clock for two days at the Shearman & Sterling conference center. Paramount was trying to bring the auction to a close by using its deadline to elicit the highest bid. Without a firm deadline, there was no reason ever to put one's best bid on the table, and Paramount refused to extend it. This was useful in our negotiating strategy with Huizenga—useful, but hairy. The pressure was almost crushing. No one slept, and except to go home and take a shower and then come back, no one left that room for forty-eight hours straight.

We still refused to make concessions to Huizenga we did not feel were appropriate. We weren't going to sacrifice our company's interest simply to obtain Paramount. When it got to be one in the morning on the day of Paramount's final deadline, my guys told me, "Why don't you go home, Sumner? This is going to go on all night." I went back to my apartment, and as soon as I got there I called. I asked Philippe, Tom and Frank individually whether they thought we should really go ahead with the deal. Each man said yes. When I asked how it was going, they told me Huizenga was up to his old tricks. I was disgusted.

"We've had enough," I told them. "Let's not make another concession. Be prepared to walk. Any more garbage, walk out, the deal's off!"

In any negotiation, at the point of no return you have to be prepared to walk. Through the process of negotiation, you determine what that point is and how much you can get. If the price is too high, you walk away. We had tremendous confidence in our ability to take the various businesses of Paramount and build them and make them more successful. No analyst could quantify that confidence. But we were a responsible company, we were not going to do the deal at *any* cost. We were going to do it only if it made sense. We recognized that, as much as we wanted to win Paramount, we might not be able to produce the winning bid. We were prepared to walk away.

We made the deal that night. The companies would be merged. Blockbuster would buy $1.25 billion of Viacom common stock at $55 a share to give us the financing necessary to raise our bid for Paramount. The $1.25 billion worth of stock was subject to a set of price protection provisions called contingent value rights, or CVR (which we changed to VCR in recognition of Blockbuster's core business—and just to be cute), which would require Viacom to pay Blockbuster hundreds of millions of dollars if the price of our stock dipped below a certain level within one year of purchase.

We consummated the Blockbuster deal only hours before the Paramount deadline. Because of the time constraints, the lawyers performed prodigiously to get all the details of the merger agreement on paper. The stakes were very high. If we didn't get that done to the satisfaction of both parties, we didn't get the money. No money, no bid. No bid, no Paramount. Among the items on which we insisted was one in which Huizenga agreed to obtain "agreements to vote" on the shares of some of the principal stockholders; we would control the votes not only of his shares but also of several substantial Blockbuster shareholders. We went down to the wire and made our new bid for Paramount almost literally at the last minute.

We changed the terms of our bid slightly. Where previously we had offered stockholders $85 a share for 51 percent of the company and QVC had offered $92 per share, we now raised the cash portion of our offer to $105 per share for 50.1 percent, just enough to obtain control.

That was a cash increase of 23.5 percent. If Barry Diller thought he was going to run Paramount, he had another *think* coming.

However, there was trouble. Wall Street did not react favorably to our merger with Blockbuster, wondering whether it was indeed "value added," and despite personal appeals to analysts by both me and Huizenga, our stock plunged 6.7 percent in a day. At the same time, we roadshowed the Blockbuster deal, traveling from city to city and meeting with Blockbuster shareholders to encourage them to accept the merger. The constant complaint we heard from them was that we were buying their company too cheaply. The press also questioned the soundness of our investment and everywhere I went Blockbuster stockholders were angry at me—one guy in the Midwest actually wanted to belt me—because I had made too good a deal.

While our cash component was indeed larger than QVC's—"*Cash is king!*" I told the annual Smith Barney Shearson Media Conference—we had reduced the back end, and the overall value of our package was very close to the one QVC had previously topped. We took some heat for that in the press.

Acting on his stockholders' behalf, Martin Davis urged the Paramount board to recommend the QVC deal, and it rejected our new offer. Not that the board's recommendation mattered much at this point. We were in a bidding war and it was going to be decided by the shareholders, who would tender their shares to the side that clearly had the best bid.

We didn't have any more money. If the shareholders were to vote that day, and cash was indeed king, we would not rule the Paramount kingdom. How could we bring the shareholders to us without adding another dime to our offer? What did we have that Barry Diller didn't?

We had Viacom and our certainty that, with Paramount, we were going to succeed. But how could we translate that confidence into dollars?

We could guarantee success to our shareholders.

I spent many days plotting the scenario with our bankers Bob

Greenhill and Ace Greenberg, Philippe, Tom and Frank, and also with Michael Levitt, a partner of Greenhill, who played a major role in developing the guarantee. What kind of guarantee were we prepared to make? What would be too much, what would not be enough? And what would be the downside of guaranteeing success if we failed?

Again, as we had with Huizenga in the deal to acquire Blockbuster, we decided to offer a CVR. David Heleniak, Steve Volk and Creighton Condon of Shearman & Sterling, all of whom had advised on the creation of the original CVR plan for DuPont and then for Rhone-Poulenc in its acquisition of Rorer Pharmaceuticals, were probably the first to suggest the idea. Viacom B shares, which we would issue to Paramount shareholders in the merger, were selling at $37⅝ per share. Under the CVR plan, we would guarantee all Paramount stockholders that if the fair market value of the Viacom B shares they received was below $48 per share on the first anniversary of the merger, we would issue additional shares or cash to make up the difference, up to $12 per share. At our discretion, we could choose to measure the difference on the second or third anniversary, with the minimum price increasing to $51 on the second anniversary and $55 on the third. (The maximum payout would increase to $14 on the second anniversary and $17 on the third.) Shareholders could choose to keep the CVRs or sell them on the stock market.

This was the ultimate "Put Your Money Where Your Mouth Is" offer. We believed so firmly that we would succeed in raising the value of Viacom-Paramount that we were willing to bet billions of dollars on it. We simultaneously raised our cash bid to $107 a share. In a best-case scenario, we were offering kingly cash and an insurance policy against loss. At worst, if in one year we were unable to make the company prosper and Viacom stock fell, we would have to deliver an enormous amount of additional stock—approximately $1.5 billion worth. Paying out that amount could do immense damage to the company, my investment and the tangible results of my entire life's work.

I was willing to take that $1.5 billion risk—not happily—but we saw the CVR as a critical instrument. We were convinced that the value of our company was real. Viacom, the sleeping giant, had awoken. QVC and Barry Diller, as I was saying every day, were in the business of selling zircon jewelry.

Because the CVR itself was a tradable instrument like an insurance policy (it could be bought and sold in the options market), it had an actual monetary value. But we were confident we would never have to pay off on that policy. The patient was not sick; it was in very good health. We felt we were offering something that would cost us nothing, for which we would get a lot of value credit, and which we would never have to deliver on. Outside of the potential $1.5 billion loss, it sounded like a good deal. Would Diller top it?

On February 1, the day the bids were to close, Philippe, Tom, Frank and I stood before the Quotron and waited for Diller's final offer to appear. The tension was almost unendurable. Then, at 4:59 p.m., one minute before the deadline, his offer crossed the tape. QVC raised its top cash offer to $104 a share but adjusted its back end until the sum of the offer was basically the same as the one it already had on the table. We studied every element of the bid and waited for a CVR or an equivalent guarantee to the stockholders. It never appeared.

How did Diller raise the money for this most recent bid? By selling more of his stock to BellSouth. I would bet that by this time BellSouth had a bigger piece of QVC than Diller did. It appeared to me that, this late in the day, Diller was carrying on this battle with virtually no equity. Diller was done. He simply did not have the confidence to gamble his future on the success of a merger between the home of cubic zirconia jewelry and Paramount.

At the same moment, we improved the back end of our offer while leaving our per-share offer for the front end at $107 cash. Under our new terms, shareholders would receive up to $12 per share if our share price fell below $48 per share. If it fell below $51 in the second year, they would get up to $14. If it fell below $55 in the third year, they would get up to $17. "The moves left the rival offers far closer than they had been," said the New York Times reporter.

In fact, the offers were not close at all. QVC refused to add a CVR to its bid. Diller was unwilling to guarantee success. The failure to understand the significance of a guarantee to the stockholders was that reporter's great error. Diller's unwillingness to offer the stockholders that level of security, we felt, was a telling statement.

"It is still a tough call," the *Times* wrote, quoting one anonymous analyst, "because, with the cash amounts similar, you have to evaluate the stock of each company, and reasonable people can differ." That was nonsense. Only a fool would fail to understand the difference between merging Viacom and all its powerful networks with Paramount compared to merging Paramount with a shopping channel.

The arbitrageurs understood the difference—we hoped.

The ten-day waiting period after this round of offers had been submitted was excruciating. Both Diller and I lobbied Paramount's major shareholders in intense roadshows.

Wayne Huizenga was suggesting that we pull out of the Paramount deal. Viacom stock had dropped precipitously during the Paramount endgame. Investors looked at the amount of debt we would have to service and apparently decided we were not up to it. Huizenga, Blockbuster's major shareholder, informed his fellow Blockbuster stockholders that he was not able to support going forward with the Paramount merger.

Why? The battle for Paramount had turned into a cash bidding contest, and Viacom had the potential to prevail only by committing to spending a tremendous amount of money. We were willing to extend ourselves and take on such a huge amount of debt for the Paramount acquisition because we were investing in the long-term future of Viacom. But Viacom shares had lost much of their value because the company was proposing to go so heavily into debt. The Viacom-Blockbuster merger was a share-for-share deal and this indebtedness would be charged against the company in which Huizenga would be getting stock. If, however, the Paramount deal fell through, the billions of dollars we had raised would not be spent and the newly combined Viacom-

Blockbuster company would be largely debt-free, and in the course of the upcoming year, Huizenga would be able to cash out his Viacom shares not at the present debt-depressed level but at their highest price.

Here was the man who only days before had urged us to "dare to be great." Now he was telling his stockholders not to dare vote for this great idea. He was trying to scuttle the Paramount deal!

Huizenga was knocking the deal all over town, in the press and to the analysts. With the price of our stock falling from a high of 59⅜ to a low of 21¾ during the struggle, he also wanted more stock to make up the difference. But Huizenga was legally committed to supporting the Paramount deal; we had negotiated those "agreements to vote," voting options on his stock. "You are required under the terms of the agreement to support the deal," we told him. So there was a strong conflict between his legal exposure and his opposition to the Paramount acquisition. I did not take a legal position but I certainly suggested one; if he violated his agreement, there would be serious legal consequences.

Meanwhile our roadshow was being received warmly, while the newspapers reported that Diller was having a hard time. Analyst Emanuel Gerard said, "Everyone in the group told Barry that if he doesn't do anything, he's going to lose." If the media didn't fully grasp the power and significance of the CVR, the market did. And when Diller, having had one opportunity already, showed no signs of matching it, we said to ourselves, "We think we've got it." But we were not 100 percent positive. Diller had ten days to pony up the money, the fortitude, the courage.

Throughout the battle, whichever company appeared to be the front-runner in the race for Paramount saw its stock go down. Investors felt that the company that ultimately won control of Paramount would be paying such a high price that it could never make it back. Conversely, the prospective loser's stock price had risen. Bottom line: The Street thought Paramount wasn't worth what we were paying. Two days before the deadline was to expire, Diller announced that QVC would not raise its bid. "A few experts pointed out," wrote the *Times'* Fabrikant, "that

Mr. Diller's statement may help raise QVC's stock and, in turn, the value of its offer."

On the evening of February 14, the expiration date of both tender offers, we repaired to "21" to have dinner while waiting for the votes to be counted. At eight-thirty I got a call from our proxy solicitor. "Sumner, you now have 50.1 percent of the votes."

It had been a cruel, abusive, sometimes ridiculous battle. A war, really. When you consider the risks we had taken; the stress we had lived under day by day, month after month for almost an entire year; the unpleasantness of facing off against someone who was supposed to be my friend, and who I felt had betrayed that friendship; the enormous disappointment of losing the Delaware court case when we knew we were right; the attempts to besmirch my reputation; the favoritism of the press—it had been a brutal hardship to fight this war. I raised my glass and toasted the men who had fought it with me.

"Here's to us who won."

Diller, when asked, said, "They won. We lost. Next."

T W E L V E

THE SHAKEOUT

I woke up the next morning exhausted, exhilarated and the owner of Paramount. I spoke with Philippe, Tom and Frank. We were all on top of the world.

"It's been a long, strange trip," I told *The Hollywood Reporter.* MTV was a Viacom company; it was within my realm to paraphrase the Grateful Dead.

A number of people called to congratulate me, including Vice President Al Gore and Gerry Levin, who as Time Warner's chairman, president and CEO ran the world's number-one media and entertainment company, a position in the marketplace that I coveted.

Barry Diller also telephoned. I had no qualms about taking his call. It is a serious mistake to let the past get in the way of the future. I knew he wasn't going to be hostile. He was too smart for that. "I'm sorry you won," he said, "but congratulations."

I accepted his congratulations but I wasn't going to let him off the hook. "Thanks," I said, "but I'm sorry you cost me $2 billion."

I met Barry several times in the months following the Paramount battle and it seemed to me on each occasion that he tried to justify his actions. At the next Allen & Company conference he told me, "I know you think that what I did was inappropriate, or wrong, but I saw it differently." From that point on, over the course of several years, I kept re-ferring to him as my "$2 billion ex-friend." Finally he said, "Lay off, will you, Sumner? Enough is enough."

He was right, but I'm not going to forget our battle. That would be foolish. But now I once again consider Barry a good friend. I have a lot of respect for his talent and abilities, and I think the feeling is mutual. Who knows, maybe we'll do some deals together in the future.

(We haven't done any deals yet. In fact, Viacom recently won the rights to the World Wrestling Federation, something both Diller and I coveted, and used it to transform TNN almost overnight into one of cable's major channels. There was nothing personal in this big victory for me; however, I do enjoy winning.)

Wayne Huizenga continued to be a problem and now began to push for a termination of the Viacom-Blockbuster merger agreement altogether. We called him on it and proposed to indeed terminate the merger if he paid us $100 million for our time and trouble. We had analyzed our finances and although we would have been reluctant to do so, we found that if we sold certain Paramount assets, we could still safely swing the deal. But we really did not want to relinquish Blockbuster; its cash flow was going to be valuable to us. The point was moot, however, because Huizenga would not go above $50 million to terminate the merger and we came to no agreement.

As we roadshowed the Paramount merger to fund managers around the country, trying to persuade them to vote for it, Huizenga was dragged along to these sessions rather unwillingly. One presentation, to a fund in Boston, was going nowhere when we both took a break and went to the men's room. Standing at the urinal next to mine, Huizenga chose that moment to harangue me once again about increasing our bid for Blockbuster. "Sumner," he said, looking straight ahead at the wall, "this deal is not rich enough. Give me more stock. I want you to add a dollar." He spoke as if he were the only man with shareholders to satisfy.

"Your stockholders have a fair deal," I told him. "I can't guarantee the movement of our stock. That wasn't a condition of our deal."

Huizenga became very agitated. "My stockholders are depending on me," he protested.

I washed my hands and turned to face him in the middle of the men's room. His demand was absurd and now I started to grow heated.

"You don't get it!" I told him. "You're complaining because the price of our stock is down. *You are driving it down!* Every time you criticize, every time you talk about the price of our stock, every time you say it is not adequate for Blockbuster stockholders, it goes down some more. *It is a self-fulfilling prophecy!*

"How can you do this?" I roared. "You're double-crossing us. We did everything you wanted. We cooperated with you, we made a deal that you liked, and it was all premised—*and you know it!*—it was premised on your commitment to the Paramount deal."

Huizenga simply growled in response. He was willing to take the risks involved in knocking a deal which he had a clear, unequivocal commitment to support. He wanted the Blockbuster board of directors to take a position not to support the deal, not even to take it to a shareholder vote. We said no and stood firm, asserting legal claims under the merger agreement that required him to hold a shareholder vote.

By the middle of the summer, our stock had started to recover, and Huizenga addressed the Blockbuster stockholders' meeting in Fort Lauderdale at which the merger vote was to be taken. "Is today a sad day?" he said. "Yes, of course it is." He had created Blockbuster from nothing and now he was giving it over. "Why are we doing this now?" he asked. And answered, "The numbers were compelling." But clearly, no matter how much money he was making in the deal, he did not want to part with the business he had built from the ground up. He was being made vice chairman of Viacom and would sit on our board of directors. "I plan to provide direction to the company and its management for many years to come," he proclaimed. "I thank our franchisees and their commitment to build the Blockbuster brand. . . . Our officers and our 55,000 employees. I thank you." And with that he broke down in tears.

We voted his proxy shares in favor and, in a vote that was closer than it should have been, the Blockbuster shareholders approved the merger.

When the time came for the Viacom board of directors to vote on the Paramount merger, Huizenga abstained. On July 7, 1994, in spite of him, the merger between Viacom and Paramount was completed. My experience with Wayne Huizenga was extremely painful. With the *Business Week* story, I felt at that time that he had ruined my life. Still, I carry no grudge. He worked hard for Blockbuster shareholders and I have a lot of respect for that. It is water over the dam and I wish him no harm.

Because the Paramount deal had evolved from a merger of equals into an auction, Martin Davis, through no fault of his own, could no longer be assured of his position in the new company. He retired with his significant stock options and Stanley Jaffe negotiated a severance package. I remained chairman of Viacom and Frank Biondi was president and CEO.

One of the first things I did once the acquisition was complete was involve myself in the Paramount studio. I met with Paramount Motion Picture Group chairman Sherry Lansing, whom I hardly knew at the time. We had previously met at an Academy of Excellence symposium where I heard Sherry arguing with John Grisham about which was better, the book or the movie—they were, of course, talking about *The Firm*. Today Sherry and I are not just business associates, we are extremely close friends. She has turned out to be clearly the best studio head in our industry.

Sherry and I would often chat about my views of the motion picture business, although I always deferred to her. At one of our early meetings I said, "Sherry, I don't intend to make movies. You're going to make the movies. My job is to run Viacom. But one thing I know is that you cannot make a great movie without a great script." She put her arm around me and said, "Sumner, I swear to you that I'll never start a movie unless I'm in love with the script." And I believe that, over the years, she has lived up to that promise.

We needed someone to head up all of our Paramount entertainment divisions. I thought immediately of Jonathan Dolgen. I had known Dolgen off and on over the years when I was a motion picture exhibitor, even before I gained control of Viacom. He was with Columbia Pictures and I remember sitting with him in one particular meeting that became rather heated and thinking, Boy, there is one smart guy. I ran into him occasionally after that. We never became friends; I viewed him not as someone I knew well but whom I knew well enough.

I discussed Dolgen with Frank Biondi, who had known him in the movie business. We agreed that Dolgen was a viable candidate and called him in for a preliminary talk, which went well. We were both impressed and told him we would get back to him. Two weeks later, having heard nothing, I called Dolgen myself and asked, "Has Frank called you to work out the details?" He said he hadn't heard from anyone at Viacom. Odd. I picked up the ball, brought the negotiations to a head and hired Jonathan Dolgen as chairman of Viacom's Entertainment Group.

Sony owned Columbia, and Sony Pictures chairman Peter Guber called and began to chew me out. "Peter," I told him, "the man is not under contract. He has no chance to get this kind of job at your studio, even though I understand he's played a significant role there. He has a right to move up when he's not under contract and we have a right to get the best talent we can. If he were under contract, I would certainly have talked to you first, but he wasn't." Peter was pretty upset with me.

Sherry Lansing and Jon Dolgen would turn out to be a remarkable team, extraordinarily effective in furthering the interests of Viacom in the entertainment business. Dolgen and I often discussed potential means by which we could make Paramount an even more successful studio. My idea was to cut motion picture production industry-wide, not increase it. My background as a theater owner told me that a glut of pictures was great for exhibitors but the studios got killed. Why? There were three reasons. One, too many pictures means you can't get adequate playing time for any of them; if there are five pictures running against you, your opening gross is affected because only so many people are going to the movies. Two, too many pictures chasing the talent means they can then raise their fees accordingly. And three, too many pictures means more unsuccessful films because, quite simply, it's hard to make a successful motion picture.

Dolgen gets credit for the risk-limiting agenda we instituted at Paramount. He is a master negotiator and he arranged in some instances for us to receive distribution fees before we split the proceeds, hedging our potential losses against the longer shot of a blockbuster success. We opened ourselves up to a variety of transactions and began to share financing with other companies—split-rights deals, distribution-only deals—also in order to minimize the potential for loss. Dolgen found a way to make failure less likely and less costly. He saw that it was better to be at bat twenty times—with some risk limitations, but without giving up too much of the upside—than to take forty swings from the heels.

It was Dolgen's idea that we treat our films not unlike an investment portfolio in the stock market; we would own 100 percent of some films, 50 percent of others, lesser parts of others still. If you were in the stock market, would you buy only one stock? No. (Unless it's Viacom.) We remained within our realm but we diversified, and our portfolio of films had a sense of balance. At the same time, it was important not to interfere with the creative process. A good deal won't make a bad movie good. We tried to separate the creative judgment about making the films from the amount of money we had to risk. We also tried to lessen the amount of cash we invested while maximizing the potential for profit.

We were almost immediately criticized for this policy, accused of not having the courage of our convictions and needlessly giving away the proceeds of our success. "You're too risk-conscious," critics said. "Sure, you cut your risk, but look at what you're giving away." In our defense, we made it a policy to analyze every picture and adapt our strategy accordingly. It was not that we wanted the pictures for which we shared financing arrangements with other people to fail; of course we wanted them to succeed. But if we were really sold on a script, we tried to produce it ourselves, as with *The Truman Show*. We would have made *Saving Private Ryan* by ourselves; we loved the script but so did Dream-Works, and by sharing the financing, we got Steven Spielberg and Tom Hanks, so that was a good business decision.

In connection with *Saving Private Ryan*, both DreamWorks and Paramount wanted domestic distribution even though, in economic terms, it was immaterial because the companies split the profit from both domestic and foreign distribution evenly. I can recall the tension when Spielberg, Jon Dolgen and I stood around and I tossed a coin with Steven for domestic distribution. Unfortunately, I lost. Dolgen was not happy. However, there was a redeeming feature; on the next Paramount/DreamWorks joint venture, *Deep Impact*, we received domestic distribution and DreamWorks got foreign distribution, and *Deep Impact* was an unexpected hit.

Even though we got beat up by the media for our risk-averse decisions, we stayed the course—and prospered. It taught us a lesson: Listen to your critics, but if in your heart and mind you know there is a path you should take, never let yourself be deterred by the possibility that you will come under their withering fire. It is not easy advice to follow but it is worthwhile remembering.

That strategy has proved very effective for Paramount. Since 1994, when we took over, the studio has produced a string of hits, including *Clear and Present Danger, Clueless, Mission: Impossible, The First Wives Club, Star Trek: First Contact, Beavis and Butt-Head Do America,*

Face/Off, The Truman Show, The Rugrats Movie, Varsity Blues, The General's Daughter, Runaway Bride, Double Jeopardy, The Talented Mr. Ripley, Rules of Engagement, M:I–2, Rugrats in Paris, Save the Last Dance, Down to Earth, What Women Want and so many more. We won the Oscar for Best Picture three times in four years, for *Forrest Gump* (1994), *Braveheart* (1995) and *Titanic* (1997). We have had the best years in Paramount's history while cutting our investment by hundreds of millions of dollars. Now everyone is trying to emulate our strategy.

I developed a very supportive working relationship with Sherry Lansing during the preparation of the film *Congo*. We had a Michael Crichton book and distinguished producers Frank Marshall and Kathy Kennedy. Marshall was also directing, and it was a costly picture, primed to be our big summer movie. The first preview was awful. If things stayed the way they were, we were in for a large and expensive disaster. Sherry told Dolgen the bad news and Dolgen called me. I called Sherry immediately. "I heard about the screening," I said.

"Yes," she replied and there was a pause. I don't know what she expected. Perhaps she thought I was going to chew her out.

"Look, Sherry, don't lose confidence in yourself," I said. "Above all, remember that I have total confidence in you. You made all the right decisions. It was a best-selling book, you hired the best producers, a terrific director. You did everything right."

They were going to spend the week in the editing room trying to fix the picture. "Do you mind if I call you from time to time," I asked, "to see how it's going?" She said of course not.

I called about once a week after that and she told me, "It's getting better." Was it chickenshit or chicken salad? "I don't know," she said, "but it's getting better."

A second preview proved that the work was worthwhile. The picture found its core young male target audience and ultimately went on to become a huge hit. At 2 a.m. on the morning after it opened, I got the numbers, just as I had done each morning at National Amusements, and called Sherry to congratulate her. It was the first call she got. "You see, I knew you could do it," I said. "You've fixed it!"

At a recent dinner at Sherry's house in Bel Air, she recalled that story and said that from that moment on she knew she would follow me into battle wherever I went. I was touched. Today, Sherry and Jon remain among my best friends and most valued advisors.

Another of my close friends in Hollywood today is Bob Evans. When I had only a few drive-ins, Evans ran the Paramount studio. He was a great leader with superb taste. Among his many historic hits were *The Godfather, Love Story, Lady Sings the Blues, Serpico* and *Chinatown*. In those early days, notwithstanding my lack of economic clout, Bob gave me total access to the Paramount studio.

Sometimes you do things for friends. In 1983, Bob was producing *The Cotton Club,* which was shooting in New York. The picture was being independently financed and some of Evans's minority investors were not bankers or a consortium of international businesspeople but fellows you really don't want to get involved with if things go badly. And things were going very badly. The picture was going way over budget and the guys who were putting the money up were, as Evans said, "not kindly disposed" to losing this kind of capital. They held him and director Francis Ford Coppola responsible. Personally responsible.

Several years earlier I had helped Evans get a loan from a bank in Boston, so he had some experience coming to me regarding financial matters. Bob appreciated my help then. Now he called me in desperation. A team of five very tough-looking "auditors" had been sent to New York to control the budget. They had taken up residence and were monitoring the overages, and things were getting worse each day. Evans had no control over the flow of money, he told me, as Coppola had total creative control of the picture.

But these guys couldn't have cared less about explanations; all they cared about was their money. And as the money continued to disappear, tempers were reaching a crescendo of hostility. Having been in New York for almost a month, they were making it very clear that if something was not done, and done quickly, Evans was dead meat. Evans, mind you, had been the producer of *The Godfather;* he knew these guys weren't going away.

"Sumner, I don't know what to do," he told me. "I'm afraid for my life." I said, "Hold on, I'll come down there."

We met in what Evans called his "crisis center," a town house on the Upper East Side of Manhattan that he had rented for the production. Years earlier, I had sat with Bugsy Siegel and his team of attorneys. This was an entirely different crew. These were not investor types. I walked in that morning and found some lounging in the big living room upstairs, others standing around on different floors. Five men in their fifties. No kids, these guys were dead serious. It was just a normal day of looking after their investment for these "auditors"; they were waiting for that day's figures, they didn't know I was coming. I gathered them together around a table. Some sat, others stood. I remember standing beside a fireplace. They were looking at me and they were not friendly.

I wasted no time. I told them, "If you do anything to Bob, I'll go to Washington and have the attorney general climbing all over you. I want to make it real clear to everyone here: I am very involved with the government. If I hear one thing that happens wrong to Bob—I want to make it real clear to everybody here! I mean *real* clear!—I'm going to the FBI and I'll get every one of you. I'm leaving now, but do you hear me?!" I walked out.

The threats stopped. The "investors," so I'm told, got most of their money back. And Bob went on to make many more films.

As we walked out of there, I had a moment to consider the potential consequences of my actions. I said to Evans, "How the hell did I ever do that?" Neither of us knew. "Promise me one thing, Bob," I told him. "Never again!"

———————

Not every division of Viacom functioned as smoothly as Paramount. We almost immediately ran into trouble with Simon & Schuster's CEO

Richard Snyder. He was, like many others in the far-flung Paramount Communications world, heading up his own operation and extremely entrenched in it, and we couldn't even find out what was happening in a business we owned. It was understandable that in a company of our size, without a conscious combining of forces, the corporate chiefs would have their own agendas, even their own fiefdoms, but this went beyond anything we had anticipated. Dick Snyder shut his door and discouraged other S&S executives from talking to us. He reminded me a little bit of Terry Elkes.

We discovered there was much hostility toward Snyder within Simon & Schuster. You can't keep a thing like that a secret. People didn't like him. He was very despotic and often verbally abusive with some of his workers. It was said that when he got on the elevator in the S&S lobby, other employees were often not allowed to ride up with him. He was charming to me on a personal basis—I actually liked him—but he obviously treated me differently than he treated the people who worked for him, which was part of the problem. To them he behaved like none of us ever behaved, volcanic and abrasive. He was a tyrant.

Dick Snyder deserved a great deal of credit for the growth that had taken place at Simon & Schuster, which was a very successful publishing house, but we put a premium on collegiality, communication and teamwork and Snyder seemed to feel that Simon & Schuster belonged to him. He was formal and arrogant around the conference table while the rest of our executives, myself included, were rather casual. We would ask for an update on the state of S&S and he as much as told us, in word and attitude, "Why are you asking me these questions? *I'm* running the company." On those occasions when he seemed to have a more constructive point of view, it was not manifested in his behavior. He appeared to think of himself as irreplaceable—not an attractive attitude, in my estimation, and not one that works with me. The situation finally got to the point where we were totally frustrated with him and knew he had to go. It would be a difficult decision to make, however, one that Martin Davis had made earlier but never had the guts to act upon.

At the same time that we were considering letting Snyder go, he was renegotiating his contract. Snyder seemed to think he was the personification of Simon & Schuster and he tried to leverage us. His attorney approached us about the terms of his agreement and it was this overture, combined with Snyder's complete culture clash with the rest of Viacom, that precipitated our making the decision to fire him. Frank, Philippe, Tom and I all agreed.

We derived some comfort from the fact that we had an extremely able person to take his place. Jonathan Newcomb, who at the time was second-in-command at Simon & Schuster, clearly knew the business. Educational publishing had become the largest segment of the S&S operation and the field was becoming increasingly technologically oriented, which was not Snyder's original background. From the operational standpoint, Newcomb was the man at Simon & Schuster who was making things work. If he had less flair than Snyder, he was critical to the company's success and was fully capable of taking us to the next level of publishing excellence. His even temperament and personality also fell well within our comfort zone.

When Snyder entered Frank Biondi's office, I believe he thought he had us where he wanted us, that his strength and leverage were at their highest and renegotiating his contract was a mere formality. Philippe was also in the room, and Frank was very low-key when he told Snyder that we had decided not to renew his contract. Snyder just sat there. There was no conflagration, no confrontation. He appeared stunned. Frank said we felt there was a culture clash, we thought Jon Newcomb was ready to lead the business and we were going to present this change in leadership to the public in the best way possible for all concerned. "We've drafted a press release but we would welcome your comments," Frank said. "If there's anything you would like to add to it, or any quote from yourself, just let us know. We're going to make the announcement later today."

We gave Snyder a copy of a draft press release and told him that his lawyer should get in touch with Philippe. We were going to honor the remaining part of his contract fully, we said, and would give him every-thing he was entitled to. We told him he could keep an office in one of our buildings, we offered him a consulting job, we offered him ways to preserve his stock options. Ultimately he turned all our offers down and cost himself a lot of money. At that moment, however, he did not say much of anything.

Some authors expressed concern when the announcement was made, and I called several of them personally, but in the aftermath the major authors stayed. Jon Newcomb took over and both he and Simon & Schuster have flourished.

One of our top priorities was to bring down the debt involved in acquir-ing Paramount. The banks wanted us to sell a minority stake in MTV, and although the media said the plan was under consideration, it wasn't. We had a clear vision of what was good for the long-range inter-ests of Viacom and MTV was directly in the middle of it. My response was clear: MTV was at the beginning of a period of sustained growth. Why would I sell it? Not a chance. Not a remote possibility. We did end up selling our cable systems and our 50 percent interest in USA Net-works, the latter under litigating duress, but MTV was never for a mo-ment in play.

A week after we bought Paramount, I was asked by Katie Couric on national television whether we were going to sell Simon & Schuster. I said, "No, it's not for sale." Had we sold it at that time, we might have gotten $2 billion for it. But I knew that was not the time to sell.

One asset we were willing to part with was the Madison Square Gar-den properties. They could have been considered entertainment soft-ware in some fashion, but they were in demand and we were not hesitant about putting them on the market.

In the spring of 1994, just after we had assumed control of Para-mount, the New York Rangers were on their way to winning hockey's

Stanley Cup for the first time in fifty-four years, while the New York Knicks were heading for the National Basketball Association finals. The MSG Network broadcast the games of both teams plus the New York Yankees and was a potent cable presence. Madison Square Garden was hot. Of all the Paramount assets, the Garden and the two sports teams with their combination of public relations sizzle and sports franchise turnover profit were the most likely to sell. In Hollywood parlance, they were "sexy." At that stage of the game, however, my main interest was not sex but money. The Blockbuster deal had not yet gone through and looked chancy, and while I enjoyed going to the games and found it a pleasure to meet Knicks coach Pat Riley, I had no second thoughts about selling these high-visibility assets if we could get the right price.

I was happy to involve Herb Allen in the sale. He had been upset with me over the Paramount matter and here was an opportunity to mend some fences as well as do a good deal. Herb is a very effective investment banker. Again, I wouldn't let the past get in the way of the future.

According to the press, the potential buyers of the MSG properties were NYNEX, Time Warner, Disney, Rupert Murdoch, George Steinbrenner, a list of billionaires including Jack Kent Cooke, James and Robert Nederlander, football's Boston Patriots former owner Billy Sullivan, Boston Garden owner Jeremy Jacobs, Reebok's Paul Fireman, and Larry Tisch, whose brother Bob was half-owner of the New York Giants. We were glad to have the press speculating on the number and identity of the suitors. Potential buyers of sports franchises are inherently competitive people and it helped our bargaining position for them to think they would be bidding against a large number of other buyers. We sent out a lot of material to potential suitors and some may have given us early indications of interest, but in fact the only serious bidders to emerge were Rand Araskog's ITT, Chuck Dolan's Cablevision, and Liberty Media, which was about to be reacquired by John Malone's TCI.

It is essential, when negotiating, to understand not only your own position but also the needs and desires of the people you are negotiating with. How important to their future, their aspirations and their vision for their companies is the asset which you possess? ITT, which had once been a telephone and communications company, had moved into the entertainment/hospitality field and, according to the *New York Post*, "probably controls more New York hotel rooms than any other chain." Owning the Garden, the Knicks and the Rangers would increase its visibility and make it a "player" again. ITT was also heavily involved in the gaming business. It had recently bought the Desert Inn in Las Vegas and was planning the construction of a $750 million hotel and casino adjacent to it. An ITT spokesman said the company was "interested in opportunities in the gaming business, if and when New York makes the decision to permit it." ITT may have thought that gambling was going to come to New York City and that Madison Square Garden would be an excellent center for its operations.

Liberty Media was a front for John Malone's TCI, and Malone's penchant for empire-building in the cable industry was well known. TCI was the nation's largest cable system; it had just bought Prime Ticket, the MSG parallel in southern California; it had interests in more than a dozen regional sports networks around the country, and in combination with MSG Network it could create a whole even greater than the sum of its parts. TCI's confidence and arrogance were renowned. Liberty's president, Peter Barton, told the media that it would sell off the teams and the building, but "There is a sense of manifest destiny. . . . We are going to end up owning [MSG Network]." As for our price of $1 billion, he said, "That's way too expensive. We are not going to pay that much."

In the mid-1960s, Chuck Dolan had been the first person in the cable industry to strike deals with professional sports teams. He now owned Cablevision, the country's fourth-largest cable operator. Cablevision's subsidiary, SportsChannel, broadcast the New York Mets, the

New York Islanders, the New Jersey Nets and the New Jersey Devils. SportsChannel had lost the rights to New York Yankees baseball to MSG Network six years earlier. If Dolan acquired the Garden, the Knicks, the Rangers and MSG Network, he would have a lock on New York sports broadcasting and become, as one columnist put it, "King Kong of New York sports." That was a lofty goal.

The media initially put a price of approximately $500 million on the MSG package. They published financial analysts' reports that the MSG cash flow was in the neighborhood of $25 million annually and then multiplied by 20, the standard formula for calculating business worth. They weren't helping us much. Every time I heard "$500 million," I said, "Over a billion." When I was asked whether we would accept bids in the range of $600–$700 million, I responded, "That's a price that wouldn't even begin to interest us." We had just acquired the MSG properties and saw all kinds of cost-saving possibilities by which we felt we could increase the cash flow to the $50 million level just by running the Garden more efficiently. Add in the sizzle factor and the ego gratification of owning a pair of media-spotlight New York sports teams—"There's no question an NBA title or a Stanley Cup would have an impact," said NHL Pittsburgh Penguins owner Howard Baldwin, who bought his club between its two Stanley Cup seasons. "This is an emotional, not a rational business"—and a billion dollars was not too much to ask. Besides, why shouldn't I reach for the moon?

There was a suggestion that we sell each MSG asset separately but we quickly realized that letting buyers pick and choose was not the way to get maximum value. If they want it, take it all. The first bidder was ITT. Chairman and CEO Rand Araskog sent over a floor bid of $650 million with an option to top any further offers. We then went through the usual Frank Biondi routine.

"Let's take it," he advised.

I had great respect for Frank, but he still had no concept of how to negotiate a deal.

"Why, Frank?" I asked. "I've got to get at least a billion. Why is that bad?"

"They'll walk away."

I disagreed, and Frank and I had a rather heated discussion. "Frank, I've done a little negotiating in my life," I said. "If somebody wants something, why the hell would you think they'll walk away because you say it's a lot more valuable than they want to pay? It's called negotiating!"

Frank didn't have an answer. He wanted to get the deal done and move on. I thought that was a terrible idea.

I rejected the offer. I told Araskog, "A billion-plus or go away."

Nobody took a walk.

The TCI/Liberty people now entered the arena. We were still in the midst of suing them regarding their restraint of Showtime/The Movie Channel, but the fact that we had a lawsuit pending should not have prevented them from showing interest in our asset. It did not. And it certainly did not stop us from treating them as a serious bidder.

Why should it? They wanted to buy at the best price they could. We wanted to sell at the best price we could. What did that have to do with the fact that we had a major lawsuit against them? They were separate issues. Perhaps we had cultivated the ability to compartmentalize in business over the years. There was talk in the press that we might include a settlement in the price of a deal with Liberty, but that was not in the cards and we never seriously considered it. We did not intend to have them "do us a favor" by buying the Garden as a way of getting out of the lawsuit. We were going to sell the Garden for what it was worth and at the same time pursue our legal rights. And while the media speculated on the peculiarity of conducting normal business relations with a party we were simultaneously suing, I didn't see any problem.

We set a deadline for the bidding. Liberty's Peter Barton, apparently in an attempt to back off his competitors, said, "It is foreordained that we will own the Garden."

I was telling everybody, "It's not going to go for less than a billion-plus. If you're interested, fine. If you're not, go away." I was serious, and it was important that the potential bidders knew I was serious. I let it be known that it would not be the end of the world if we operated the Garden ourselves. We could increase the cash flow by putting Christmas shows and Nickelodeon and MTV shows in there to compete with Radio City Music Hall. We probably could have done a good job of raising admission prices and cutting expenses, which would be the way to increase profits. "We're not sure we're doing the right thing by selling it," I kept saying. That was my line.

Believe me, we were doing the right thing. We really wanted to sell because we needed the money to trim our debt. But I was holding the line with at least apparent great confidence. "A billion-plus. That's it." I went out on a limb, but if serious bidders wanted this property, they had to believe me or risk going home empty. Knowing how important local sports was to TCI/Liberty and how important this piece of New York was to Cablevision's Chuck Dolan, I thought I had a good chance to prevail.

At the last minute, ITT and Cablevision combined forces and made a joint bid. On deadline they came in with a verbal offer of $1.055 billion. Also on deadline, TCI/Liberty came in at very much the same price but with conditions. They sent us a contract full of loopholes which, if we signed it, would have given them merely an option to buy with many easily available means of scuttling the deal. If you sign a contract that gives the other side that many ways out, forget it, it's worthless. In arrogance, Liberty sent us this contract and said, "If you don't accept these terms by three this afternoon we are withdrawing it."

It was a naked threat. We were being leveraged. If Liberty withdrew, we would have no leverage with Dolan. No leverage, no deal. Both TCI/Liberty and Cablevision considered each other a serious bidder, and both wanted the property, so at least that conflict was to our advantage. But to hold an auction with only one bidder is hardly an advantageous way to do business—although, under those circumstances, you would never let the one bidder know he is the lone bidder. The Liberty offer was not dismissible, and its people were threatening to announce their withdrawal from the bidding publicly, so we had to act quickly.

I met in my office with both Cablevision's Chuck Dolan and ITT's Rand Araskog. As I was sitting down with them, discussing the terms of their bid, my office was getting calls from Liberty's attorneys: "If you don't sign this contract the way we gave it to you, we're going to withdraw it." They really thought they had us. Peter Barton was running the show but I was certain John Malone was operating behind the scenes. Here I was trying to conclude a deal with Dolan and Araskog and their competitor was demanding that we accept an offer we didn't like—or else.

I tried to keep the meeting light; I was friendly and warm but inside I was churning. I wanted to tell Liberty, "Beat it!" but I didn't dare until I could wrap up a deal with the two men sitting in front of me. I stood my ground.

"We don't have a deal at $1.055," I told them. "You're not the only one in the game here." It was pure brinksmanship. I really did not want to deal with Liberty but at the same time I had to sweeten the ITT/Cablevision offer. That was my job.

"If you come in at $1.075, we've got a deal," I said. "And I will commit to making that deal, no matter what anyone else comes in with."

I had two reasons for asking for that extra $20 million. First, I wanted the $20 million. Second, I thought it would fortify our chances of getting at least the $1.055 billion which Dolan and Araskog had offered but which we did not yet have in writing. Sometimes people are foolish. Sometimes after you have agreed to accept a negotiated price or condition, the other side comes down with negotiator's remorse and feels it has offered too much. This was a way to make it clear that they hadn't offered too much.

Dolan and Araskog walked out of my office uncertain whether we had a deal at all. What they knew was their offer was not enough. Now it was up to them.

I had to stall Liberty until I got an answer. The people at Liberty thought MSG was their "manifest destiny"; if they couldn't have it neither could anyone else, and they were preparing to announce their withdrawal from the deal to the world. We could not allow that to happen. My mission was to keep the Liberty deal alive and at the same time move Dolan and Araskog to a higher level. If either Liberty or ITT/Cablevision announced it was pulling out, the game was over.

We kept niggling the Liberty people about small points in their contract. They, of course, were bluffing about the 3 p.m. deadline. We amassed a list of picayune items—we didn't like one provision, we needed clarification on another—each of which had to be fully negotiated before we would accept their contract. We kept them going for forty-eight hours.

Finally, Araskog and Dolan agreed. I would get my $1.075 billion. "We each kicked in another $10 million," Araskog said.

But a deal isn't a deal until it's a signed deal. We already had the ITT/Cablevision contracts in advanced stages but there are always certain provisions that have to be finalized. We worked around the clock.

It seems that important negotiations always end in the middle of the night. That's because when you're close to finalizing a deal, you never stop simply because night falls. You want to get it done, and keep at it right up until the final minute. You don't say, "Time to go to sleep. See you Monday." Some people apparently do say that, but that's not the way I do business. You can go to sleep and wake up the next morning to find that the other side has pulled out or has found a better deal elsewhere. If you have what you want in theory, the smartest thing to do is stay on the case until the deal is signed.

I was pacing the floor of my apartment at the Carlyle, sweating, worrying. I knew we had a deal with ITT/Cablevision but I wanted to get it in writing as soon as possible. Who knew what Barton and Malone were up to? We signed the agreement at 4 a.m. on a Saturday and announced it later that morning.

Liberty and TCI were in a state of shock. Their "ordainment" capacity had been inadequate. They couldn't believe we had kissed them off. But they had made a mistake, they had overplayed their hand. Viacom, meanwhile, rather than the $500 million that the business community said we could expect from the sale of MSG, was in possession of $1.075 billion to put toward paying down our debt.

As so often happens in deal post-mortems, one side was accused of having paid too much. This time it was ITT/Cablevision. But Chuck Dolan said, "The opportunity to acquire a world-class property like Madison Square Garden comes along once in a lifetime, and we were determined it would be ours." I understood. I had felt the same way about Viacom's acquisition of Paramount. Cablevision acquired ITT's interest and eventually came to control 100 percent of MSG. And Dolan would truly make it work, which pleased me. The best kind of deal is one in which you get the highest possible price and the people on the other side still ultimately succeed. When you walk away from the table, you must not let them think for a minute that you've got the better of them. It is acceptable for them to think you made a great deal for yourself, but they have to feel good about their end of the agreement as well. Chuck Dolan and I have since done several deals that were mutually beneficial. He paid top price for properties that became, by dint of his own skill, worth even more than the high price he paid for them. That kind of shared success is particularly helpful when you find yourselves across the negotiating table again.

I believe in taking every penny off the table. Absolutely. If it's there to be had, you might as well have it. But you need a good understanding of how to conduct a negotiation and how far you can go. You should never act in a way that is inconsiderate of the other side. Style and grace are important. You can be an aggressive negotiator while at the same time deal with people in a fair, honest and appropriate way. A negotiator should always be conscious that there is a life beyond the deal, not only for morality's sake but for business reasons. One deal often leads to another and the way you conduct yourself will have concrete consequences when you do business again in the future. Your reputation does indeed precede you.

But, yes, we get the best price possible for everything we buy or sell. Why not?

THIRTEEN

WE ARE ALL VIACOM

I n *November 1995*, Wayne Huizenga resigned from the Viacom board and stepped away to form another company, Republic Industries. He left us with Steve Berrard in charge of Blockbuster and we felt secure in this natural progression of management.

I was not so secure in other areas of the company, however. In 1995, Paramount studio's earnings were less than we had anticipated. I wanted to know why and how to fix the problem. I would have preferred that Frank Biondi go to California and do it, but he didn't, so I spent the better part of three months there, involving myself intimately with the studio's workings, meeting with marketing and production executives, and truly immersing myself in all its operations.

Frank's ideas were good, but it was increasingly clear that if there was a problem he did not have that hungry commitment to solve it, which made it difficult for him to get to the bottom line.

In December 1995 we were pursuing a ten-year, $1.2 billion deal with European broadcaster Leo Kirch to license Paramount product in Germany, our largest European market. Rather than involve himself directly, Frank had let the studio people handle the negotiations, but they just couldn't close the deal. We commissioned an up-and-coming young Viacom executive to develop a fact-finding report on the European market. We sent Tom Dooley and Philippe Dauman to Europe for a round of talks, and when they returned, we scheduled a meeting to discuss their findings.

Our young executive had spoken with various consulting firms and investment bankers and now presented his report, which was thick with facts. In essence he said, "This is what's happening in Europe. Things are moving fast. People are making deals with one another." He cited examples and named names. "If we don't involve ourselves, we will be left behind." The people who owned the broadcast companies, he said, were essentially my peers and would deal very differently with me and the Viacom CEO than they would with anyone even slightly further down the corporate ladder. After laying out the facts he said, "In order to finalize this deal, it would be advisable to send Mr. Redstone and Mr. Biondi to Europe to meet with the principals."

Within minutes Frank was dismissing the report and its recommendations. He consistently appeared to resent any idea, agenda or scenario that had not originated with him. Not only was he dismissive, he did not seem to be on top of the matter and made several statements that were factually inaccurate. Wrong people, wrong places. The young man tried very politely to say, "Well, you know, so-and-so actually owns . . ." but Frank was having none of it. A lot of work had gone into this report and he summarily rejected it.

"But tell me, Frank," I asked incredulously, "what is the harm? What's the downside of you and me meeting with these people? Maybe we can work up some competition for Paramount's product." Frank could not see it. He brought the meeting to an abrupt close and went back to his office.

We sat there in disbelief. The young man who had prepared the report was very upset and Philippe tried to calm him. Frank's behavior and judgment made no sense to me, certainly no business sense. It was the last straw. I decided then and there to say goodbye to Frank Biondi.

When I told them of my decision, Tom and Philippe were in a state of shock. We had held several meetings over the years in which I discussed letting Biondi go, but I had never been able to pull the trigger. He was extremely knowledgeable and valuable or too popular or too entrenched, I had felt. Now they told me, "Absolutely the right move for the company, but we never thought you'd have the guts to do it." And frankly, until then, despite my growing misgivings about Frank, they were probably right.

I held a meeting with board members Ivan Seidenberg and Ken Miller and our outside directors, and when Miller walked in and saw who was there—and who was not—he immediately said, "So you finally decided to fire Frank Biondi." He was not displeased.

I knew it was a move that was without a doubt in the best interests of Viacom; Frank's method of operation was ultimately working against us. I also knew I was going to be crucified by the media. Reporters loved Frank. He was open to them, friendly and honest, but they really did not know what went on inside our company. As far as management went, the financial analysts frequently did not know either. As unpleasant as I knew the following weeks would be, however, I resolved to move ahead with my decision.

I took the holidays off to consider my alternatives. Frank had brought the company a long way and taught me much about the entertainment industry, but the time had come to let him go. He never seemed truly committed to immersing himself in the issues and opportunities that were now so important to Viacom. While it is acceptable to delegate authority, there is a limit. When a problem arises, you have to jump all over it along with your management team and the people responsible. I needed someone in the position of CEO who was hands-on. That person was me.

We worked up a press release in which I said, "Frank has a different vision than I do about how the company should be run. . . . [An] entrepreneurial, aggressive, responsive, hands-on management style is the most effective way to capitalize on the enormous opportunities at Viacom. The changes I am announcing today will create just that kind of management." On January 17, 1996, I said goodbye to Frank Biondi and replaced him in the position of CEO.

Frank took the news calmly, almost as if he expected it. But I was shocked to learn that the first person he called was not his wife but his lawyer to determine his rights under his contract. We were prepared to honor his contract to the fullest, so that was not an issue, but I found this implicit statement of his priorities to be revealing.

As I had anticipated, I took a lot of heat. My "strong will" was mentioned by *The Wall Street Journal*. As far as my assuming the role of CEO, "Considering Mr. Redstone's age," the *Journal* wrote, "that raised a few eyebrows." (Bob Dole was my age exactly, seventy-two at the time, and was running for President of the United States. I told reporters, "If he can run America, believe me, I can run Viacom.") In *Newsweek*, Frank was "genial," I was "tough." Under the headline "Redstone's One-Man Show Opens at Viacom," the *Journal* said I had "grabbed the CEO post" for myself, and wrote that "an iron-fisted autocrat may not always have the right answers in the increasingly competitive media world." The paper opined that Viacom now had no one who commanded the same respect as Biondi in the film and investment industries. However, many people inside those industries called to praise my decision. Some asked why I had waited so long. The press also commented on my "use of Murdoch as a role model." People kept saying that. Granted, Rupert Murdoch was an entrepreneurial guy who went where the trouble was. But he was not a great negotiator—he overpaid for everything. Still, he always made it work; and I admire him greatly to this very day. I never wanted to emulate Murdoch. As good as he is, I just wanted to beat him.

The New York Times quoted "a former senior executive at Viacom, who asked not to be identified": "Viacom's stock price is a reflection of Sumner. It's not just his net worth. It's a reflection of his ego."

Our stock plunged, hitting a fifty-two-week low, and I was getting hammered by the press every day. Under a headline that read "Sumner

Redstone Makes a Bad Thing Worse," *Barron's* wrote, "Clearly the investment community liked Biondi's unassuming management style and extensive knowledge of the media industry." The *Los Angeles Times* headlined, "Wall Street Gasps," and quoted a professor of management at the University of Southern California: "Sumner has made an unfathomable mistake. I have always used Biondi and Redstone in my lectures as an example of why you need both an entrepreneur and a manager at the top of a company. An entrepreneur's lust needs to be counterbalanced by a manager's prudence and discipline."

I was at a disadvantage because I wanted to defend myself but I had no desire to say anything derogatory about Frank. I held my tongue because of my admiration and respect for him. As much as I insist that you should not be distracted by Wall Street or the press, this entire experience was, indeed, painfully distracting. I felt abused but I refused to be deterred.

I did not want our major investors to become alarmed by the press reports so I called several of them to explain our actions. Mario Gabelli was among my first calls. He was a smart fund manager, smart enough to have invested with us from day one. "Sumner," he said, "I'm going to be a partner of yours for the rest of my life." Our largest investor, Gordon Crawford of The Capital Group, Inc., was also supportive. I was surprised at the number of people inside the industry, including Murdoch, many closer to the operating issues of Viacom operations than was the press, who said, "I can't believe it took you so long."

I have immense affection for Frank. He has many talents and we accomplished great things. But Viacom had grown into a global media giant requiring skills and a sense of urgency he could not provide. It was, sadly, time to part ways.

Within a month of taking control of Viacom, I flew to Europe to handle the Paramount licensing negotiations. Why wait? Accompanied by

Philippe, I began my journey in New York, then flew to Florida to speak at a financial conference and from there to London, where I addressed another group. We then flew to the continent. Among the parties who had expressed interest in licensing Paramount product were the billionaire media giant Albert Frère, who controlled CLT-UFA; the German media conglomerate Bertelsmann; Philips Electronics NV and Leo Kirch. I was also in daily communication with Murdoch. We scheduled meetings with each and hit four cities in one day. Noting my schedule, Jonathan Dolgen later told me, "Sumner, please never do that again." "Why?" I asked. "Because you're going to kill yourself."

We met with Bertelsmann in Germany at a place called Gudeslow in the middle of nowhere and had to land on a rather intimidating former Nazi military airfield. I spoke with Chairman and CEO Mark Woesner and Michael Dornemann. I also spoke on the telephone with Rupert Murdoch, who was in negotiation with Bertelsmann to be a potential partner in the licensing deal and was also a potential licensor negotiating separately to control all the product.

We had lunch with Albert Frère, who was the number one broadcaster in Europe at the time. He served us an impressive three-star meal, cooked by his private chef at his château in Belgium. Frère was a noted wine connoisseur and our lunch was accompanied by bottle after bottle of excellent vintage from his private collection. There were millions of dollars' worth of art on the walls, and I couldn't help but marvel at his lifestyle. It was certainly a far cry from the way I lived.

That day I also met with the chairman of Philips. But despite the fact that there were other American studios that were licensing their product, and all these deals were being made very quickly, at no time and in no place throughout that day were we ever in an obvious negotiation. Not once did I say, "Look, we are going to make a deal with someone. We would like to get this done and here is your deadline." Never. We spoke about our company and the fact that we were probably going to do a deal with Leo Kirch, with whom the studio had been negotiating and with whom we were scheduled to have dinner in Munich that evening. Of course we didn't tell our other suitors that we were stuck at $1.2 billion and didn't have a signed agreement. "I'm sure we are going to end up making a deal with Leo," I told each of these men. "We've had a relationship with him for many years and I doubt that you could come up with a figure that would make you a serious contender. But I just felt that I should come by because we haven't closed the deal with Leo. I'm not suggesting you do become involved, nor am I suggesting that you could prevail, because I really think the deal is going to end up with Leo . . . although we are having some issues with him. And since we are, if you have any interest, that's fine. If not, that's okay too." I said the same thing every place I went—and left it at that.

The last meeting of the day was with Kirch. We had dinner in a Munich restaurant and over Wiener schnitzel talked about his long and friendly relationship with Paramount. Even though he and I had not yet gotten to know each other, I said it was important to us to continue that relationship. I told him I knew how strong his ties were with our company, but on the other hand, Leo, you can't blame us, there is interest in Paramount product from several other people. We never misstated the facts; we simply put them in the best light possible.

The message got through. The studio people originally negotiating this deal had had a long-term relationship with one player, Kirch, whereas we simply wanted to get the best deal we could for the company. Kirch knew we had no particular preference for him, that we just wanted the most money possible, and that we had met with his competitors. He no longer had a steal.

In negotiation, as I have said before, you must understand the people with whom you are dealing. You must understand their objectives. You must know what the upside is in their making a deal and what the downside is in not making it. I knew that Leo Kirch had built his professional life on controlling the product of the major studios in Germany. The entire rationale for his company, his entire empire, was built on this control as a fundamental premise. I knew he was not going to let Paramount get away, and I played off that assumption. We had met with his competitors and would certainly entertain any offers they might make, but they were all a prelude to the offer we were convinced Kirch would ultimately come up with. He no longer had the field to himself; he now had competition and his vision of his company was on the line. How much was that worth?

The European businesspeople I had met that day did not disappoint. Not only were they in a position to license Paramount product, now they were also in the new and equally enticing position of having a chance to take it away from Leo Kirch. In making their offers, they had to ask themselves two questions: What was the product worth, and what was it worth to them to hurt Kirch? Not only had we created an interest, we had created an interest *with a bonus.*

Where a day earlier we had had only Kirch involved, now new offers came in and we began to pit one buyer against the others. The net result: our lawyers at work full-time in Los Angeles and New York negotiating with four different potential buyers for the Paramount product. We were able to get the major players in Europe, whom we had never met, to compete with each other to our benefit.

My assumption was correct. Kirch ultimately came in with the highest bid. The deal Frank Biondi could not close at a billion two we closed at two billion. It was among the best deals we ever negotiated, a turning point for Paramount that has continued to pay off ever since. Kirch has also done well with the deal, which has formed the basis for a good and continuing relationship between us.

Afterwards, I called all the bidders and thanked them for their interest. I told Albert Frère, "I know you did not prevail. It was close. Obviously Leo was willing to go further, and maybe you were right to stop where you did. But I have enjoyed the contact we've had. And who knows, the day may come when there will be another opportunity that you might be interested in." Sure enough, the next deal we made was with Frère and his associates for Paramount Pictures in France.

We were running Viacom in a new way. But don't think that I don't miss Frank. He has many talents, just not those that are required to be a CEO.

Among the first steps I took as CEO of Viacom was to create and convene an executive committee consisting of the heads of the company's many divisions. Jonathan Dolgen of the Viacom Entertainment Group, Jon Newcomb of Simon & Schuster, Tom Freston of MTV Networks, Steve Berrard of Blockbuster and Edward Horowitz of Viacom Interactive Media were all on the committee, as were Tom Dooley and Philippe Dauman. I promoted Tom and Philippe to the position of deputy chairmen. We all sat around a conference table to discuss each other's businesses—and we began to get to know one another better than we had.

One industry executive said in *Electronic Media,* "This is a way for Sumner to get in the face of his executives, remove a layer of management, and push, push, push." That was not entirely accurate. Outside of Viacom there was undoubtedly the perception that I was "too hands-on," but inside our company people knew better. There is no company in the world that has the kind of environment we've had. There is not one Viacom executive who can't challenge me, and I welcome it. I am not interested in being surrounded by yes-men or yes-women. I want active people who are happy and willing and ready to express their ideas. Anybody who operates on any other basis is a fool.

Unfortunately, Gerry Laybourne had left Viacom some months earlier. She had *been* Nickelodeon and ran it with extraordinary success until she made what I believed to be an extraordinarily bad career move, leaving Viacom for Disney. She would soon find out that the world was different at her new workplace. At Viacom when she had a problem, she would walk into my office and we would discuss it. We were not just business associates, we were friends. She and Frank had not seen eye to eye very often, and she later told me that if she had known I was going to fire him, she would not have resigned. Who knows?

I was now CEO but I did not think of myself as anyone's boss. I wanted to make that clear. As I've said, years earlier I had run National Amusements as a family and I wanted Viacom to work the same way. I wanted us to work together. "Anybody in this room who thinks he's in the cable business, in the book business, in the studio business, in the network business is in the wrong room," I told the members of the executive committee at our first meeting. "We are in the business of Viacom."

As we sat around the table, I asked each executive to review his division. "Jon, what's going on at Simon & Schuster? Bring us all up to date. What are your strategic plans?" They were not being grilled; they were being given a stage and encouraged to perform. I knew most of what would be said, but the other people around the table were busy running their own operations and hadn't had the time or the opportunity to involve themselves in the full range of company operations. Through these meetings, each person would acquire a knowledge of the major issues and agendas of the other divisions. Apart from the fact that this was informative, it was also necessary to move the company forward. It was important to me and to all of us to be aware of the projects and problems of the far sides of Viacom. We had smart, enthusiastic and committed people whose opinions and skills could easily provide solutions and direction outside their individual realms and find ways to benefit one another.

The idea worked in concept and in reality, with few exceptions. As months went on, the people around the table began to acquire knowledge of one another, which strengthened their focus on Viacom not simply as a conglomeration of divisions but as a team. Simon & Schuster, for example, was well positioned to publish hundreds of thousands of Star Trek books, a Paramount franchise, as well as Nickelodeon and MTV books. How could we do that if we did not have collaboration?

While I was always available to deal with problems, I did not meddle. Short of the major issues like going to Germany to deal with Kirch or traveling to Dallas to deal with Blockbuster, I most often got involved in solving individual difficulties when the head of a division said, "Sumner, help me."

As an illustration, only recently Matt Blank of Showtime/TMC was having a big problem with Chuck Dolan and Cablevision. Dolan had bought MSG and we were on good terms, but more recently he had also bought a large number of cable subscribers from John Malone and TCI at what appeared to be a very cheap price. However, part of the deal had apparently been an agreement for Cablevision to give tremendous support to TCI's pay services. All of a sudden we were getting indications that Cablevision was going to take Showtime and The Movie Channel off the air or, at best, cut them to the bone. Why? To make room for TCI's Starz and Encore. Matt came to see me and said, "We've done everything we can, Sumner, but we have a real problem here and I'd like you to get into it."

"If that's what you want, I'll do it," I said. "Give me a memo, give me all the facts." Once I had fully acquainted myself with the situation, I called Dolan and we had a series of meetings.

"Chuck," I told him, "I really want to emphasize the long and successful history we've had together. We have sold you many assets, and yes, we have done well in those deals. But on the other side of the coin, you have done terrifically. Our Long Island cable system has turned into a bonanza for you and has been critical in your growth. To use that system to harm Showtime is really not something you ought to do."

Dolan did not appear to be moved by this moral suasion.

"Look, Chuck," I continued calmly, "this isn't much different from what we went through with Time Warner and TCI, and we were compelled to file major lawsuits." I think that got his attention. "Don't misunderstand me. That is not what I want to do. But what you're doing is a very serious threat to us, the consequences of which we can't and won't accept." I let that sink in. "Chuck, I'm saying this as gently as I know how. You may not understand the legal ramifications of what you are doing. One of the provisions of the FTC decree that we obtained during the fight for Paramount—it's amazing how few people know about this—is that you cannot discriminate against an independent program-mer in favor of your own programming. Now, you may say that Starz and Encore aren't your own, but that provision applies to companies which are affiliated and it is clearly applicable to you. I have to tell you again that we can't accept what you're doing, but I'm telling it to you in the context of a friend talking to a friend, and I mean it that way."

I believe I made my point. "Sumner," he said, "I've got to say one thing. When it comes to talking about the law, I've got to pay a lot of at-tention to you."

No further pressure was necessary. We resolved our difficulties by entering into long-term agreements that were even better for us than the ones preceding them. Cablevision, for its part, got good value in Showtime and The Movie Channel plus the absence of an expensive and time-consuming legal battle. Chuck was an important customer and a good man, I had treated him with respect and restraint, and I wanted him to be satisfied as well. I believe he was. He continues to be an ad-mired friend.

Michael Saperstein, a partner at Bear Stearns, is another. He and I are constant dinner companions. Michael was deputy head of the Secu-rities and Exchange Commission under Richard Nixon. He is charming and articulate, but I do have to ignore his extreme right-wing views, and sometimes I have to remind him that every member of Nixon's cabinet whom he gave as a reference to Bear Stearns when applying to the firm was in prison by the time he got the job.

The Viacom executive committee meetings sometimes produced differences of opinion among our own members. There were, for exam-ple, serious differences surrounding the *Rugrats* movie. *Rugrats* was a children's animated TV series, an extremely popular Nickelodeon fran-chise that was ready to expand its viewership by crossing over into feature-length film. Of course it would be a Paramount picture. Tom Freston of MTV Networks wanted to spend $25 million on the project. Jonathan Dolgen of Paramount wanted to spend only $13 million. They simply could not agree.

Jon insisted that in *Rugrats* we were dealing with a limited demographic and therefore a limited upside not worth spending an extra $12 million to pursue. He said, "Look, you've got young kids up to, what, ten, twelve years old? That's all you have."

"Yes, but you're going to get their parents too," Tom replied. "Besides, this is a very important franchise."

"Jon," I asked, "don't you think that by making this movie we are going to expand the franchise?"

"You only have cable presence," Jon argued. "Tom, you're a giant in the cable business, but Disney reaches the broadcast business and cable only reaches 70 percent of the homes."

It was a major difference of opinion between two very important Viacom executives whose intelligence and loyalty I valued highly and for whom I had the same loyalty, trust and respect.

It was not the first difference of opinion that had ever arisen at an executive committee meeting. Normally I was able to do whatever was necessary to persuade the members themselves to resolve the matter. But this was a crucial Viacom moment; we were talking about our first full-length animated movie, and the argument went on for a long time. Jon and Tom simply could not agree on how to handle it, who would spend the money and what the rewards might be. Even though in the final analysis Viacom was all one company, both men got extremely territorial. They were powerful leaders of strong individual fiefdoms. Jon was speaking for Sherry Lansing and the whole of Paramount. Tom was speaking for a big gang of people at MTV Networks.

They were not afraid to express their opinions in the strongest possible terms, which was good. I needed to hear them. Voices were not raised but both men stuck firmly to their positions. The disagreement stretched on for months. Neither man could convince the other and neither man would yield. I did not view it as a battle of egos; ego enters into so much of what we all do and there is nothing wrong with that. What I saw were two forceful men who truly believed in their divisions and their ideas. Finally, I realized that this was one of the rare instances in which I would have to make the decision.

After considerable deliberation, I announced, "This has nothing to do with the validity of the views that everyone has expressed here, because I respect them. I am not even going to begin to try to take a position based on the relative merits of the arguments that each of you has made. One can make the case either way." By saying that I showed my respect for both Tom and Jon, and hoped perhaps to temper any disappointment on the part of the man whose position had not prevailed. "But we're going to go with Nickelodeon and spend the $25 million. Why? Not because I love them more than I love you, Jonathan. It's because it is *their* franchise, something they spent their lives building. And they feel it's necessary to spend that amount of money commensurate with their view of how the picture should come out."

So it was settled. Dolgen, although disappointed, accepted the decision with good grace and did everything in his power to make the movie a success. That is why I love Jon and all the rest of our management team.

The success of *The Rugrats Movie* was historic. It was the first non-Disney animated picture to break $100 million in domestic revenues. It is now in foreign distribution and home video—our first undertaking. We now have four full-length animated pictures in various stages of pre-production and will release at least one every year. We hope ultimately to release two or three annually. We didn't just make a movie, we created a new high-growth business for Viacom.

In running Viacom I do not insist on consensus. I don't think consensus is reasonable to expect. If we are going to embark on a major agenda, I feel much better about it when we have the full support of all our managers, but there are exceptions. Reasonable people disagree. We still have differences of opinion between Paramount and MTV about which movies to make. My general point of view is, "You should make only what you both agree on," and that has been the norm in what has become a very good working relationship. But continual agreement is virtually impossible. You can't run a company like Viacom and expect everyone to see eye to eye; if they did, there would be something wrong in that world. I think our company has been brought closer together by our disagreements and their resolution. Confrontation is a good thing. It usually leads to the truth. I was and remain very proud of Viacom's achievements. MTV continued its growth into continent after continent. VH1 developed nicely. We sold our radio stations. No analysts valued that asset at more than $780 million. We got $1.075 billion. We were able to deliver on our promises to our investors and to ourselves to grow the businesses we bought.

Anyone who suggested that I alone was responsible for Viacom's success would be totally divorced from reality. Viacom is a giant company operating many divisions all over the world. If I deserve any credit it is for assembling a terrific management team and creating an environment in which they can work with maximum effectiveness.

So I was feeling pretty good until Blockbuster tanked.

FOURTEEN

THE TURNAROUND

S o there I was in Dallas in April 1997. Steve Berrard—who with Wayne Huizenga had built Blockbuster from scratch and who was his second-in-command and operations guy, the man we had given a big contract and a lot of responsibility when we named him Huizenga's replacement as Blockbuster's CEO—had jumped ship. Bill Fields, the Wal-Mart heir apparent we hired to run Blockbuster with great hopes and great expectations, was gone as well.

Fields had recommended that Blockbuster headquarters be moved from Fort Lauderdale to Dallas at precisely the same time that, unbeknownst to us, he was becoming disengaged from the workings of the company. Those who made the move to Texas, some of them new hires, did so in large part because of Fields's leadership, and when he lost interest they lost interest. Then he left, and an almost total implosion of management took place with such remarkable speed that we didn't fully comprehend its dimensions.

When I arrived at our Dallas headquarters with Tom and Philippe, we found a total wasteland. We had a brand-spanking-new distribution center but because of the turnover, not too many people fully understood the distribution system. We were fortunate to have retained the executive who had handled distribution for Wal-Mart, Gary Peterson. But there was no corporate history, no corporate memory whatsoever.

People with no experience in the business had been promoted four or five rungs up to positions of responsibility which they had to learn on the job. They were without strong leadership and were almost uniformly pessimistic about the present and future of the company they worked for.

Blockbuster was without leadership. Not only were *The Wall Street Journal* and *The New York Times* beating up on us, we had spent a lot of money moving to Dallas and even the Dallas newspapers were killing us. I don't want to use the word "hopeless" because I have never been hopeless. Hopeless means the world is out of control, and to me, an important part of life is having the confidence that you can affect the world around you. Otherwise you are lost. So, from my standpoint the situation at Blockbuster was not hopeless. But it was a disaster.

We needed someone to lead the organization. This time I decided to conduct a thorough and painstaking search. If that meant leaving Blockbuster temporarily without a commander, it was better than repeating my earlier mistakes.

Meanwhile, the business was taking a beating. Blockbuster's EBITDA—earnings before interest, taxes, depreciation and amortization—was down approximately 20 percent from the year before. Despite an EBITDA of $800 million, Blockbuster had not performed as well as expected and, according to the Street, was worth less than zero for Viacom. That assessment had sent our stock plummeting.

The whole of Viacom was being punished for the failures at Blockbuster. Our managers, so important to the excellence of Viacom, saw the value of their stock options plunge in direct correlation to Blockbuster's difficulties. Their investments and their financial future appeared in real jeopardy and they were clearly concerned. In that atmosphere, our competitors were trying to hire away our most talented managers, telling them, "You don't have any money in your options, the company is going nowhere, you can do much better with us." The crisis was pervasive.

With this in mind, I addressed all our Viacom managers at our management conference held at a resort in Arizona. My principal job was to rally the troops, to instill a new confidence, to make them feel and realize that this was a disaster we would overcome. I spoke to them forthrightly.

"There is no denying that we have had our difficulties this past year," I told them. "Let's make no mistake about it—the issue is Blockbuster.

"One of the basic tenets of the financial markets is that they don't like surprises. Unfortunately, we have had to deliver some big surprises regarding Blockbuster and, understandably, those surprises have led some to question our credibility. Did we knowingly mislead the Street? Absolutely not. The Street was surprised because *we* were surprised.

"Investors and analysts are upset because we gave them an indication of where Blockbuster would be, based on what we were told. When we surprised them with a downward revision, they had a right to be angry. I am just as angry! That is why we made changes and that is why I am spending several days a week in Dallas. We are not going to let ourselves be surprised again.

"I also know that the management of Viacom—my management—is being questioned. Have I made mistakes? Yes. To begin with, I should have taken action sooner. We knew there were problems at Blockbuster but we did not know the extent of them. And I would like to address another criticism that has emerged—namely, that the problems we are having were somehow caused by the changes in management I have made. Anyone who thinks that is misinformed. The problems we are having *required* the changes in management. What we did, we had to do.

"We are going to continue to spend time working with Blockbuster and dealing with the issues over the next several months. We are very encouraged not only about the soundness and potential of the business but about the quality and capability of the people who are running it.

"There is no denying we have had a tough year. But I want you all to know—and I want those who work for you to know—that I am committed to working to the point of exhaustion to turn Blockbuster around, to restore the confidence of the market in us, and to making

Viacom everything it should and can be. It won't happen tomorrow, or next week, or next month, but it will happen.

"I leave you with a few simple thoughts: We must refocus our attention on even the smallest details of the individual businesses and work even more closely together to achieve our common goal. As we do that, our rewards will come and we will be recognized once again for being on the winning team. Something I know we all want. And something I know we will all get."

In Dallas, I was taking the closest possible look at the inner workings of Blockbuster. It was dismaying. I saw warehouses piled high with unsellable items. Our stores were cluttered with junk and we were stuck with merchandise that it would take years to get rid of. I involved myself in everything, even down to the nitty-gritty of screening new television spots, which wasn't exactly my job. I met with the best of our people and began asking them a lot of questions.

It appeared to me that there were two fundamental flaws in the video rental business. First, we were paying more for each copy of each movie than we could afford. Blockbuster typically paid $65 per videotape, and each Blockbuster outlet carried approximately 10,000 individual tapes. That was $650,000 in inventory at every location. Blockbuster operated nearly 6,000 video and music stores worldwide. We had to rent each movie between thirty and forty times in order to get an acceptable return on investment and turn a profit. It was simply too expensive to stock enough copies of every movie the customers requested. Customers were not getting what they wanted, and that was the second fundamental flaw in the video rental business. Thirty percent of the people who walked into Blockbuster stores were walking out with nothing. The Blockbuster management had a phrase for it: managed dissatisfaction.

In the beginning stages of the business, when video rental stores were still a relative novelty, a customer might come in with a list of films he or she wanted to see, and if the store operators had just ten copies of a popular movie and had run out, they would "manage" this "dissatisfaction" by renting the customer a second choice. But times had changed. Now people had many other entertainment alternatives, and if they couldn't have what they wanted, they could move on and find something else to do. They would walk out of our stores empty-handed. Then they started dropping out of the rental market altogether and the business began rolling downhill rapidly.

"What other business treats its customers like that?!" I asked. *Managed dissatisfaction?* "Is there any other business where you advertise something you don't have? It's like walking into McDonald's for a hamburger and being told all they have is french fries!"

I brainstormed with Tom and Philippe and the people in Dallas. We had to have more tapes in the stores, but we could not afford to pay for even the ones we did have. We had to create some arrangement under which we would get them for a lot less. In short, we had to come up with some way to fundamentally alter this business.

That was by no means an easy task. We were faced with the necessity of changing long-held practices on both sides of the table. Blockbuster had worked with the studios under the previous economic model during the infancy and ascendance of the video rental explosion, and everybody was wedded to it. Blockbuster had never complained about the price of tapes. I couldn't believe it. Now the people to whom the company would normally have turned for leadership had no new insights. The studios had no incentive to change the deal; they thought it was pretty good for them. They were getting $65 a tape times 6,000 stores times 10,000 tapes per store. That was $3.9 billion in the studios' pockets!

We developed charts and statistics and tried to cost out different scenarios. What would happen if we got the price lowered to $30? What would happen if we got more tapes? At one point after crunching the numbers, we determined that if we could come up with 40 percent more tapes without increasing the total price we were paying, we might satisfy customers, generate sales and make a go of it. We had to change the dynamics of the entire video rental industry or it was going down the tubes. And I was not a mere bystander but a major participant. Block-buster was taking Viacom and me personally down the tubes with it.

I scheduled a trip to Hollywood to meet with some of the studios to discuss creating a new model for the video rental business. I had made these trips before, beginning forty years earlier while negotiating for National Amusements, and this time I went with passion if not over-whelming confidence. I'm sure the studios thought I would be wasting their time. The extremely skeptical business media said I was going "hat in hand," but they had it wrong. Going begging at the studios is like wav-ing a flag of failure, and in neither attitude nor demeanor did I feel I was a supplicant; I felt I was bringing news of an impending disaster to a sleeping populace.

I met with the head of video distribution for Warner Bros., Warren Lieberfarb, and his entire crew. Warren is a flamboyant film industry character in his own right, but during our meeting he behaved with ex-traordinary restraint, considering the message I brought. "I don't know what spell you put on Huizenga and Berrard," I said. "Anything you wanted, they agreed to. They did a good job building that company but it was a disaster in operations.

"We have been paying you $65 a tape. Forget it! We're not going to pay! If we continue that way we will destroy our business—and you will go down with us. The studios can't live without a video rental busi-ness—we are your profit—and this business is going into the toilet. I'm not here only on behalf of Blockbuster. I'm here because this entire business is going to tank—it's tanking now—and my job is to save it. If I save it for Blockbuster, I'm going to save it for you. We've got to get the tapes a lot cheaper and we've got to have more of them!"

Warren just listened. I am absolutely convinced he thought I was off the wall.

I saw Columbia and Fox on the same trip and some of the conversa-tions grew rather heated. "If Blockbuster fails," I told them, "you fail. And if you don't have a video rental industry, you don't have a studio!" I asked for 40 percent more tapes with no raise in the total cost. "We are not going to continue paying these prices. I'm telling you it's not going to happen!"

No one said, "Great, Sumner, we're going to change the way we do business for you." They were all very polite but they as much as pushed me out the door. I suppose some portion of my message must have penetrated, however, because we did come home with 20 percent more tapes with no increase in total cost. Even so, according to our projections, that would only prolong the agony and death throes of the video rental industry.

I could not remain the sole leader of Blockbuster. My first priority was Viacom and we needed a strong and innovative CEO at Blockbuster. The name of John Antioco had come across my desk during the executive search that yielded Bill Fields. Now here it was again. Antioco had an excellent résumé. At that time in his late forties, he was chairman and CEO of Taco Bell Corporation, a division of PepsiCo. Previously, he had served as chairman and CEO of The Circle K Corporation, successfully leading that company out of Chapter 11 and eventually taking it public. I called my close friend Ace Greenberg of Bear Stearns, which had roadshowed Circle K with Antioco, and he told me, "He's five A's." I also spoke with several others in the industry, including the large retailer Invescorp, and got the same reaction.

A recruiter approached Antioco, but, unfortunately, he was not particularly interested in making a move. Taco Bell was about to do a spin-off from PepsiCo and he had some fairly substantial financial incentives holding him in place. Antioco was reluctant even to enter into a conversation with Viacom, but the recruiter convinced him that if we really wanted him, the price and those incentives would not be a problem.

Antioco first met with Tom and Philippe and he passed that audition. I was going to be in California on a Friday night and we suggested that he meet me for dinner. "I can't make it on Friday night," he said. He explained that he lived with his family in Scottsdale, Arizona. "My daughter is going to be in a play that night and it's important to me that I see her in it."

Tom and Philippe reported this information to me and then got back to Antioco. "Sumner wants to know," he was asked, "do you want the job or not?"

"I'm not sure," Antioco replied. "But I'll tell you what. I can't meet him on Friday night but if he wants I'll fly back to California on Sunday and see him for lunch at his hotel."

I was prepared to be impressed by the man's résumé when I met him, but at that point I wasn't certain about the man. While I admired a father who put aside work to see his daughter perform, I wanted someone who would commit himself heart and soul to the job at Blockbuster, not a mercenary executive who was looking to make a killing. As for Antioco, he had just read the *Business Week* piece about me and half expected to be lunching with a tyrant.

We hit it off immediately. Antioco, I was surprised to find, was a casual man with a very pleasant way about him. He had come from humble beginnings, which I empathized with. He had learned his earliest business skills from his father, who was a milkman, and had begun work as a manager trainee at 7-Eleven, rising through the ranks to become the Southland Corporation's vice president of marketing and senior vice president of operations. Furthermore, he had performed a corporate turnaround with Circle K, which was an apprentice approximation of the scope of the job he would face at Blockbuster.

Antioco had also done his homework. On his own time he had taken the trouble to walk into not only our Blockbuster stores but also those of our competitors, including Hollywood Entertainment. He already had substantial knowledge about the problems we confronted.

On top of that, I found I liked him. We sat and chatted in Bungalow 8 at the Beverly Hills Hotel, had lunch, came back and chatted some more. What had been planned as a one-hour interview session stretched long into the afternoon. As the conversation flowed comfortably, we got to know each other and discussed the depth of the problems we would face in turning around Blockbuster. Personal empathy is a very important quality to be factored in when deciding whether to work with someone, and I felt John was a person I could trust. I indicated to him the possibility that I would offer him the job and it was clear to me that he would probably accept.

However, I was still being cautious. I set up a dinner meeting with John, Philippe and Tom. That, too, went well. We all agreed that John was our man and we brought him aboard. We appreciated the fact that he was taking a large gamble, leaving an extremely important and lucrative job at the thriving Taco Bell to attempt one more business miracle.

Taco Bell's corporate parent was PepsiCo, which could have posed a sizable problem. I was friendly with PepsiCo's chairman, Roger Enrico, and the company was obviously important to the theaters of National Amusements. I did not want to create bad blood between us but I wanted Antioco. After Berrard and then Fields, I knew I could not afford to make another mistake. Fortunately, John did not have a contract with PepsiCo so there were no legal restrictions to prevent my hiring him, only corporate social ones. The word had gotten out by the time I reached Enrico on the phone, and having just lifted one of his top executives, it's fair to say I felt quite some trepidation.

"Roger," I said, "I hope you're not too upset. But, you know, here's the point: I need John worse than you do!" Enrico was less than pleased but he had no recourse other than to accept the situation gracefully. He was in the process of holding meetings with Taco Bell franchisees and asked me not to make any public announcement of Antioco's departure until those meetings were completed. I agreed, but I wanted Blockbuster and Viacom to announce this successful hire themselves. It was a positive move for us, and the addition of Antioco would be seen on Wall Street as a large step in the right direction. While not happy about it, Enrico did not stand in my way or Antioco's.

Once John was in place and had moved to Texas, I spoke with him several times a day, seven days a week. He took immediate charge. We established a routine in which I called him every Sunday morning, when I knew he would be going over the numbers on his computer at home. He could read inventory levels for every movie in every Blockbuster store. One Sunday he looked at the screen and sighed. "You know, Sumner, if we ever had in-stock inventory and customers weren't dissatisfied, we might be able to really move this business. What do you know about this revenue-sharing deal?"

The concept of revenue sharing between video rental stores and the studios had existed in a limited form for several years. Under a revenue-sharing arrangement the studios provided free or cheap tapes and the video rental stores, the retailer, provided a percentage of each rental in return. A company called Rentrak was trying to make a go of it, acting as a middleman, but Rentrak did not have all the studios under contract and shared revenues only on selected titles.

There were, however, several problems with a revenue-sharing setup. Because the retailer was cherry-picking a studio's releases instead of taking them all, the deal he would get for the more successful movies was less advantageous. And because some studios were represented and others weren't, the customer became confused. Why were there many copies of some movies and few copies of others? More significantly, under the Rentrak arrangement the studios' split was higher than the retailer could afford and Rentrak's cut was a further 10 percent, which would drop the profit margin so low the store could never make it up in volume. Blockbuster had previously disregarded this economic model because the company had embraced the concept of "managed dissatisfaction" and didn't think sharing revenues with the studios was the right way to run the business.

I knew revenue sharing worked in other industries. Motion picture exhibitors, for example, shared revenues with the studios as a matter of course; that's simply how the business was run. At National we didn't buy a copy of every movie we screened—that would have been insane. We licensed each copy and shared the proceeds from ticket sales with the studio. But when I canvassed Blockbuster franchisees, I had consistently been told, "Revenue sharing doesn't work."

I discussed the idea with Antioco and he said, "Sumner, it depends on the deal you get from the studios. If we get the right deal, I think revenue sharing *can* work."

John brought in Blockbuster's executive vice president of merchandising, Dean Wilson, who ran all the company's buying and whom John described as a "very quantitative kind of person," and together we developed a new revenue-sharing model which we felt would turn around our company and the entire video rental industry. It was both revolutionary and simple.

We knew we could not afford to pay $65 per tape, nor could we afford to advertise what we did not have in our stores. We needed several times the number of tapes that we had in each store and we needed to pay a lot less for them. Thus the new revenue-sharing model, under which Blockbuster would be given enough copies of every studio release to satisfy customer demand. No more walking into Blockbuster stores and walking out empty-handed. If a million customers wanted, for example, a *Titanic* or a *Shakespeare in Love* or a *Men in Black,* they were all going to get *Titanic* or *Shakespeare in Love* or *Men in Black* and everyone would go home happy.

Furthermore, rather than buy copies of each tape at $65 apiece, Blockbuster would pay only duplication costs of around $2 per tape plus a few dollars more—average cost, $6 or $7. In return, instead of receiving no money whatsoever from the rental, the studios would participate in essentially a 60/40 split of the revenues, with the retailer—Blockbuster—getting the 60 percent. Since they participated in supply and were getting a piece of the revenue, the studios would supplement our own advertising by advertising the release dates of their videotapes, adding to demand. When demand for a given movie diminished beyond the level of profitability, the used tapes would be sold at retail, usually for more than we paid for them, the revenue going to Blockbuster. Not only would we receive the tapes at a modest price, at the end of the day we could recoup or even make a little money over our costs. In theory, with enough copies of every movie available to our customers, satisfaction would rise, rentals would rise, and income would rise.

This was one attractive model! But how could we sell it to the studios? They certainly would not take us at our word; they would want proof.

John suggested we simulate a revenue-sharing environment. An experiment. "Let's take six test markets," he said, "and buy enough inventory through the traditional method to simulate the copy depth. Then we advertise that we have unlimited copies of every movie and, for the first time, Blockbuster will give people what they want."

Between the added inventory, the advertising and the monitoring process, it would not be an inexpensive proposition. But the future of Blockbuster was on the line, and with it the future of Viacom. I gave the project the green light. We approached the studios about helping us with this experiment and working with us on some price reductions, but for the most part we footed the bill ourselves. It cost us approximately $50 million.

The experiment was an extraordinary success. The figures came back better than we expected and we were excited to present them to the industry. John spearheaded the drive. My role was to support the concept fully. We went to the Disney people first. They were number one in the field, representing 20 percent of the home video market, and John felt they were the most businesslike of the studios. If we could sell them, we would have leverage elsewhere. John, Dean Wilson and I had lunch with the head of Disney Home Video, Michael Johnson, because they thought he was most inclined to give us a sympathetic hearing. While most of the home video people at the other studios had, as Philippe put it, "been there forever," Johnson was relatively new to his position, a young man not buried in the past and more open to a fresh outlook on the business. Rather than the gloom-and-doom approach I had used earlier, our pitch was basic: We can make you more money.

Our figures bore us out. We developed graphs and charts to illustrate our case, but what we had found was in itself stunning. We told

Johnson, "If you put enough inventory into our stores and help us market it, we can increase your revenues by 15 percent across the board—at a minimum—and maybe even more." Our test markets showed that we could, in fact, produce an upside of close to a 20 percent increase—and keep it there. We crunched the numbers and demonstrated for Johnson that under the revenue-sharing model Disney stood to realize a significant increase in revenue over the system currently in place.

Johnson, to his credit, got it. He took the proposal upstairs to Disney chairman Michael Eisner.

I did not really know Eisner. I had had dinner with him a few times, mostly several years ago when he was running Paramount with Jeffrey Katzenberg and Barry Diller and I was an exhibitor. What I did know about him was that he had been nice to me during the *Business Week* fiasco and that he was smart and that, like me, he was a risk-taker. He had been a great risk-taker when he bought ABC, as I was when I acquired Viacom and Paramount. But I did not have a personal entree into Disney's decision-making process, so we just had to wait and hope that our presentation and Michael Johnson's enthusiasm would sell the idea.

Eisner proved that his reputation was well founded. He understood our concept and he bought it. Disney signed a long-term revenue-sharing agreement with Blockbuster. Because it was the first one in, we gave the studio a good deal and were happy to do it.

We were exultant. With Disney on board our new economic model had to be taken seriously. Paramount Pictures, as part of Viacom, would also participate. But we did not want Paramount to be the second studio to sign on. Its participation would be discounted by the other studios because it was a Viacom company. We needed one more studio to reach the point at which all the others would come aboard or be at a competitive disadvantage with their number one customer, Blockbuster, if they didn't.

We went back to Warren Lieberfarb at Warner Bros. It quickly became clear that Warren had his own agenda, and that was DVD. Time Warner had an active interest in this new technology, and if Viacom and its affiliated businesses, Paramount and Blockbuster, would support it, he said, Warner Bros. would be agreeable to a revenue-sharing deal. It was a call I had to make. Jonathan Dolgen was not yet geared up for DVD and I had to take Paramount's position into account, but when it came down to the wire, I felt it was in the best interests of Viacom as a whole to support DVD and enlist Warner Bros. in the new Blockbuster plan. The studio signed a short-term deal with a caveat that it could pull out after a year.

Warner Bros. was indeed the linchpin. With Warner, Disney and Paramount we had 50 percent of the market and we knew that Columbia, Universal and Fox had to play. But even if they didn't we could still manage the entire process.

At the same time we were importuning the studios to join us in our new model, we were cutting our videotape purchases of the non-participating studios by approximately 25 percent. Blockbuster was still bleeding and we had to perform difficult business surgery to stanch the flood of money out of our operation. The studios that were not participating with us in the revenue-sharing plan, I believe, thought we were pressuring them: Share revenues with us or else see our orders shrink significantly. Fox was the last studio to sign on. Imagine, if you were Fox, walking into a Blockbuster store and seeing massive quantities of other studios' films, provided at cost, and only a few of your own, purchased for $65 apiece. We had to explain to Fox that our decrease in purchases was based on economic necessity and the realities of our financial position, as opposed to simple negotiating hardball. The last in a group negotiation is not the best position to be in. Fox ultimately accepted our explanation and soon we had all the studios on board.

It was not long before the business began to come around. Antioco and Wilson's model had proved to be 100 percent accurate. With the studios advertising their videotape release dates and our own new excellently conceived ad campaign—"Go Home Happy!"—rental revenues ceased their nosedive and started to move in the opposite direction. Not only was Blockbuster not going to fail, it was well on its way toward major success.

A short time after we had signed Warner's original short-term agreement as a result of the DVD trade-off, Warren Lieberfarb called me from Japan and said, "Sumner, terrific. Everything is great!" But he was blowing hot and cold about signing a new agreement. As the end of the old agreement approached, we met again with Warner and proposed a long-term deal. We never seemed to get an answer. I would call Antioco regularly: "So, have we heard from Lieberfarb yet?"

"No, we haven't, Sumner."

Lieberfarb had a variety of excuses. "We'll get to a deal but we're very busy now. We can't do it until September." Then, "We're over our heads at the moment. We can't really meet with you guys and solve any of this until January." The economics of our agreements with each individual studio were very similar but not exactly the same. Clearly Lieberfarb was moving the date to frustrate us, trying to box us into a corner and force us to sweeten our deal to get Warner on board for the long haul or else lose the studio altogether. He used his influence to encourage a New York stock analyst to issue a report that said we were not making headway in closing the deal and there was some possibility that Warner's participation might not continue. Warner's absence, it was implied, would threaten the entire revenue-sharing system as well as the independent public offering of Blockbuster stock which we were planning in the near future. Lieberfarb was literally trying to leverage the IPO and use it for negotiating purposes.

We needed Warner.

Or did we? We looked around and that studio was the only holdout. Everyone else had signed on. We got in touch once again, but this time we said, "You're threatening to go public with the fact that you're not revenue-sharing with Blockbuster. That's fine. But you're overreaching. We have everyone else and we can live without you. In fact, if we don't have an agreement by this Monday, we'll make the announcement that we have long-term revenue sharing with all the Hollywood studios except Warner and we're very comfortable with that. We are prepared to leave you out. That's the deal. If you want it, great. If you don't want it, that's fine, too. We have an agreement or we don't have an agreement. Your call."

That was on a Thursday. Warner executives got on a plane, flew down to Dallas, and we had a deal by Monday morning.

Sometime later I had dinner with Michael Eisner and we talked about our revenue-sharing arrangement. "Sumner," he said, "it's spectacular for us. How is it for you?" "Obviously," I told him, "it's great for Blockbuster, too."

Revenue sharing changed the face of, in fact saved, the video rental business. All of us at Blockbuster, but in particular John Antioco and Dean Wilson, deserve tremendous credit for conceiving and enacting the revenue-sharing model. I will say it again: Success is not built on success. Great successes are built on failures, on frustrations, even catastrophes. If there is one single accomplishment which I believe had the greatest significance and in which I take the greatest pride since I became involved with Viacom, it was my recognition of the fundamental economic flaws of the video rental business, and my participation in and support of the revenue-sharing model that saved Blockbuster.

Business kept getting better. Viacom's debt load, which the press said would be crippling, had been cut by two-thirds. Blockbuster began to thrive, although it does have challenges from new technology. The acquisition of Paramount, for which it was said we had overpaid, was also looking good. We sold half of USA Networks for $1.7 billion, while keeping the ever-growing TV Land. We also sold the educational, professional and reference book-publishing units of Simon & Schuster, which in its entirety had earlier been valued at around $2 billion, to the British media group Pearson PLC for $4.6 billion, making Pearson the world's largest educational publisher and leaving us in proud possession of the flourishing Simon & Schuster consumer book-publishing division. Factor in the sale of the MSG properties for $1.075 billion and I had recouped what I paid for Paramount and still owned the television stations, the theme parks, the television production operation, the studio and the library. Add up their value and it came to approximately $4 billion more than I had paid, and in addition I got the Paramount studio, the Paramount television production operation and film library for nothing—with about $4 billion to boot!

I have found that if you pay too much attention to the press, or even to Wall Street, you will fail and your company will suffer for it. For better or worse, I live my life in a fishbowl under public scrutiny because of the work I have chosen and the success of my company. I took punishing criticism for my executive management decisions, particularly the firing of Frank Biondi, and I do not deny that I take what is said about me and the company personally. I find it difficult to adequately describe the pain I felt when Viacom was not doing well. Walking into a room full of my colleagues, knowing that all of them had read the *Business Week* piece that had savaged me, was excruciating. How did I put that aside? I didn't. But what I did tell myself was that my critics could write whatever they want about me; that was their opinion and they were entitled to it. Yes, *I* had been distracted, but I was not distracted from doing my job.

And now that Viacom, including Blockbuster, was doing well, the press started to come around and the abuse was turning into accolade. *Forbes* ran a major story entitled "The Vindication of Sumner Redstone." *Vanity Fair* published a laudatory article entitled "Fort Sumner." *Fortune* labeled me the "king of the moguls." The crowning touch was when *Entertainment Weekly* labeled me the most powerful person in the entertainment industry.

Among my major successes was the excellent management team I put together, and now they were finally being recognized. After the barrage of criticism, *Forbes* wrote: "All the major divisions of Viacom are stronger and more profitable today than they were under Biondi." And even more recently, I received perhaps the greatest honor in my life when in a poll (of which I was not even aware) six hundred top CEOs in the United States voted me as their most inspirational person, after their mothers. I will admit I took that personally, too.

FIFTEEN

EYE ON THE FUTURE

*I*n 1997, unbeknownst to me, the CBS Corporation analyzed the marketplace to identify possible candidates for a merger. After all the facts were gathered, numbers reviewed, and economic and social issues factored in, the only company to make the cut was Viacom.

CBS CEO Mel Karmazin had said publicly and repeatedly that he was going to buy Viacom, but interestingly, he never mentioned it to me. Nevertheless, I kept hearing reports that he was going to purchase my company, and I would remark to our people, "Does he think he can buy it without talking to me?"

Karmazin made several attempts to set up a meeting but I put him off, not out of inconsideration but because it was a time of tremendous activity in the life of Viacom and I was often traveling and going a mile a minute. Time passed and finally Merrill Lynch analyst Jessica Reif, who was deeply involved in our industry and had a strong buy recommendation on both Viacom and CBS stock, asked me, "Why won't you meet with Mel Karmazin? Why won't you get together with him and at least listen to what he has to say?" Apparently she saw some potential advantages. In fact, enough time had passed between overtures that I was unaware that he was trying to reach me.

For decades the concentration of broadcasting powers in the hands of a few companies was seen as an anathema to the public interest.

However, times change, and in August 1999 the FCC revised its regulations to allow a single company to own two television stations in the same market, an arrangement known as a duopoly. CBS and Viacom both owned and operated stations in Boston, Detroit, Dallas, Miami, Philadelphia and Pittsburgh, which until now had meant that a merger between the two companies would have run into serious regulatory difficulties. The new regulations made those objections moot and provided a good excuse for Karmazin to try to contact me again.

This time I did not put him off. In fact, what went through my mind was, We do a lot of business with CBS. Two of its hot shows, *JAG* and *Becker,* are Paramount-produced with more to come. I should get to know this guy. I had heard wonderful things about him so I invited him to Viacom. Only a few weeks after the FCC regulations were altered, he and I were sitting at a table in a dining room off my office having lunch.

Karmazin looked friendly and jovial but it was soon apparent that he was quite sharp and down-to-earth. We talked broadcasting business generalities, conditions in the industry, how we were doing, how he was doing. Finally he said, "I thought there might be several possibilities for us to discuss."

I was very attentive. "With the new rules," he began, "you and I are in a position to put our stations together and get the benefits of creating duopolies. Either we buy some of your stations or we swap some or joint-venture them."

"Sounds interesting," I told him. "I'll talk to Jon Dolgen." Our seventeen broadcast stations reported to Jon.

"We have two cable networks," Karmazin continued, "TNN and Country Music Television, and it also occurred to me that we could swap our cable networks for your television stations."

"You know something," I said, "that also sounds interesting. With MTV, Nickelodeon, VH1 and TV Land we are very strong in cable."

"That's what I had in mind," Karmazin said. "They would become much more valuable to you because you could get a lot better distribution from the cable industry than we could. On the other hand, having your stations would create five or six duopolies for us."

That was worth pondering. "Okay," I said, "let me think about that."

"I have another idea," Karmazin went on. "I don't know if you have the slightest interest, but I've given a lot of thought to a merger between our two companies."

That idea had also occurred to us from time to time, and we had discussed it among ourselves, but found it undesirable. The paradigm was Disney's acquisition of ABC, and that had faced severe challenges. "I have told the financial world over and over again that I am not interested in a network," I told Karmazin.

"I know, I know, I'm just throwing the idea out," he replied. "But today we are a lot more than a network." Karmazin gave me a brief outline of what CBS had become. The corporation owned radio and television stations, the network, outdoor billboard advertising, and had a stock-swap merger with the King World syndication network in the works. Karmazin's presentation was casual but effective. His brief outline was actually quite expansive. The CBS Corporation was considerably more diverse than I had given it credit for.

"Let me chat with my associates here about your ideas," I told him, "and I'll get back to you." It was a friendly lunch and we went our separate ways.

I talked to Philippe and Tom and we agreed that what interested us were the CBS cable channels. Good cable channels were difficult to acquire, there were few on the market and CBS had two. Their acquisition would be very beneficial for us. Let's play along, we decided, and entertain Karmazin's other proposals, with the idea that what we really want to do is zero in on the cable channels. "But if we have another meeting with Mel," I said, "let's also at least pay attention to his Big Picture. I'm not saying we should merge, but as I listened to him discuss CBS today, it certainly might be a lot more advantageous than I had thought.

"For one thing, CBS would bring us a whole lot of mostly nonoverlapping businesses, and even when they do overlap, they're powerful. That's only one of the differences between this deal and the Disney/ABC deal. We've always thought that if it didn't work there, why should it work here? Now I'm having second thoughts. All I'm saying is, listen. Listen to everything." I admonished them to consider that by acquiring CBS, Viacom would stand firmly in the four fastest-growing areas of the media business—radio, outdoor advertising, cable and broadcasting—and that we would, therefore, have a chance to be, among other things, the preeminent advertising company in the world.

We set up another meeting with Mel and I said, "How about going through, just as you did with me, each of the three agendas you have in mind." I didn't tell him that we were only interested in Agenda No. 2, and it didn't take us long to realize that as far as he was concerned, Agendas No. 1 and No. 2 were to a large extent a charade. Agenda No. 3, a merger, was what he really had in mind. It was pretty obvious. Mel had come with a video presentation, much as he would bring to Wall Street analysts, about the power and promise of CBS. He showed it and it worked. I was beginning to be sold.

I had never been interested in buying a major network. I would rather gamble millions on growing an independent network like UPN, of which we already owned half, than spend billions on CBS. But as Karmazin's presentation made clear, the CBS television network was just one part of a conglomeration of assets owned by the CBS Corporation. As I sat there watching the video, I could see what it would mean to Viacom to add CBS's syndication operation Eyemark and King World to our Spelling and Paramount production houses; and what it would mean to MTV, in terms of cross-promotion and cross-selling, to own CBS's radio stations. Mel detailed CBS's advertising position and I realized that, together, we would have over $10 billion in advertising revenue *that year*. The closest to us would be Fox—still well behind us—and that number would grow. Before Mel and I even began to explore his three agendas together, I could see some real upside potential in a merger of our two companies. Of course, I didn't express that to him as strongly as I was beginning to feel it; after all, we were negotiating.

When the lights went up Mel said, "I want to make one thing clear. Just in case you're really thinking about a deal. I know very well, Sumner, that you're not going to part with control so I'm not going to ask for what I can't get."

I thought that sounded reasonable. "If we're talking about the possibility of a merger," he continued, "obviously it would be an acquisition by you. I would pay a lot of money if I could acquire you, but I know I can't."

I told him he was right on that account. Any amount he might be willing to pay was a value we believed we would attain on our own, so why would we want to sell? "There are others who have been interested and I've told them the same thing," I said. "You would have to offer me such an astronomical figure that we would be talking about something that could not happen with us for many, many years in the future. Then I would have to listen as a moral matter. Because I control the company I really don't have to listen to anything, but I would have an obligation to our stockholders to entertain a number that was extraordinarily high and not otherwise attainable."

A CBS acquisition of Viacom was not one of Mel's agendas and we never seriously pursued the idea. "I expect that you would maintain control of the merged company," he said matter-of-factly.

At that moment I thought to myself, Maybe we're going somewhere. But what I said out loud was, "And we will not pay a premium."

"We understand that," Mel replied.

So here I was in a position to acquire CBS, maintain the same control I had at Viacom and not pay a premium. This was indeed an unusual deal.

We had several subsequent meetings in my office. People saw Karmazin come and go and began to wonder what he was doing there. Tom Freston mentioned it, as well as some others. "We'd better not continue meeting here," I finally told Mel. Now that I was seriously considering the acquisition of CBS, I didn't want to start rumors, spread stories or cause our own people to begin worrying. We met thereafter at his apartment in what used to be the Paramount building, now a Trump operation, on the north arc of Columbus Circle. Mel later said that he knew I was serious when our talks moved out of my place and over to his.

In fact, I knew I was going to do the deal before Mel knew I knew I was going to do the deal. I saw the creation of an advertising juggernaut, number one in the world. I also saw that we would be the number-one creator and purveyor of television programming to the networks, cable and syndication—a syndication giant. I saw explosive growth. We would be by far the fastest-growing media company in the world.

"All I'm after is what would be in the interest of our stockholders," Mel told me as our talks progressed. "As far as I'm concerned, I'll go away if you want."

I knew better than to take that seriously. Mel hadn't ascended to the top of CBS just to disappear. And I'm quite sure he knew that wasn't what I had in mind either. I told him what I felt—that I would not do the deal without him. "I don't know you well," I said. "But I know your reputation and what you have accomplished. To take on all these new assets without you would be unthinkable."

Mel and I negotiated the deal without investment bankers. Most important were the governance issues: Who would run what?

Mel would have liked to be the CEO of our merged companies, and I had sufficient respect for him that I would have considered giving him that position as long as I was chairman and in control. But I truly loved the job I was doing at Viacom; I was proud of having built the company from a few drive-ins to one of the major media companies in the world, and I have never wanted to give up the job of CEO.

We solved this problem by agreeing that I would remain CEO while Mel would become chief operating officer with some specific powers, normally falling in the CEO's province, that would be his only for a period of three years. I gave him the power to hire and fire. Everyone in the company would report to Mel. Mel would report to me. I gave him the power to spend autonomously on all projects under $25 million. Projects exceeding that limit would require board approval, and it was my board, 10–8. There was an exception made for radio, where I gave Mel more leeway because he had come from that industry and been such a hotshot in developing Infinity Broadcasting.

We also agreed to lock Mel into his job. This clause in our agreement, I believe, came from the CBS board of directors. Here we were taking them over without a premium, they had a dynamo CEO and they wanted to make sure he kept his job for three years. I had no problem with that; it would have been absurd for me to bring Karmazin aboard as chief operating officer and say goodbye to him a year later. That would have been contrary to the interests of the company. The agreement also locked in eight members of CBS's board for three years.

I was satisfied. If I didn't have absolute control of the company *forever*, I would not have been. Mel and I both covet control and there might be areas where we would collide. But as he and I said at the time, if we ever had to look at his contract, we were in trouble. I viewed him as a partner, and I am sure he saw me the same way, working together for our mutual advantage and the advantage of the company. There would be talk that we were both tough guys and wouldn't get along. That was nonsense. We both wanted the same thing: to drive the company forward.

I often had occasion to say that Mel and I were kindred spirits. Both of us had started with nothing and ended up in control of major corporations. Mel had built up a great fortune, worth about $500 million in CBS stock, and other than his being permitted to sell 10 percent of his holdings in the second and third years of his contract, his stock was locked up with him. That was important to me; he would be gambling almost everything he had acquired over the years on the success of the merger.

CBS approved the deal. Now it was up to us. I held a meeting of the

Viacom board, including my children, Shari and Brent, Ivan Seidenberg, Fred Salerno, Bill Schwartz, Ken Miller, George Abrams, Tom Dooley and Philippe Dauman.

We went through all the issues carefully. First, we concluded, one of the major strong points in favor of the merger was the fact that neither company *had* to do it. There was no weak link; we were both going strong. Viacom was growing faster than any other media company in the world—by ourselves. We didn't need CBS. CBS, for its part, was also performing very well.

Second, we certainly weren't making the deal to get bigger. Bigger is not necessarily better, although it is certainly true that bigger is better than smaller. But this merger was not about bigness; it was about putting together two groups of assets that would produce an extraordinary company. Being number one has been my objective ever since I was a schoolboy—and the new Viacom would be number one in radio, number one in cable programming, number one in outdoor advertising, and would own the number-one audience deliverer both nationally and locally in television. It would also own a great studio, which as far as I was concerned was number one in its field. And we would have a first-rate publishing operation and thriving theme parks. We would continue to own the most powerful brands in the world. Add that all together and no other company would have our depth and array of assets. I had always said content was king, but there is nothing wrong with being king of content as well as king of distribution.

The board discussed the merger well into the night. The governance issues were considered at length. If everyone at Viacom reported to Karmazin, would I become so isolated that I would lose my relationships with the management team with whom I had lived for thirteen years? That was clearly a potential source of concern and I had to find a means of allaying it. I was routinely on the phone many times a day with Jon Dolgen and I was sure there would be nothing to prevent that level of involvement from continuing with all of Viacom's top executives. Jon,

Tom Freston, Sherry Lansing, Herb Scannell, Judy McGrath, John Sykes, Matt Blank, Jon Newcomb and the others would remain as powerful after the merger as before and would not lose their relationship with me. There was no distance between us; I would still be available to discuss the significant issues. "Look," I would tell them, "Mel understands that you people are tremendously important to me in two ways: first, as my friends and, second, to the business. I assure you he's not going to do anything that would harm you or the company. He wouldn't do that."

But Karmazin was CBS's CEO and we could not have a merger without his playing a powerful role in the management of the new company. It would be a trade-off and, I trusted, a positive one. It was a great leap of faith to invest him with such important responsibilities, but I would remain in control. I understood that if Viacom's top executives came to me every time Mel made a decision with which they disagreed, it could cause problems. I believed that they were too smart to disrupt the company in that way, but meanwhile they would maintain the personal and business relationships that they and I had built up over the years. There would be no distance between us, I would stress. I could guarantee I would not be isolated from them.

With those reassurances, finally the consensus was clear. The board members were in favor of the merger. We were acquiring CBS without paying a premium. As for the governance issues, there was no reason for me or anyone else to be concerned. Because Karmazin would report to me or to my designees, I would maintain control of the company. "This is a great deal," they told me. "You have to do it."

Tom and Philippe sat with me. Philippe said, "You understand, Sumner, that the only way Mel will agree to come in as COO and not CEO is if Tom and I leave as deputy chairmen."

I was shocked. "I don't get it. Why?" I could not believe what I was hearing.

"Because if we stay," Tom explained, "we would get in the way of your relationship with Mel and would be perceived by him as diluting his authority."

I was truly upset. "But I don't want you to go," I said sincerely. "Let me discuss this with Mel. I'm positive there's an important role for both of you in the new Viacom."

Another thought occurred to me. "We don't have to merge with CBS," I told them. "If either one of you has the slightest reservations about the merger—not both of you, either one, and I don't care what your reasons are—this deal will not fly."

Like the other board members, they insisted that buying CBS without paying a premium was a fantastic opportunity for Viacom, a coup, and I had to take it. But they could not play a part in it. "You're not going to lose us," Philippe said. "We'll be here to advise you in every way," Tom added. "We're on the board, we'll know everything that's going on."

"And we'll remain friends," Philippe assured me. "There's no reason for you to be concerned. We're not going to lose contact just because we're not in the next office."

But I *was* concerned. When it came to negotiating the major deals of my life, for Viacom, Paramount and now CBS, both Philippe and Tom had been of enormous help, but that was not what bothered me. "You've been part of the creation of this giant company from day one," I said. "And now you tell me you won't be playing a role in what I consider to be our greatest achievement, the drive to be the largest and, more important, the best media company in the world. We'll start out as number two but we'll close in on number one, take my word for it. There's no way I can accept that you aren't going to play a role in this incredible adventure."

I got nowhere, and I would remain very dissatisfied with the fact that doing this great deal for our shareholders meant losing Philippe and Tom as executives. I admired their work and took pleasure in having them around me. I enjoyed the freedom they took in popping into my office and I enjoyed walking down the hall into theirs. I would miss their daily involvement in the affairs of the company and in my life. I would miss them both professionally and personally. "But you're not going to lose us personally," Philippe insisted. "We'll both be around anytime you want us." But they wouldn't be down the hall.

They were, of course, right. The job they had been doing would be taken by Mel Karmazin and they refused to stand in the way of my relationship with him. Today, Philippe and Tom not only have their own successful private equity firm, but Philippe also remains on the boards of Viacom and Blockbuster. They are still my close friends and trusted advisors. And, incidentally, they are very, very rich. And they earned every penny of it.

On September 7, 1999, Mel and I announced the merger. Viacom would acquire the CBS Corporation for $37.3 billion. There was our picture, in color, on the front page of *The New York Times*, both of us smiling. "We will be a global leader in virtually every facet of the wonderful, diverse media and entertainment industry," I said. Mel added, "This is the deal I have wanted to make from the time I was bar-mitzvahed."

Response to the Viacom-CBS merger was overwhelmingly positive. Government approval went smoothly, as planned. And I would soon come to know Mel Karmazin as a superb executive. As much as I expected from him, Mel has exceeded my expectations. He is tireless. He learned every detail of our business overnight. He has formed solid relationships with the other Viacom executives and, to his credit, has urged them to maintain the same business and personal relationships which they have always had with me. Together we all remain an effective and successful team.

Mel also brought with him some outstanding additions to the Viacom team: Fred Reynolds, our CFO; Les Moonves, who is doing such a wonderful job running the CBS network; Farid Suleman, the superb manager of Infinity; Joe Abruzzese, the supersalesman; Sean McManus, head of CBS Sports; Nancy Tellem, head of CBS Entertainment, and so many others. I have come to enjoy and respect the directors who came from CBS. They are intelligent and warm, and I am glad to have them on the Viacom board.

At almost exactly the same time that the CBS deal was being developed, my wife decided to divorce me. She had filed a similar suit during the struggle for Paramount but had ultimately withdrawn it. This time, however, a picture of me appeared on the front page of Rupert Murdoch's *New York Post*, strolling down a Paris street with a beautiful woman. It was hardly the clandestine tryst of two lovers; the woman's mother and children were walking a few steps behind us. When I spotted a photographer snapping a series of shots from across the street, I had joked, "That's Phyllis and her lawyer." I wasn't far wrong.

Her divorce action hit me like a bullet. Phyllis and I had been married for fifty-two years, and despite the fact that our marriage had been rocky for a long time I could not believe that she wanted to end it. I've always been an extremely private person and did not relish any publicity about my personal life. I take responsibility for my part in the dissolution of our marriage but it is a shared responsibility. She also had a great deal to do with it. I am happy to say that I continue to be on intimate terms with our children and grandchildren. I still care a lot about Phyllis and I wish her happiness.

Of course, divorce settlement or no, my interest in Viacom's parent company, National Amusements, had been structured in such a way that events in Phyllis's and my personal life would not affect the ownership, control or management of Viacom. I had suffered a deep personal loss, but in strictly business terms there was little that I could lose.

What a company we have! Beginning with MTV and Nickelodeon and growing into VH1, TV Land, Comedy Central, UPN, TNN, Country Music Television, Showtime/TMC and CBS along with Paramount Pictures, Simon & Schuster, Blockbuster, Infinity Broadcasting, outdoor advertising, Paramount Parks and thousands of screens in Canada and overseas, the Viacom brands reach and influence tremendous numbers of people around the globe from the cradle to the grave. And we run it for the good of our shareholders and the good of our consumers.

The crossover benefits among Viacom divisions are almost endless. We can take the number-one children's brand in the television world, Nickelodeon, and bring our viewers to the Paramount movie studio, supported and promoted by every other division in our company. We can show those movies on thousands of screens around the world, including our own. We can turn our books into movies, our movies into television shows, our television shows into movies, and we can sell, air and syndicate those television shows on our stations as well as others. We can publish the music on the sound tracks and advertise and merchandise it all over the globe. We can cross-sell across the MTV Networks, CBS, Infinity; we can cross-promote, as MTV did for *Survivor* on CBS; we can be the best place for advertisers since we have the best platforms in outdoor advertising, radio, cable and television. We are the only company that can reach every demographic. We are already the number-one creator and seller of television programming to the networks, cable and syndication. We can extend and expand our brands to create new characters and new ideas and new revenue streams, supported by consumers with a lifelong affiliation with and affection for the programming they have grown up with and been influenced by. We have made Viacom a place where financial discipline lives side by side with artistic freedom, where aggressive executives work together as friends, and where the best interests of the entire company are our ultimate goal.

As I have said, I firmly believe there is more to life than the bottom line. I think many people would like to make some kind of dent in the world, leave as large and indelible a mark as they are able, and Viacom is in the position, no matter how indirect the path may sometimes be, to affect the world around it. All of us at Viacom are not saints—far from it—but I am surrounded by people who believe they have an obligation beyond the bottom line, who know where the bottom line ends and social responsibility begins.

I am proud to say we at Viacom are purveyors of ideas and ideals that, once established early, will last a lifetime. If you watch the highly successful Nickelodeon, for example, you will find no difference in the way white and black children are portrayed. We don't have to lecture our young viewers about race relations. We simply present a world in which kids of different colors play together in complete harmony, they see this paradigm in action—and are likely to follow it in the real world. MTV plays music by all races and nationalities, a diversity that is implicit but undeniable. Viacom has also spent tens of millions of dollars through our networks and other divisions to fight more overt battles against intolerance, racism, violence and drug abuse on a worldwide basis. We have a major campaign against drugs under way in China, where MTV is already in 56 million homes.

Viacom has the extremely important opportunity to affect change for good. It is part of the fiber of the company. And as much as we are doing, we probably should do more—and we will.

For example, a group of schoolchildren in Colorado read about the present-day buying and selling of slaves in the Sudan and determined to do something about it. They raised money in their community to purchase the freedom of people who had been sold into slavery. They also wrote to politicians, talk show hosts and other people they thought could help their cause, but they got no results. Among the people they wrote to was me. As it happened, my granddaughter Keryn was living in Colorado and called this effort to my attention. I, in turn, called it to the attention of all the Viacom divisions. Nick News, the young people's news division of Nickelodeon, produced a segment designed to bring the world's attention to the situation and effectively jump-started an enormous campaign to end this international outrage. We made a difference.

When *Time* magazine ran a story about the effort, it praised Viacom and me. In actual fact it was Keryn who got the job done and I wrote a letter to the editor which said, "Her persistence and tenacious focus on this international atrocity convinced me that I should spotlight the children's extraordinary effort. The credit belongs rightfully to Keryn and other youngsters. This tale reminds us of some sage advice: Listen to your children. It is frequently they who show us the power of an individual to make a difference in this world."

I was so very proud of my granddaughter. I am proud of my other grandchildren, too. Kimberlee, my first grandchild, went to school in Israel and took a summer job at Nickelodeon, just as Keryn had worked at MTV. Kim made it clear to me that she did not want to work here unless she had a real job, could make a real contribution and be treated like any other employee. She has gone on to study at a prestigious university and Keryn has done the same. I have three other grandchildren, Brandon, Tyler and Lauren. They are all strongly motivated to achieve their goals. I believe that I, along with their parents, have been able to play a role in instilling in them the value system in which I believe.

I consider it an achievement to work as hard as I do and still maintain an intimate, loving relationship with my children and grandchildren. My daughter, Shari, mother of Kimberlee, Brandon and Tyler, is deeply involved in both my personal and business life. Today, she runs the National Amusements theater chain—the job I had before Viacom. She has become a leader, if not *the* leader, in the motion picture exhibition industry. I was very touched when on Father's Day, in the midst of an extremely contentious divorce between her mother and me for which Shari could have found me totally responsible, she wrote me a note which I will always treasure. She said, "Dear Dad, I cannot tell you how proud I am of you and how happy I am to have had you for a father."

My son, Brent, and his wife, Annie, are equally dear to me. Brent was one of the top prosecutors in Suffolk County, Boston, where he had the best record of wins on the homicide squad. He is now working at MTV Networks, with the desire to learn everything he can about Viacom's business. I admire the way he has dug into a world that is new to him.

I was brought up in an environment where the protection of the rights of the underprivileged, whether we were talking about child labor or the minimum wage or the right to vote, was extremely important. That is why I was first drawn to the practice of law. And now one of the greatest pleasures in my life comes on the days each year I spend teaching students at Brandeis and at Boston University and Harvard University Law Schools. There I feel I am truly making a difference.

So, what will I be doing five years from now? That is not a question I concern myself with. Nor am I particularly concerned about my age, although a great many others appear to be. If I am not yet ready to talk about succession, I am always very ready to talk about success. My enthusiasm for my job will not recede. The will to win is the will to survive and I continue to have a passion to win. In that way I will always feel young.

I like to think about President Franklin Roosevelt's cabinet during World War II, many around the age of seventy. Who is among the most admired in today's financial community? Chairman of the Federal Reserve Board Alan Greenspan, a man in his mid-seventies. Age is overstated as a factor in the ability to run a company. Instead of measuring a person by the amount of energy he devotes to his work, or by the quality of his recent accomplishments, some people focus on age and consider it a negative factor. That's nonsense. Judgment, commitment, competence, attitude, vision—these are the important elements to be considered, not age. I can't do anything about age!

Chronological age has little to do with intellectual capacity, the ability to work, the ability to lead. In fact, I often surprise my younger colleagues by being the first to accept and, indeed, suggest new ideas and new agendas when the assumption is I will hold on to the old ones like a bulldog.

What am I going to be doing five years from now? My industry is changing with the speed of light and I can say only that I want to continue in its brilliance. Now my concern is about what I will be doing tomorrow, next week, next month. There is work to be done and I am determined to do it the best way it can be done. I still want to be number one.

INDEX

A.G., 192
ABC, 62, 230, 293, 301, 302
Abrams, George, 306
Abruzzese, Joe, 309
Academy Awards, 251
Academy of Excellence, 247
Adams, Bert, 62
Advance Publications, Inc.,
    209, 230
Aldrich, Jeff, 79
Allen, Herb, 177, 178, 183,
    193–94, 208, 257
Allen, William T., 223
Allen & Company, 177, 193,
    195, 205, 244
Allied States Association, 83
Andrews, Julie, 95
Antioco, John, 287–92, 294,
    296
Araskog, Rand, 257, 259, 260,
    262, 263
Army, U.S., 50–55
Associated Press, 151–52
AT&T, 192
AutoNation USA, 29, 30

Baldwin, Howard, 259
Bank of America (BOA), 119,
    121, 129, 139–41
Bank of New England, 71
Bank of New York, 214
Barkan case, 221
Barron's, 270
Barton, Peter, 258, 260–63
Baruch, Ralph, 148
Bass Group, 220
Bear Stearns, 124, 154, 277, 287
Beatty, Warren, 172
Beavis and Butt-Head (TV
    show), 174, 191
*Beavis and Butt-Head Do
    America* (movie), 250
Becker (TV show), 300

Before They Were Rock Stars
    (TV show), 165
Behind the Music (TV show),
    165
Bell Atlantic Corporation, 206,
    209, 215
BellSouth Corporation, 207,
    214–17, 230, 240
Bennett, Danny, 169
Bennett, Tony, 116, 127,
    169–70
Bergson, Herbert, 62, 74
Berrard, Steven, 25, 26, 28–30,
    34, 230, 236, 266, 274,
    281, 289
Bertelsmann, 192, 271
Beverly Hills Cop (movie), 176
Bingaman, Anne, 203
Biondi, Carol, 147
Biondi, Frank, 144–51, 156,
    159, 163, 164, 172,
    184–86, 197–98, 208, 217,
    230, 236, 239, 240, 244,
    247, 248, 255, 259–60,
    266–70, 273, 274, 297, 298
Björk, 176
Black, Hugo, 64
Black Hole, The (movie), 89, 91
Blank, Matt, 33, 276, 307
Blockbuster, 23–40, 192,
    205–7, 212, 230, 233–35,
    237–39, 241–42, 245–47,
    266, 274, 275, 280–97,
    309, 310
Boasberg, Charlie, 176–77
Bonaparte, Napoleon, 230
Borkland, Herbert, 62
Boston Garden, 257
Boston Latin School, 43–50,
    55, 56, 81
Boston Patriots, 257
Boston University Law School,
    151, 314

Boucher, Marion, 215–16
Boyz II Men, 176
Brandeis University, 35, 151,
    314
Branson, Richard, 205
Braveheart (movie), 251
British Telecommunications,
    162, 166
Brotherhood, The (movie), 83
Buena Vista Distribution
    Company, Inc., 90
Bullitt (movie), 83
Burke, John, 17, 37
Burton, Harold, 64
Bush, George, 171
Business Week, 35, 37, 228, 247,
    288, 293

Cablevision, 154, 257, 258,
    261–64, 276, 277
Candy (movie), 83
Capital Group, Inc., 270
Carson, Johnny, 171
Caskey, John, 75
Castaldi, Alex, 79
Catholic Legion of Decency, 96
CBS Corporation, 23, 174,
    299–311
Cheers (TV show), 175
Chicago, University of, Law
    School, 57
Chicago Tribune, 53
Children's Television Work-
    shop, 145
Chinatown (movie), 252
Cinemax, 155
Circle K Corporation, 287, 288
Citibank, 119, 140–41, 214
Clark, Thomas, 60, 64
Clear and Present Danger
    (movie), 250
Clendenin, John, 207
Clinton, Bill, 171–73